ARTICULATING
DESIGN
THINKING

ARTICULATING
DESIGN
THINKING

First published in 2012 by Libri Publishing

Copyright © Libri Publishing Ltd.

Authors retain the rights to individual chapters.

ISBN 978 1 907471 51 3

The right of Paul Rodgers to be identified as the editor of this work has been asserted in accordance with the Copyright, Designs and Patents Act, 1988. All rights reserved. No part of this publication may be reproduced, stored in any retrieval system or transmitted in any form or by any means, electronic, mechanical, photocopying, recording or otherwise, without the prior written permission of the copyright holder for which application should be addressed in the first instance to the publishers. No liability shall be attached to the author, the copyright holder or the publishers for loss or damage of any nature suffered as a result of reliance on the reproduction of any of the contents of this publication or any errors or omissions in its contents.

A CIP catalogue record for this book is available from The British Library

Book design by Carnegie Publishing

Printed in the UK by Ashford Colour Press

Libri Publishing
Brunel House
Volunteer Way
Faringdon
Oxfordshire
SN7 7YR

Tel: +44 (0)845 873 3837

www.libripublishing.co.uk

CONTENTS

FOREWORD vii
Nigel Cross

INTRODUCTION 1
Paul A. Rodgers

1 GETTING TO GRIPS WITH DESIGN THINKING IN INTERACTION
  DESIGN: LESSONS FROM ARCHITECTURAL PRACTICE 9
  Parag Deshpande

2 WORK DRESS DESIGN: A CASE STUDY ON THE EMPOWERMENT
  OF HUMAN ABILITIES 27
  Maria Antonietta Sbordone

3 STUDENTS' RESPONSES TO INCLUSIVE DESIGN 39
  Richard Herriott and Birgitte Geert Jensen

4 THE DESIGN THINKING APPROACHES OF THREE DIFFERENT
  GROUPS OF DESIGNERS BASED ON SELF-REPORTS 55
  Gabriela Goldschmidt and Paul A. Rodgers

5 THE EFFECT OF EMPLOYING DIFFERENT DESIGN METHODS ON
  THE DESIGN COGNITION OF SMALL DESIGN TEAMS 73
  John S. Gero, Morteza Pourmohamadi and Christopher B. Williams

6 TOWARDS A LIVING FUTURE OF CALM 89
  Rachael Luck and Ian Ewart

7 'WE WANT TO ADD TO THEIR LIVES, NOT TAKE AWAY...' 107
  Katja Fleischmann, Gemma Visini and Ryan Daniel

8 SKETCHING PROFILES: AWARENESS TO INDIVIDUAL DIFFERENCES
  IN SKETCHING AS A MEANS OF ENHANCING DESIGN SOLUTION
  DEVELOPMENT 135
  Shoshi Bar-Eli

9 LEARNING NATURAL USER INTERFACE DESIGN THROUGH
  CREATIVE DRAMA TECHNIQUES: NEW APPROACHES TO
  DESIGN EDUCATION 157
  Adviye Ayça Ünlüer and Oğuzhan Özcan

10   THE FACETS OF DESIGN THINKING   171
Oliver Breuer, Agnese Caglio, Frederik Gottlieb, Sergejs Groskovs, Anette Hiltunen,
Miguel Navarro Sanint and Brian Schewe

11   CRAFTING 'SOLVABLE' PROBLEMS IN THE DESIGN PROCESS   189
Janet Kelly

12   DIFFERENT PERCEPTIONS OF THE DESIGN PROCESS
     IN THE CONTEXT OF DESIGNART   207
Michael Leitner, Giovanni Innella and Freddie Yauner

13   CONCEPT DRIVEN INTERACTION DESIGN RESEARCH IN THE
     DOMAIN OF ATTRACTIVE AGEING: THE EXAMPLE OF WALKY   227
Elena Nazzi, Naveen Bagalkot, Arun Narargoje and Tomas Sokoler

AUTHOR INDEX   246

Nigel CROSS

FOREWORD

The series of meetings that has become the Design Thinking Research Symposia (*Articulating Design Thinking* results from the ninth meeting) was initiated by Nigel Cross, Norbert Roozenburg and Kees Dorst at Delft University of Technology, The Netherlands, in 1991, with what was initially expected to be a one-off international meeting on 'Research in Design Thinking'. But the content and format of that meeting were felt by the participants to be so good as to warrant more of the same. So a second meeting was also held in Delft, in 1994, focused on the use of protocol analysis as a research tool for analysing design activity. This became known as the 'Delft Protocols Workshop'. For the first time in design research, a common data set (videotapes of both individual and team design activity) was provided to researchers around the world, for their own analyses, presented at the workshop.

A third meeting was held at the Istanbul Technical University, Turkey, in 1996, on the topic of descriptive models of design, and the fourth meeting was held at the Massachusetts Institute of Technology, Boston, USA, in 1999, on the topic of design representation. It was there that the organisers introduced the term 'Design Thinking Research Symposium' as the generic title for the series. The fifth meeting was again in Delft, in 2001, on the topic of design in context and developing an interdisciplinary approach to studying design in a broader social context.

The sixth symposium, at the University of Technology, Sydney, Australia, 2003, returned to somewhere near the focus of the original meeting in Delft in 1991 on the nature and the nurture of expert performance in design and again brought together a relatively small, international group of active researchers. The seventh meeting, on analysing design meetings, was held at Central St. Martin's College, University of the Arts, London in 2007. This was another small, focused workshop meeting, again providing researchers worldwide with a common data set for analysis – this time video recordings of meetings within architectural and engineering product design teams. Throughout this series of symposia, the small workshop format has been found to be a successful way of synthesising the contributions of an international community, of reporting current work and of identifying and promoting necessary further research.

Another workshop meeting adopting the same principle of analysing a common data set was held as a National Science Foundation Workshop at the University of California, Irvine, USA, in February 2010, on 'Studying Professional Software Design'. The data provided were video recordings of pairs of software designers tackling the same design task.

The eighth DTRS meeting, 'Interpreting Design Thinking', was again held in Sydney, Australia, in October 2010, and invited interdisciplinary contributions linking design to other disciplines. This meeting acknowledged the growing role of design thinking in business, industry, social services and elsewhere.

The ninth DTRS meeting, 'Articulating Design Thinking', at the School of Design, Northumbria University, Newcastle-upon-Tyne, introduced another variation on the theme of a shared approach and an international range of analyses. The organisers invited researchers to set up studies based on designers' responses to a common design brief. This novel approach brought a different perspective to the analysis of design thinking, complementary to previous analyses. This perspective is explored in the essays contained in *Articulating Design Thinking*.

Nigel Cross

PREVIOUS PUBLICATIONS

The series of DTRS meetings has produced a substantial set of publications in books and journals, with significant research results, and has helped to foster an international community of scholars and researchers focused on design cognition.

The published output from the symposia series includes:

DTRS1

Cross, N., Dorst, K. and Roozenburg, N. (eds) (1992) *Research in Design Thinking*, Delft, The Netherlands: Delft University Press.

DTRS2

Cross, N., Christiaans, H. and Dorst, K. (eds) (1996) *Analysing Design Activity*, Chichester, UK: John Wiley & Sons.

Dorst, K. (ed.) (1995) 'Analysing Design Activity', special issue of *Design Studies*, vol. 16, no. 2.

DTRS3

Akin, Ö. (ed.) (1997) 'Descriptive Models of Design', special issue of *Design Studies*, vol. 18, no. 4.

Akin, Ö. (ed.) (1998) 'Models of Design', special issue of *Automation in Construction*, vol. 7, no. 2/3.

DTRS4

Goldschmidt, G. and Porter, W. (eds) (2004) *Design Representation*, London: Springer Verlag.

Goldschmidt, G. and Porter, W. (eds) (2000) 'Visual Design Representation', special issue of *Design Studies*, vol. 21, no. 5.

DTRS5

Lloyd, P. and Christiaans, H. (eds) (2001) *Designing in Context*, Delft, The Netherlands: Delft University Press.

Lloyd, P. (ed.) (2003) 'Designing in Context', special issue of *Design Studies*, vol. 24, no. 3.

DTRS6

Cross, N. and Edmonds, E. (eds) (2003) *Expertise in Design*, University of Technology, Sydney, Australia: Creativity and Cognition Press.

Cross, N. (ed.) (2004) 'Expertise in Design', special issue of *Design Studies*, vol. 25, no. 5.

DTRS7

McDonnell, J. and Lloyd, P. (eds) (2009) *About: Designing – Analysing Design Meetings*, London, UK: Taylor & Francis.

McDonnell, J. and Lloyd, P. (eds) (2009) 'Analysing Design Conversations', special issue of *CoDesign*, vol. 5, no. 1.

Lloyd, P. and McDonnell, J. (eds) (2009) 'Values in the Design Process', special issue of *Design Studies*, vol. 29, no. 2.

SPSD

Petre, M., van der Hoek, A. and Baker, A. (eds) (2010) 'Studying Professional Software Design', special issue of *Design Studies*, vol. 31, no. 6.

DTRS8

Stewart, S. (ed.) (2011) 'Interpreting Design Thinking', special issue of *Design Studies*, vol. 32, no. 6.

Paul A. RODGERS

INTRODUCTION

As Nigel Cross has clearly described in the Foreword of this book, the meetings that have become widely known as the Design Thinking Research Symposia (DTRS) have been running fairly regularly since the first DTRS at Delft University of Technology, The Netherlands, in 1991. Arguably, the second meeting held again at Delft in 1994, which focused on the use of protocol analysis as a research tool for analysing design activity and is commonly referred to as the 'Delft Protocols Workshop', is the best known of the DTRS series. It was here at Delft in 1994 that, for the first time in design research, a common data set (videotapes of both individual and team design activity) was provided to researchers around the world, for their own analyses. The researchers then presented their papers and interpretations of the designers' work at the workshop.

DTRS 2012, held at Northumbria University's School of Design, the ninth meeting in the DTRS series, will again be run along similar lines (with some key differences) to the workshop-based events that we have seen in past DTRS events such as the Delft Protocols in 1994 and the 'Studying Professional Software Designers' workshop held at the University of California, Irvine in 2010 wherein a number of workshop delegates were asked to respond to a given common set of data (i.e. video recordings and transcripts of design-team activities).

DTRS 2012 introduces a variation on the theme of the shared approach and an international range of analyses of data provided. This time, invited researchers were asked to set up their own studies based on designers' responses to a common design brief. The aim here in this novel approach was to get a diverse set of different perspectives on the analysis of design thinking and action that would be complementary to previous analyses. That is, we were interested in articulating not only different analyses of a common set of data but in different approaches to design activity via a common design brief. In other words, we were interested in using a generic design brief to generate a variety of data sets and their subsequent analyses and articulations.

The design brief set asked the main question: 'How can the design of products, spaces and services make growing old seem more attractive and inviting?'

As background information, researchers were reminded that 11 per cent of the world's 6.9 billion people are over 60 and by the year 2050 that figure will have doubled to 22 per cent. Thus, if we are to support a growing number of older people, we need to produce products, spaces and services that allow them to stay healthy and well, in and around their own home. So, each team of researchers was asked to design a domestic product, living environment or service for older people that surpasses conventional expectations. For the purpose of illustration, the following would all be viable responses to the brief:

- A piece of furniture or furniture system
- A domestic tool, product or appliance
- An architectural intervention
- A decorative item or scheme
- An interior design or living environment
- An adapted bathroom, kitchen or workshop
- A new domestic service.

Every DTRS 2012 participant in the book made their own arrangements as to how they approached and tackled the set brief. Some DTRS 2012 participants chose to undertake the design activities as part of a small or large team (made up of academic and industrial partners); some chose to observe and record others undertaking the design task; whilst the design task was undertaken by a single designer in other cases. The time taken for the participants to undertake the design activity and generate a 'designed' outcome was left entirely open. Some participants observed design activity that lasted days, whilst others took weeks to complete. Upon completion of the design activity, each DTRS 2012 participant wrote up their observed design activity and submitted it as a paper.

As such, this book contains 13 papers from researchers based in eight different countries – Sweden, Italy, Denmark, Israel, the UK, USA, Australia, and Turkey.

At the outset, DTRS 2012 was particularly keen to include novel papers that described collaborations between industry (small SME-style enterprises, medium-sized companies or even global players), design students, academics and researchers from design disciplines and other relevant areas such as computing, the humanities, the arts and sciences and/or a combination of all of these.

Each chapter in this book has been subject to a double-blind review and assessed for inclusion in the DTRS 2012 event. Each author was asked to consider focussing their chapter on relevant design research issues including understanding and articulating design thinking, the role of context in design, disciplinarity and socio-cultural roles in design, amongst several others. A final special mention is well deserved by all the reviewers who conducted such excellent reviews in good time. The reviewers, who must take a large part of the credit for this book, are:

Robin Adams, Purdue University

Linden Ball, Lancaster University

John Clarkson, University of Cambridge

Nathan Crilly, University of Cambridge

Nigel Cross, The Open University

Ken Friedman, Swinburne University of Technology

Gabi Goldschmidt, Technion Israel Institute of Technology

Graham Green, University of Glasgow

Ann Heylighen, Katholieke Universiteit Leuven

Peter Lloyd, The Open University

Rachael Luck, University of Reading

Ben Matthews, University of Southern Denmark

Janet McDonnell, University of the Arts London

Rivka Oxman, Technion Israel Institute of Technology

Norbert Roozenburg, TU Delft, The Netherlands

Nick Spencer, Northumbria University

John Stevens, Northumbria University

Cameron Tonkinwise, Parsons, The New School for Design

Bob Young, Northumbria University

The 13 chapters that make up this book all deal with articulations of design thinking from a variety of disciplinary perspectives including inclusive design, architecture, work-dress design, industrial design and interaction design.

The first chapter, 'Getting to Grips with Design Thinking in Interaction Design: Lessons from Architectural Practice', written by Parag Deshpande, contributes to the debate on design thinking within interaction design research by introducing a view of design thinking originating from the practice of architectural design. In his chapter, Deshpande adopts the role of designer *and* researcher where he works with clients and others to address the design brief aforementioned and later writes up his observations and reflections on the design activities he has undertaken. Deshpande's key claim in this work, he states, is that an understanding of design within the field of interaction design can be enhanced through a closer study of an architectural view of design thinking. In this sense, he proposes a number of characteristics commonly associated with an architectural view of design thinking, such as, 'separation of the stages of envisioning and making, taking a design by drawing approach, rejection of the given design brief and solution-first strategy'. Deshpande suggests that these common characteristics inherent in architectural design practice have yet to be fully or adequately acknowledged in the practice of interaction design.

Maria Antonietta Sbordone's chapter, 'Work Dress Design: A Case Study on the Empowerment of Human Abilities', describes advanced research on materials and technologies in the area of work-clothing design targeted for elderly women. The overarching aim of Sbordone's project, originating from her observations of the changes and strains that a woman's body has to cope with in elderly and pre-elderly age, is to improve the life conditions of women through the creation of specialised clothes for the safety and comfort of women performing their everyday activities such as shopping, preparing food, lifting things, climbing step ladders and so on. The chapter describes the use of photographic analysis in the daily activities of elderly women. The photo sequences collected reveal both the main activities performed by elderly women and how, over the years, these everyday activities contribute to problems with posture and other diseases that lead to irreversible changes in the body.

Herriott and Jensen's chapter, 'Students' Responses to Inclusive Design', explores how the use of inclusive design methods affects students' design working processes. Using work diaries, the students broke down their projects into a variety of tasks including problem solving, data gathering and ideation. Herriott and Jensen's work provides a valuable insight into how the design problem is resolved in design solutions by offering a number of quantitative insights into how the design students' time is allocated during their design processes and how the allocation of their time changes as the project progresses. Rather than simply conclude that design processes are 'messy' and 'disordered', Herriott and Jensen's study visualises it and finds patterns underlying a process that is perceived to be chaotic. The chapter provides a rough measure of the dynamics of a project in the form of the 'switch between' ratio from the start to the finish of a project.

Goldschmidt and Rodgers' chapter, 'The Design Thinking Approaches of Three Different Groups of Designers', compares the design behaviour of student designers on the basis of their design ideas and their self-reported design activities, especially the sequence of their design activities and the time each student allotted to them. Goldschmidt and Rodgers found that most participants did not follow a linear process and skipped some of the conventional activities prescribed in design methods, and that a large chunk of the students' time was devoted to preparing final presentations.

On the basis of their findings, Goldschmidt and Rodgers pose questions regarding design methods in the era of 'Design Thinking' where designers are asked to adopt an entrepreneurial frame of mind. Are designers and design educators ready to let go of an adherence to rigid 'methods'? They finish by claiming that learning to 'let go' will be one of the major challenges facing design education and practice in the years ahead.

John S. Gero et al.'s chapter, 'The Effect of Employing Different Design Methods on Design Cognition of Small Design Teams', presents the results of a comparison of design cognition between two design teams employing different design methods while they design assistive technology devices. The design cognition of the teams of designers is obtained through protocol analyses of two sets of design sessions – brainstorming and morphological analysis and the protocols segmented and coded using the Function–Behaviour–Structure coding scheme. The preliminary results reported in Gero et al.'s chapter show that there are statistically significant differences in the design cognition of the designers when using these two design methods. The chapter's findings from the experiments conducted include the observation that brainstorming does not produce more structure design issues than morphological analysis, brainstorming has less expected behaviour design issues than morphological analysis, designers involved in brainstorming do not conduct less analysis design processes than when performing morphological analysis, and less description design processes do not occur during the brainstorming sessions compared to the morphological analysis sessions.

Luck and Ewart's chapter, 'Towards a Living Future of Calm', outlines several challenges for designers of future homes in the UK. Their chapter reminds us that we live in a built environment that we know could be improved, and we have many ideas how to design homes and neighbourhoods to be more accessible for all; but what do older people think about where and how they live, their local environments, service encounters and the material stuff they use as they go about their daily lives? They report the findings of a 'Living Futures' participatory design project where older peoples' testimonies and visual materials were collected to examine the ways domestic surroundings, local environments and routine encounters feature in their lives. Luck and Ewart's chapter reflects on these conversations and posits a number of considerations for the ways the future might be designed for older people. In particular, their chapter shows how the participants' framing of everyday interactions with people and things as potential design problems and their awareness of their future needs might provide valuable insights in the consideration of how all our future lives might become calm.

Fleischmann et al.'s chapter, 'We Want to Add to their Lives, not Take Away…', discusses the proliferation of mobile devices across a wide range of ages, from the very young to the elderly, but also the neglect of mobile devices (apps) specifically aimed at the older generation (60+). Fleischmann et al.'s chapter asks whether apps specifically designed for the elderly are even available. If so, do they help make growing old seem more attractive and inviting? Their chapter describes a multidisciplinary approach known as the POOL model (where design students collaborate with other students from disciplines such as IT, journalism and photomedia). The authors report that, while the

POOL approach has brought various benefits to the students involved, such as greater understanding of teamwork and other diverse disciplines, many of the students' project outcomes have lacked a focus on the end user. Fleischmann et al.'s chapter describes how a team of twenty students approached the design of a product for a mobile device that makes growing old seem more attractive and inviting and reports reflections on the extent to which the design thinking process employed in the study led to a greater sense of empathy amongst the student designers.

Shoshi Bar-Eli's chapter, 'Sketching Profiles: Awareness to Individual Differences in Sketching as a Means of Enhancing Design Solution Development', looks at design processes as derived from an analysis of their sketching and design behaviour. The chapter reports different ways in which sketches are used as a tool for thinking and communicating throughout the conceptual phase of the design process and how in each of these profiles the designers interact differently with their sketches, which helps the designers to develop solutions. Bar-Eli's research emphasises the need to examine sketching in a more flexible and dynamic way that broadens the notion that designers read new information in their sketches, and that the manner in which designers look at and translate their own sketches can be used to distinguish between them. The chapter suggests that a better understanding of sketching and design behaviour patterns may serve as a basis for the development of various pedagogical concepts, strategies and tools, and may allow students to understand better the relationship between their world of thought and experience, and their design process.

Ünlüer and Özcan's chapter, 'Learning Natural User Interface Design Through Creative Drama Techniques: New Approaches to Design Education', describes the Natural User Interface (NUI) approach, a contemporary concept in Interactive Media Design that lets users interact with devices through the use of everyday actions and gestures – thus differentiating it from a standard Graphical User Interface (GUI) approach. The authors report that learning to design NUIs requires exploring a variety of subjects and technologies as well as embracing user-centred design principles. Their central observation, however, is that students who are used to working with the more stereotypical technologies of GUIs typically have a hard time adapting to such a large and flexible field. Through their studies, the authors conclude that creative drama techniques are a convenient way of developing NUI-based design thinking because these techniques support the use of body language, on which NUIs depend. Ünlüer and Özcan's study aims to answer questions regarding the ways in which techniques inspired from creative drama can be implemented into interactive media design education in order to derive innovative ideas for NUI-design through commonly used methods such as role-playing, improvisation and mime as a way of deriving a diverse range of creative games that may be applied to different phases of design education.

Breuer et al.'s chapter, 'The Facets of Design Thinking', seeks to contribute to the panorama of design thinking based on multiple perspectives. Their chapter describes a number of different responses to the 'making aging more attractive' brief that was undertaken by a design team applying design thinking practices. The chapter presents four design concepts that give the reader an understanding of the final outcome, a description of how the design team initially addressed the brief and the processes involved in describing and analysing these concepts according to four different dimensions. The four dimensions described in the chapter are (i) the role of design – exposing the provocative, proactive or visionary results, (ii) the rationale – going beyond expectations as a confrontation of the fieldwork conducted, (iii) design approximations – responses to a specific user, the relational scale and the societal scale as a holistic approach to the problem, and (iv) the outcome of each of the four design concepts that correspond to increasing awareness, establishing a different social order, creating user self-awareness and materialising memories in a tangible system.

Kelly's chapter, 'Crafting "Solvable" Problems in the Design Process', is an attempt to explicate how a 'wicked' problem is addressed in a design process in order to construct it in such a way as to be 'solvable'. Kelly's chapter demonstrates how aspects of a problem space were selected in a way to allow a corresponding solution space to be defined and then shows how both this problem space and solution space evolved through design exploration. The case presented in this chapter comprises two design projects, which were run in parallel, performed on behalf of two medical device manufacturers. In this case, Kelly reports that, in order to respond to the varied and sometimes contradictory interests of the various stakeholders, the design problem that defined the starting point for exploration was crafted from aspects of the problem space where these interests overlapped. The chapter shows that the resulting proposals are concepts that aim, not to surpass conventional expectations, but to change them to be better aligned with the actual experience of using the technologies.

Leitner et al.'s chapter, 'Case Study: Different Perceptions of the Design Process in the Context of DesignArt', investigates the emerging area of DesignArt with the aim being to research how design knowledge, design processes and coherence with the design brief are perceived and valued by relevant stakeholders. The chapter describes a single case study wherein the well-known Dutch gallery Droog invited a designer to submit a proposal for an exhibition on the 'future of living at home in old age' and over the course of three weeks how the designer produced deliverables to update the client on his progress. The authors report how they followed the designer's work over the course of the three weeks, gathering data from the designer, the client and from their neutral perspective, using interviews and questionnaires. The chapter attempts to reproduce accurately the interactions between a designer and a client in as unbiased a way as possible. The authors report that their results suggest that intuition-based decision-making and factual knowledge are valued differently by each of the parties. Moreover, the chapter reveals that the client and designer understand 'the process' not so much in observable and logical steps towards the final proposal but rather as a sum of creative thinking and work represented by, and visible in, the outcome itself.

In 'Concept Driven Interaction Design Research in the Domain of Attractive Ageing: The Example of Walky', Nazzi et al. present the design exploration of an archetypal senior-citizen product (i.e. the trolley bag) that is mainly used for shopping and how this humble product might open up new opportunities for social interactions. The authors describe how a set of theoretical perspectives that include embodied interaction, the role of social interaction in ageing and the phenomenon of microblogging combine to inform the design and development of Walky. The authors report how a co-designing situation with senior citizens living in a local community in Valby (a suburb of Copenhagen), AKPDesign and other stakeholders, including members from the municipal corporation of the city of Copenhagen, explicated the process of developing interactive artefacts. Moreover, the authors highlight how this co-designing situation was instrumental in engaging with the theory–situation dialectics in designing for social aspects of ageing, which led to the senior citizens having a stronger sense of belonging to their community and therefore to a more attractive ageing.

The aim of the Design Thinking Research Symposium (DTRS) events is always to present a diverse and contemporary set of perspectives on design thinking, research and action that will build upon previous work. DTRS 2012 was interested in articulating not only different analyses of a common set of data but in different approaches to design activity, via a common design brief. The chapters in this book provide an excellent set of lessons, case studies, responses, examinations, facets and perceptions of design thinking, research and doing in a modern, complex and challenging world.

Parag DESHPANDE

Umeå Institute of Design, Umeå, Sweden

GETTING TO GRIPS WITH DESIGN THINKING IN INTERACTION DESIGN: LESSONS FROM ARCHITECTURAL PRACTICE

Introduction

While the discipline of interaction design has often been compared with other more traditional design disciplines, due to the centrality of design, the task of an interaction designer is a complex one, perhaps more complex than that of designers practising within traditional design disciplines. The ever-evolving nature of computational technology, the design material used by interaction designers, the emergence of everyday human activity areas as design settings for interaction design and the ephemeral nature of the design boundaries of the discipline point to the fact that interaction designers deal with design situations that are *complex* and that are sometimes characterised as 'wicked problem' [18].

Interaction designers require conceptual and methodological tools for design, the kind that practising designers from traditional design disciplines seem to have, to deal with such design situations. Not surprisingly, therefore, the nature of practice of traditional design has been the source of knowledge for interaction design to empower interaction designers to deal with the design situations they face. A number of design traditions associated with traditional design practice, such as its iterative design and so on, have already been incorporated within the interaction design practice [13]. However, there appears to be some concern regarding the success of such design traditions when used in interaction design practice and a probable reason for this has been attributed to the fact that such design traditions do not appear to be grounded in the holistic understanding of the nature of design practice within traditional design disciplines [20]. Broadening understanding of the nature of design practice has therefore emerged as an important agenda for interaction design research in recent years [20].

More recently, *design thinking*, the central concept that characterises the design practice within traditional design disciplines has been introduced into the broad HCI community through a number of papers in the field of Interaction Design [e.g. 7, 15, 16]. 'Design thinking', as suggested by design research in traditional design disciplines, refers to the thinking process of a designer engaged in the activity of design. It is this thinking that allows designers in traditional design disciplines to deal with complex design situations or the 'wicked' nature of the design problems they face. Given that interaction designers, like designers from more traditional design disciplines, also deal with complex design situations or 'wicked' design problems, researchers in recent years have been arguing in favour of a *deeper examination* of the idea of design thinking and its potential advantages for the practice interaction design [6, 7, 20].

The aim of this chapter is to contribute to the debate on design thinking within interaction design research by introducing a view of design thinking that I have recently developed and which originates in the practice of architectural design [5]. To bring this view of design thinking into being, I have reflected, as a practising architect and a researcher, on one of my own architectural design projects as well as on design research literature. This view therefore offers an insider's perspective on the character of design thinking in the practice of architectural design. This view of design thinking, however, is not comprehensive in its scope. My aim when developing this view was to identify and make sense of both observable (to myself and to others) and non-observable activities, initiated and reflected by my own thought process when engaged in design; and to articulate the nature and the structure of such activities. I therefore did not elaborate on a number of aspects associated with design, such as the client's involvement in the process of bringing an artefact into being, the collaboration of design teams during design, the role of expert knowledge (other than the designer's) in guiding design, the designer's role during the process of implementation of the designed artefact and so on.

In this chapter, I examine the above-mentioned architectural view of design thinking to bring an interactive artefact into being following the design brief provided by DTRS9. In the following section, I discuss characteristics of this view. In the next section, I provide a reflective account of a design project where, following the design brief provided by DTRS9, I applied the architectural view of design thinking to bring an interactive artefact into being. Finally, I conclude the chapter by discussing some of the advantages this view of design thinking appears to offers to the interaction design practice.

Design Thinking in Architectural Design

The practice of architectural design is a professional one. That is, architects, hired by their clients, design one or more habitable buildings as desired by their clients. The professional practice of architecture is carried out in two distinct stages. First, in collaboration with their client, the architect envisions and expresses the building in the form of drawings; and second, the building is constructed by builders/contractors following the drawings provided by the architects. Architects play the central role in carrying out the activities of the first stage whereas the engineers involved in the process of construction carry out the activities of the second stage. In most cases, architects involve themselves in the second stage of practice. However, barring some cases where architects are required to take on-site decisions as per the requirements of the building site, their role in the second stage of practice is generally limited to the activity of supervision of the building being built.

The architectural view of design thinking that I developed focuses on the first stage of the practice of architectural design, this being the stage in which the design solution, as desired by the client, is envisioned by the architect. But before we discuss the characteristics of the architectural view of design thinking, let's examine how design is understood within the practice of architectural design.

Architectural design has been defined as an art of designing *places* [17]. Places are spaces that are imbued with meaning [21]. Places therefore can be seen as artefacts through which our minds relate to the world. From the perspective of cognitive psychology, such places or artefacts can be seen as cognitive artefacts that allow us to extend our cognitive space outside our mind and into the real world. In this sense, such places function as external representations for our mind and help us in making sense of the world. The job of an architect, therefore, involves assisting clients to clarify, evolve and realise their internal representations (the client's vision) with an external one (reality), the characteristics of which evolve continuously during design. As this external representation occupies the real world, it is also the job of the architect to shape the real world to receive the artefact.

The following, then, are the key characteristics of the architectural view of design thinking:

1. As noted above, the architect's job is to transform a client's vision into reality; and therefore, a design brief (design problem) that conveys the vision of the client is the starting point of design in architectural design. The vision here refers to the characteristics of a *place* informed by a client's understanding of the design situation vis-à-vis an artefact, which in the client's view ought to occupy the design situation. Clients, in general, are not very good at preparing a design brief that accurately reflects their vision. Consequently, architectural design briefs typically contain very little, if any, information about the client's vision. They do, however, provide information about the constituents of the place, i.e. a description of an artefact (e.g. a habitable building) and the design situation or the real world (the building site) to receive the artefact.

Design briefs can vary significantly in terms of the level of details they provide – that is, sometimes they are very well articulated and sometimes they are open ended. However, architects, guided by the traditions of the profession, do not consider the given design brief as the final brief for design, regardless of the level of detail it provides [3, 8]. Instead, the vision reflected by the given design brief is considered as a tentative/preliminary vision that is further developed in collaboration with the client during design. This approach offers following advantages:

- Clients often do not seem to have enough information about the design setting, as well as the artefact to be designed that will be embedded within the design setting. This means that it is difficult, if not impossible, for them to think about a place or vision that will come into being by interaction of the design setting with the artefact. The above approach allows architects to apply their design expertise and assist their clients in articulating and realising their vision.
- This approach also gives architects an opportunity to explore their design ideas vis-à-vis the design setting and express themselves artistically while achieving their client's vision.

2. Design, as understood in architectural practice, is a pragmatic activity. It is dialogical in nature, both architect and client being collaboratively engaged in a constant dialogue with the proposed artefact vis-à-vis the design situation.

This is because design is intentional and involves directions of fit [9]. When confronted with a design situation, the architect visualises a solution to be embedded within the design setting (world-to-mind direction of fit). However, when the solution is critiqued vis-à-vis the design situation, information about the design situation as well as about the proposed design solution is thrown up which is often new to both the architect as well as the client (because it is the client who provides initial information about the design solution as well as the design situation to the architect). And this requires architects to modify the initial solution by incorporating the new information available or to replace the design solution with a new one (mind-to-world direction of fit). The architect, in collaboration with the client, continues to work in both directions of fit until the characteristics of the place, i.e. design solution vis-à-vis the design situation, *become* the vision of the client*.

This dialogical nature of design is reflected by the following actions that are carried out in no particular sequence:

Architects, adopting a *solution-first strategy*, develop design solutions(s) in response to the design brief [11]. Architects think about the design situation in terms of 'layers' when developing design solution(s). Typically, such layers include: the built environment the building site is part of, the building site, the

---

* This process has also been characterised as *reflective design* [19] and co-evolution of problem and solution [4].

built area that will occupy the building site, internal spaces of the built area and so on. Architects work with one layer at a time, in no particular sequence, to develop solutions.

The nature of such solutions is dictated by the architect's design philosophy [12] – that is, their view on way in which the design solution ought to be embedded within the design setting. At the same time, architects collect information about the design situation to be used as *constraints* to shape the design solutions [12]. Such constraints are also identified by carrying out a careful study of design projects (or *precedents*) of a similar nature and scale implemented by the architects themselves or other architects [12].

Architects do not physically construct the design solutions developed. Instead, they express them in the form of *sketches* and/or *three-dimensional scale models* made by hand or generated by computer aided design tools. Such sketches or models representing the design solution are deliberately left incomplete in terms of the content they depict, to assist architects in their thinking. This 'design-by-drawing' [10] approach allows architects to critique design solutions vis-à-vis the design situation, individually as well as with their clients, quickly and efficiently. Additionally, this approach also helps them modify already expressed design solutions in response to the critique and thus create new design solutions to be critiqued again vis-à-vis the design situation.

The tradition of critique allows architects to uncover information about the design situation. This allows architects to respond to the design situation by bringing their expertise and experience and to shape the design solution vis-à-vis the design situation in a desired manner.

The tradition of sketching/drawing allows architects to *communicate and share* design solution(s) developed not only with their immediate design team but also with collaborators located anywhere in the world. This enables architects to take advantage of specialised design knowledge available, regardless of its geographical location, to conduct critique sessions collaboratively.

3. The activities of *envisioning and making* (construction) are considered as separate activities in architectural design. It is only after the design solution has been fully detailed out and agreed upon with the client that it is handed over to another agency, in the form of detailed drawings, for its implementation or construction.

Applying the Architectural View of Design Thinking to Interaction Design: A Design Project

To show that the application of the architectural view of design thinking can offer benefits to the practice of interaction design, I carried out a design project following the design brief provided by DTRS9. While my primary role when carrying out the design project was that of a researcher, my background as an architect helped me in carrying out the design project. In this section, I provide a reflective account of the design project carried out to capture and analyse my own design activity.

As noted earlier, design is a collaborative activity where the designer works with their clients to assist them in achieving their vision. The design brief provided pointed to a user group, old people, as 'clients' for the design project. I therefore needed to identify my clients before starting on the design project.

The identification of the client for the design project was carried out on the basis of two aspects. Firstly, I avoided considering elderly people whose living environment and daily activities, as well as the issues they face, were well known to me (such as my parents and close relatives); and secondly, I avoided considering people who could not give me enough time during the design project. Keeping these aspects in mind I contacted family friends, as it was easier to convince them to give me time during design project. I was also careful in selecting these family friends, contacting the ones whom I knew well socially whilst having little or no knowledge of their living environment and everyday activities. While such people were appraised about the objective of the design project, I avoided discussing any specific issue(s) they faced to keep an open mind when carrying out the designing.

After initial discussions with some of the potential clients, Prabbhakar and Sulabha, an elderly couple in their mid 70s, were identified as my clients for the design project discussed here. Prabhakar is a retired professor from a local college and Sulabha, his wife, is a social worker. They live in a modern two-bedroom flat situated in the suburbs of Bhopal, India. The couple leads a healthy and active life. Their children live abroad and visit them from time to time.

The design project with the above-mentioned clients was then carried out over four days. Out of the four days, approximately two hours every day was devoted to discussions with my clients, firstly to learn about the design situation (i.e. about them, their living environment and their everyday activities) and then to discuss design solutions developed. As noted earlier, the architectural view of design thinking considers design as a two-stage activity consisting of envisioning and making. Following the architectural view of design thinking, in this design project the task of design was limited to envisioning the design solution to satisfy the design brief. In what follows, I provide a reflective account of the design activities carried out during the four days, a day at a time.

Day 1

The objective of the first day of the design project was to introduce my clients to the design brief provided by DTRS9 and hold discussions with them to learn more about them, their living environment and their everyday activities. I requested that we hold the meeting at their flat so that I could get a first had 'feel' of their living environment, the context for their everyday activities. I provided printed copies of the DTRS9 design

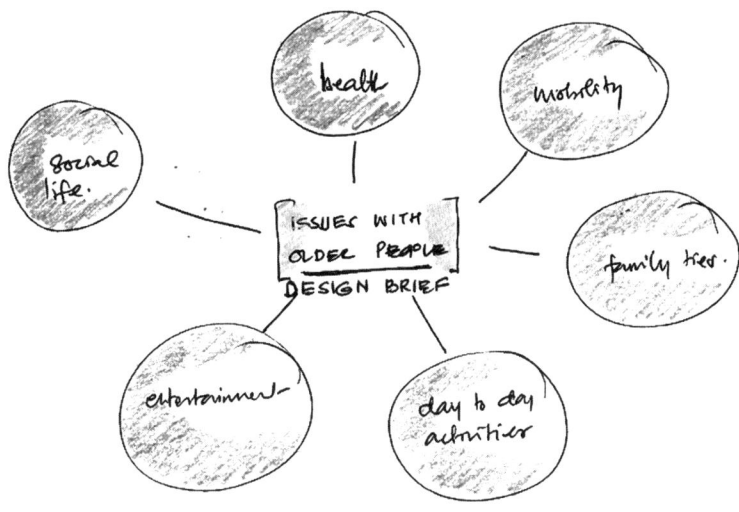

Figure 1: Decomposed sub-problems or problem spaces

brief to my clients a day before the meeting. Following the architectural view of design thinking, I requested that my clients interpret the design brief with an open mind and think about all possible issues that they face in their everyday domestic activities. The time allocated for these initial discussions was approximately two hours.

During the first hour, following the architectural view of design thinking, in collaboration with my clients, I decomposed the design situation into several areas, such as health, social life (e.g. entertaining friends at home etc.), mobility (within their living environment), family ties, entertainment and everyday activities. These decomposed areas were arrived at as a result of my discussions with my clients as well as my own understanding about the issues faced by elderly people in their living environment. The decomposition of the design situation into the above-mentioned areas allowed my clients to think about these areas one at a time and made it easier (compared to thinking about the design situation as a whole) for them to identify issues they faced.

The relevance of each such area for my clients and any issues identified by them were discussed and critiqued. The critique revealed that, out of the areas identified, the area of family ties was of immediate concern because of them being geographically separated from their children as well as their immediate family. Therefore, the area of family ties was identified for the next stage of the design process.

During the second hour, I attempted to investigate the area of family ties in detail. The visit to my clients' flat and my discussions with them allowed me to get a good understanding of their living environment as well as their everyday activities. It was noted that my clients mostly occupied the living and dining area of the flat during the day. They used this area to watch television, to have their food, to use their telephone, to read and to entertain guests during the daytime. Their *temple*, a small area of their living room designed for meditating and praying, used by them every day was also a part of this area. When asked if they missed anything in the living room, they said that it was their children and they missed being with them in that space very much. They also informed me that they have always had their children sharing this central space of the house and that, ever since their children moved out, it does not feel like the same space. Then they pointed towards their photographs and said:

> they are with us and still share the space with us, but it is not the same...

They also mentioned that they chat and talk with their children regularly, using both the phone and the Internet, but that it was their physical absence from their everyday life that was rued by them.

Developing the Design Solutions

Following the architectural view of design thinking, the next task was to develop design solutions and present them to my clients.

The information collected from my clients and their everyday environment, as well as my study of precedents from similar design situations, allowed me to think about a number of design solutions to maintain and strengthen family ties that seemed appropriate for the design situation (world-to-mind direction of fit). However, just thinking about a design solution was not enough. I also needed to think about shaping the design solutions to make them part of the given design situation.

Guided by my view about the design situation (design philosophy), I wanted my design solution(s) to merge into the central activity space used by my clients in such a way

solution 1 solution 2

Figure 2: Solution 1, Solution 2

16 Articulating Design Thinking

solution 3

Figure 3: Solution 3

that it did not stand out and did not divert my clients attention form their everyday activities. To do so, I identified the constraints offered by the design situation (i.e. furniture occupying the space, the character of activity spaces etc.) and applied them to shape the design solutions as well as identify their location of placement within the design situation (mind-to-world direction of fit). The design solutions thus developed were then expressed by free-hand sketches.

I developed a number of design solutions out of which I have included three in this chapter. All three solutions included here were developed as pair artefacts, one to be introduced within the clients' living area and another to be kept within the living area of one of their children. Both the artefacts were envisaged to be connected together via Internet and to glow when they sense presence of people around them. The idea of placing these artefacts in both these places was that both my clients and their children could sense the presence of each other in a subtle way while using their activity spaces in an everyday manner.

I developed three different versions of the artefacts to be placed in three different places within my clients living environment. Solution 1 was envisaged as a pair of lamps, one to be kept within the living area of my client and another to be kept within the living space of one of their children. Solution 2 was envisaged as a pair of artefacts to be kept in the place of worship in both residences. And Solution 3 was envisaged as a pair of artefacts to be kept in a shelf in the dining area of both residences. The places for locations of such artefacts were identified keeping in mind the intensity of activity observed in my client's living environment and it was assumed that similar areas within the residences of their children will observe similar intensity of activity.

Day 2

On the second day, I met my clients again and presented my design solutions. Using my sketches, I described the design solutions developed, one by one, to my clients. We then critiqued all these solutions collectively and collaboratively. The critique revealed that, while clients were happy with all three solutions, they were more interested in examining the advantages offered by an important aspect of such solutions: web connectivity.

> [T]he use of internet is important to us as it not only allows us to be in touch with our family through chat programs like Skype, it also allows us to pay bills and shop online. However, we find it difficult to type... particularly type in the name of the website without errors... it is extremely frustrating...

Thus, the critique of design solutions illuminated use of Internet as an aspect associated with the design situation that was missed by me as well as my clients during our previous meetings. Following the discovery of this new information about the design situation, I had another discussion with my clients and asked them about issues they encountered when using the Internet.

My clients informed me that the biggest issue they faced when using the Internet was the use of the computer. Prabhakar was a computer literate and could operate the computer in general; but he was not comfortable when using the keyboard and took a lot of time to key in any text when using the Internet. Sulabha was not a computer literate but wanted to learn and, as with her husband, it was using the keyboard that she found difficult and discouraging. Additionally, my clients mentioned that they used their computer, a desktop, from their bedroom and it required them to sit on an uncomfortable chair to operate it. They were not happy about it and wished that they had another computer, a laptop for example, that they could use from their living room and carry with them to other places as required. However, using a laptop was no different to using a desktop computer as far as the keyboard was concerned.

Thus, the issue faced by my clients was not the use of the Internet *per se*: it was the use of the keyboard, the default input device connected to the computer, to key in text when using the Internet. The identification of this issue and my knowledge of precedents addressing similar issues in a variety of design situations allowed me to think about a number of design solutions that seemed appropriate for the design situation (world-to-mind direction of fit).

Guided by my understanding of their everyday activity context, once again I wanted the artefact, the input device, to merge into their living room setting (design philosophy). Therefore, I wanted to design an artefact that was independent of the computer. At same time I wanted it to be portable, wireless and usable by my clients when they are relaxing in their living room. The artefact, however, required a screen to display it and, for this purpose, the television set, located within the living room and wirelessly connected to the artefact, was envisaged as the computer monitor. The key constraint offered by the design situation shaping the artefact was the level of computer literacy of both my clients (mind-to-world direction of fit).

Keeping the above in mind, I developed a design solution and requested another meeting with my clients.

Day 3

On the third day, then, I met my clients and discussed my first solution (Solution 1), expressed by free-hand sketches. The idea here was to develop a customised screen-based tablet, wirelessly connected to the television set that will display the output of the keyboard. I then critiqued the design solution in collaboration with my clients.

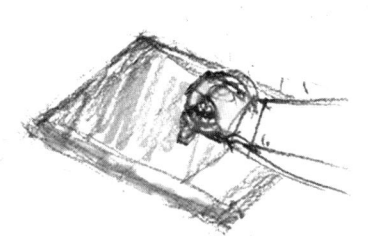

My clients were not impressed with the proposed design solution as in their view this did not really address the issue they faced. They informed me that the proposed solution is not different from a conventional keyboard and means that they would continue to have problems when using it to make text entries.

Their comments made me realise that perhaps the design solution should think of a way that minimises the usage of keys to enter any texts required.

Figure 4: Solution 1

This made me think of fiducial markers or QR codes and how they might be integrated with the input device. Fiducial markers or QR codes are essentially images that store information, such as web addresses (URLs). Such markers are beginning to appear more and more in magazines, on posters, on business cards, or on almost any object about which users might need information. Users with a camera phone, equipped with adequate reading software, can scan these codes to open a web page in their mobile phone's web browser. The following are examples of such markers/codes and their use in the field of advertising:

Figure 5

Advertisement for Greenpeace campaign http://osocio.org/message/the_big_wild_qr_codes/

Advertisement for Ralph Lauren http://blog.crowdscience.com/2011/08/qr-code-examples/

Given that such markers could be used to guide users to a particular website, I thought that they could also be used to drive an input device that could potentially allow my clients to browse the Internet with ease without the need to key in any web address (URL) at all. This approach, of course, had some limitations. Firstly, this approach assumed it would be easily possible to create marker or QR codes of the websites that were frequently visited by my clients and will be available to them in some form – either in the form of a physical book or an e-book. Secondly, this approach offered only a partial solution to the issue my clients had identified as in some cases they would still be required to use keyboard to enter various kind of text. However, this approach had the potential to visit their favourite web sites with ease and therefore I following this approach to develop design solutions. Unlike the last stage, this time I first wanted to introduce the idea of using markers/QR codes and then develop solutions along with them, and for this purpose I requested another meeting with my clients.

Day 4

After introducing the core idea of using markers/QR codes, I developed an initial solution (Solution 2) and expressed it with quick free-hand sketches. This design solution was envisaged as a lamp with an embedded web cam, located on a side table. It assumed that a book with printed markers/QR codes could then be placed under the lamp. The web cam would read the marker and display the website on the television screen.

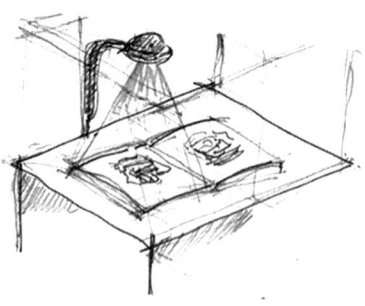

I then critiqued this solution along with my clients. They agreed that there were some positives as it eliminated the need to key in web addresses to visit their favourite websites. However, we also noted a number of negatives with this solution. Firstly, it was not a portable artefact. While it was not a major negative, my clients did not like its non-portability. Secondly, the solution did not allow navigation through the website. This means that another artefact, such as a mouse, was needed to navigate the website displayed on the television.

Figure 6: Solution 2

In response to this critique, I developed and presented Solution 3 to my clients. This solution envisaged a web cam being mounted on their reading glasses. They could then 'read' the printed marker book with glasses on. The web cam then read the markers and displayed the corresponding website on the television. Having glasses embedded into their reading glasses meant that they would interact with the artefact from any place within their living room.

Figure 7: Solution 3

I then critiqued this solution with my clients, who liked its portability. However, they pointed out that navigating the website was still a problem and an additional device was required along with this solution to browse the Internet.

At this time, I began to consider the idea of having an e-book of markers instead of a printed book. There were a number of advantages offer by an e-book as it was possible to display it on a variety of portable devices. I then developed Solution 4.

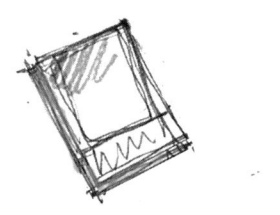

Figure 8: Solution 4

Solution 4 was envisaged as a Kindle-like device that would display the markers, accompanied by text providing a short description of the website. The user was then required to browse through the markers and select a marker of their choice by pressing a button. The television would then display the website associated with the marker. The user could then navigate through the web site by using up and down keys.

The critique of this solution with my clients revealed that they did not like the idea of navigating the website using up and down keys. This, obviously, was a major negative associated with this design solution.

Figure 9: Solution 5

At this time, I was beginning to think about using touch screen displays as they offered the required interactivity necessary for the solution. The next design solution (Solution 5) was therefore developed on a touch-screen platform. The screen displayed markers (each accompanied by information about its associated website) which could be selected by touching the screen; the television would then display the website. Once the website was displayed, the phone would work as a track pad facilitating navigation through the web site.

Figure 10: The design solution that uses touch phones to use the Internet

The critique of this solution suggested that my clients really liked it and could not envisage any negatives. However, I was beginning to question the need to display markers on screen, along with text regarding the website associated with them, as they were no longer being 'read' by a camera. Instead, the solution was using markers as hyperlinked images.

Why not replace the markers with images of the home page of the websites? I thought that this was a good idea as users could see visuals and thus get a better idea about the websites. I discussed this solution (Solution 6) with my clients, which replaces markers with images of the home page of their favourite websites while retaining all the functionality of the previous solution (Solution 5).

Once again, I critiqued this solution along with my clients and was happy to note that they accepted my design solution and were happy with it. However, they wanted to evaluate a working prototype of the design solution – which remains to be developed at this stage.

Thus, an interactive artefact, an input device to facilitate easy use of Internet, was envisioned using an architectural view of design thinking. The feedback received from my clients indicated that the envisaged artefact, if realised, had the potential to achieve the vision expressed by the DTRS9 brief.

Discussion

The design project discussed in the previous section underlines the application of some of the key aspects associated with using the architectural view of design thinking to bring an interactive artefact into being. A number of these aspects originating from architectural design as well as other more traditional design disciplines, such as early focus on users, design iterations, prototyping and so forth, have already incorporated by the practice of interaction design (even though their success has been questioned). However, some other aspects associated with the architectural view of design thinking, such as separation of the stages of envisioning and making, a design-by-drawing approach, rejection of the given design brief and solution-first strategy, have yet to receive adequate attention in the practice of interaction design. In this section I discuss how such aspects assisted me when engaged in the design project.

1. Separation of envisioning and making

    As noted earlier, the architectural view of design thinking considers design as an activity consisting of two distinct stages, envisioning and making. The separation of the activities of envisioning and making allows designer to focus fully on the envisioning stage and leave the task of implementing the design solution to others who are more competent in the process of implementation.

    Following this view, I confined myself to the task of envisioning the artefact when working on the design project. I could go through a number of iterations, critique them in collaboration with my clients and then arrive at the final solution without physically making the artefact. Limiting myself to the envisioning stage also helped because I do not have the competency to implement the design solution envisioned by me and require assistance from other professionals who are more competent than me to implement the solution.

    Given the complex nature of interaction design artefacts and the competencies required to realise them, I believe that the field of interaction design can benefit from a clearer separation of the activities of envisioning and making.

2. Design by drawing

    The separation of activities as per the architectural view of design thinking means that the designer does not actually make/implement the design solution. However, the designer needs to express the design solution in some form to critique it in collaboration with their clients. The design-by-drawing approach represents a practice in architectural design following which the designer makes sketches and drawings to represent design solutions without actually making/implementing the artefact. The advantages of a design-by-drawing approach for design have been noted and discussed by researchers [10].

    The design solutions developed during the design project were all expressed using sketches. Following the tradition of sketching in architectural design, such sketches were deliberately left incomplete to aid thinking during the process of critique. The clients reacted well to the incomplete nature of the sketches in both positive and negative manner and that assisted them as well me in moving forward with design iterations.

    Research in interaction design is beginning to acknowledge the importance of sketching for the activity of design [e.g. 2]. However, how sketching assists designers in developing design solutions is yet to receive adequate attention in interaction design research.

3. Rejection of the given design brief

   Rejection of the given design brief as such is an important aspect of the architectural view of design thinking. As noted earlier, the rejection of a given design brief allows architects to assist their clients in articulating their vision. Additionally, this approach indicates that this view of design thinking recognises the presence of multiple solutions for any given design situation.

   The brief given by the DTRS9 was an open-ended one and therefore already pointed to the possibility of several design solutions for the given design situation. Following the architectural view of design thinking, keeping the open-ended nature of the design brief in mind, the brief was considered as tentative. Then, through a development of design solutions, the brief was further articulated in collaboration with my clients.

   The design brief, known as the requirement document, is an important document within the practice of interaction design. However, unlike architects, interaction designers accept the brief as given. Doing so usually takes them towards a particular solution which may not necessarily be the right one for the given design situation. Therefore, I believe that interaction design practice can benefit by adapting this aspect associated with the architectural view of design thinking.

4. Solution-first strategy

   The solution-first strategy is an approach where the designer develops design solutions as a way to understand the given design situation [11]. It is an established way of knowing about a design situation during which designers, in collaboration with their client, are engaged in a dialogue with the design situation. Following this approach, designers do not wait for analysis of the design situation to be completed and start developing design solutions as soon as they receive the design brief. Therefore, in a way, this approach can be seen as a bottom-up approach to articulate a client's vision for a given design situation.

   In the design project carried out, I began developing design solutions after I received the design brief and had an initial meeting with my client. As discussed, I critiqued the design solution developed in collaboration with my clients and, as a result, a couple of facets of the design situation were illuminated that had been missed during our meetings. Development of design solutions therefore allowed me to make sense of the design situation effectively efficiently and allowed me to articulate my clients' vision.

   The practice of interaction design continues to work with an 'analysis first and design later' approach which has been criticised [14]. I believe that, given the nature of the design situation being confronted by the field of interaction design, the solution-first strategy could prove to be very useful. In particular, the discipline of interaction design can benefit because of its multidisciplinary nature. The solutions developed by interaction designers coming from a variety of educational backgrounds are likely to be of a diverse nature allowing us to understand different aspects of the problem space.

Thus the above-mentioned aspects associated with the architectural view of design thinking benefited me during the design project and can benefit the practice of interaction design. The practice of interaction design could also benefit by adopting the view of design informed by the architectural way of design thinking in a holistic manner. Currently, the practice of interaction design views design as craft or making and the designer as a skilled craftsman [15]. This view of design is akin to the unselfconscious view of design where the designer, guided by traditions, carries out the activity of design [1]. The architectural view of design is akin to the self-conscious view of design [1], which is more mature and holistic. I believe that this is a richer view of design compared to the view of design prevalent in the field of interaction design and can offer benefits to the interaction design practice.

Conclusions

In this chapter, I have noted that our understanding of design within the field of interaction design can be enhanced through a closer study of the architectural view of design thinking. I have illuminated some of the features of the architectural view of design thinking and have shown how the architectural view of design thinking can be applied to bring an interactive artefact into being. I have also underlined some of the aspects of this view of design thinking that appear to offer some advantages to the designer carrying out the activity of design. I believe that a deeper examination of the architectural view of design thinking could illuminate further benefits for the practice of interaction design.

References

1. Alexander, C. (1964) *Notes on the Synthesis of Form*, Cambridge: Harvard University Press.
2. Buxton, B. (2007) *Sketching User Experiences: Getting the Design Right and the Right Design*, Morgan Kaufmann.
3. Cross, N. (2007) 'Forty Years of Design Research', *Design Research Quarterly* 2, 1, 3–5.
4. Dorst, K. and Cross, N. (2001) 'Creativity in the Design Process: co-evolution of problem solution', *Design Studies*, 22, pp.425–37.
5. Deshpande, P. (2009) 'Bringing an interactive artifact into being: Examining the use of an architectural design model in interaction design', unpublished doctoral thesis, University of Limerick, Ireland.
6. Fallman, D. (2008) 'The interaction design research triangle of design practice, design studies, and design exploration', *Design Issues* 24 (3), p.4.
7. Forlizzi, J., Zimmerman, J. and Evenson, S. (2008) 'Crafting a Place for Interaction Design Research in HCI', *Design Issues* 24(3), pp.19–29.

8. Harfield, S. (2007) 'On design "problematization": Theorising differences in designed outcomes', *Design Studies*, vol. 28, pp.159–73.
9. Heylighen, A., Cavallin, H. and Bianchin, M. (2009) 'Design in Mind', *Design Issues*, 25 (1), pp.94–105.
10. Jones, J.C. (1992) *Design methods*, second edition, New York: Van Nostrand Reinhold.
11. Lawson, B. (1979) 'Cognitive Strategies in Architectural Design', *Ergonomics*, vol. 22, pp.59–68.
12. Lawson, B. (2006) *How Designers Think, Fourth Edition: The Design Process Demystified*, 4th Edition, Architectural Press.
13. Löwgren, J. (1995) 'Applying design methodology to software development', in *DIS '95: Proceedings of the 1st conference on Designing interactive systems*, New York, NY, USA, ACM, pp.87–95.
14. Löwgren, J. (2001) 'From HCI to interaction design', in Chen, Q. (ed.) *Human Computer Interaction: Issues and Challenges*, Hershey, PA: IGI Publishing, pp.29–43.
15. Löwgren, J. and Stolterman, E. (2004) *Thoughtful Interaction Design: A Design Perspective on Information Technology*, MIT Press.
16. Nelson, H.G. and Stoltermann, E. (2003) *The Design Way: intentional change in an unpredictable world*, Englewood Cliffs, NJ: Educational Technology Publications.
17. Norberg-Schulz, C. (1980) *Genius Loci: Towards a Phenomenology of Architecture*, New York: Rizzoli.
18. Rittel, H.W. and Webber, M.M. (1974) 'Dilemmas in general theory of planning', *Design Research and Methods*, 8 (1), pp.31–9.
19. Schön, D.A. (1983) *The Reflective Practitioner: How professionals think in action*, London: Temple Smith.
20. Stolterman, E. (2008) 'The nature of design practice and implications for interaction design research', *International Journal of Design*, 2 (1), pp.55–65.
21. Unwin, S. (1997) *Analysing Architecture*, London: Routledge.

Maria ANTONIETTA SBORDONE
Seconda Università di Napoli (SUN)
IDEAS, Department of Industrial Design, Environment and History

WORK DRESS DESIGN: A CASE STUDY ON THE EMPOWERMENT OF HUMAN ABILITIES

Introduction

Dress as an Experience-based System: Work Dress Design (WDD)

A strong correlation exists between the design of work clothes and the evolution of late-modern industrial products: the artefacts which entail complex systems of services available on today's industrial scene increasingly tend to include experiences as new forms of value. The experience-based commodity, or the 'ing the thing' theorised by Pine and Gilmore [5], makes design a growingly complex process, which places man in a mutual, evolving relationship with the products. Experiences transform the subjects who, in turn, transform the goods.

The aim of work dress design (WDD) is to meet the latent needs emerging from the analysis of how the human body performs as it changes due to physical strain and the passing of time. WDD introduces innovation to allow the clothes to change with their user, based on the experiences of those who wear them: they interact physically and biologically, they constantly adjust to changing situations and respond to external stimuli.

The project originates from the observation of the changes and strains a woman's body has to cope with in the elderly and pre-elderly age. The increasing ageing of the population entails a growing demand for underwear and freestyle clothes that may adjust to the everyday transformations of the body. The clothes used for this type of

WDD exert a mechanical action, which reshapes the silhouette and affects posture, thus improving the body's performances remarkably. An equally important innovation concerns the advanced textile materials used, whose thermo-regulating, antibacterial and skin-nourishing action lead to greater comfort and prevention against damage. It's an active system, which produces adjustment, protection, safety and prevention with a view to improving and intensifying daily actions autonomously.

Work clothes, therefore, no longer relate to the needs of a general worker but change to suit their users, making the workers' experiences the focus of the clothes' performances by reacting in an active, rather than passive, way.

Towards Hi-dress Design

Bio-technology today produces real innovation by making available high-utility technology which 'dilates spaces and consciousness' [1] and aims at creating an aware interaction between the user and the world of artefacts.

The collaboration between scientific research and work dress design leads to experimentations in the field of specialised clothing and advanced fabrics. The phrase 'wearable electronics' describes all those products in the area of clothing which experiment with the combination of a variety of electronic tools to be used in leisure or with a view to health and safety at work. The temporary joint ventures of brands operating in different sectors resulted in a few major achievements: Philips and Levi Strauss, for instance, created clothes combining MP3 readers and GSM mobile phones.

The most interesting innovations, however, are produced in the branch of research which combines electronic technologies and advanced fabrics: interactive dresses, for instance, make it possible to monitor the health of those who wear them remotely by means of sensors embedded in the fabric; medical dresses make it possible to deal with specific health or hygiene issues thanks to microcapsules containing medical substances. Self-cleaning fabrics protecting from extreme temperatures (Mit Lab) by means of genetically modified bacteria; threads as light as silk, like Biosteel (Nexia Biotechnologies, Quebec), which make people invulnerable; and garments that oppose skin ageing or allergies are only some of the possible applications.

In such a context, work dress design can make use of advanced technologies but also of strategies suitable for the creation of highly specialised brand-related garments. Through the strong link between biology and technology it is possible to deal with peculiar working conditions, securing work health and safety. The (WDD) work dress, originally a protective and passive garment, becomes an active protagonist, signalling health and safety problems and thus preventing accidents. Identity, safety, usefulness of the work dress (in terms of the useful technologies described by Fabris [2]) and an ethical aesthetic sense are at the heart of work dress design, which brings together new design cultures and fashion design; a sector that comes up with significant creations, inspired by the most advanced scenarios and overcoming the narrowness of hi-dress design.

Freestyling or Clothes for All

Work dress represents that part of technical clothing which expresses specialisation and comfort, producing an evident, though temporary, sense of belonging in those who wear it. Work clothes are designed to ease physical performances in terms of motor activities and to secure a high degree of health and safety at work. These can be defined as the minimum requirements that common work wear should necessarily meet.

The function of covering or protecting oneself is a sort of meta-function which, at a higher level of meaning, qualifies the dress concept by terms such as distinction, communication and identification. The higher level is established by the dress code, which affects the practices of employment, setting up a set of rules for use ranging from the combination of the various elements to wear to the recognition of the context in which they are worn and to the behaviour to adopt.

In the case of work clothes, dress codes take on the difficult task of codifying specific everyday needs, regulated by sector-specific norms; in addition, being instances of work dress design, the design inputs activated in the cognitive process lead, more and more often, to the constant interaction of different skills and expertise in the practice of the creative process.

The interdisciplinary contributions to the process enhance a knowledge transfer which stimulates design in creative groups where each member performs his or her task by sharing in the specialised skills available in the group. In this context, work dress is viewed as a field of experimentation in applied research, with a remarkable economic impact on industrial research as well. Actually, when it concerns the design of specialised technical clothes, work dress overlaps with that particular sector of sportswear which draws inspiration from technological and process innovation.

Direct experimentation on materials mostly depends on an ability to imagine innovative processes stimulated by the anticipation of new cognitive models which affects technological transfer and industrial processes, pushing them beyond their usual limits.

Work dress design led by creative groups and supported by interdisciplinary research moves away from the idea of fashion meant as a constant updating of styling. The causes for this are to be found in the gap between the two macro-sectors, which concerns the concept of time: for styling, being there before anyone else is crucial, as it means leading the game; for work dress, instead, time acquires an extra value in slowness: work clothes represent the brand and, as such, they may renovate themselves, replace some parts, use different materials or colours, but actually they do not change at all. A brand that survives through time is a most prestigious one because it rests on a strong identity, conveying solid values. Its consensus takes the shape of customer retention. Work dress as a non-product of the brand is free from styling and opens the season of freestyling, thus becoming the super-specialised dress with its own identity-marking dress code.

The Poverist Dress

Back in the 1920s, the Florence-born brothers Ernesto and Ruggero Michaelles wished to revolutionise ways of dressing using Futurist logic and introduced the unprecedented type, the 'overall'. Launched in 1911, it appeared three years before Rodchenko's 'dress of revolution for comrade workers' which also was an overall. Thayaht, a fictional name, imbued with Futurist culture, designed the poverist dress in a reaction to the high price of fabrics and clothes, taking on a revolutionary position and siding against the prevailing logic of fashion *tout-court* which was not at all part of the cultural debate that was extending to include all areas of human activity. Alongside Thayaht, progressive intellectuals and aristocrats adopted, arguably before the working class, what was viewed as the most daring dress of the time – the overall, which was shown off during 'overalls required' receptions. Later on, thousands of people adopted the overall, also because it came with the paper pattern needed for self-production – a surplus value which, once again, turned out to be a veritable invention, as it was a forerunner of the service economy that would appear on the economic scene several decades later.

In the summer of 1920, the Florence-based newspaper *La Nazione* distributed the paper pattern of the overall designed with a view to economising: 'saving energy' because it made movements easier by adhering to the main lines of the body and guaranteeing greater freedom of movement; 'saving on fabric and seams', as it was produced with very little material, few seams and buttons; 'saving on garments', since an overall doesn't need a jacket, a jumper or a shirt, collars, cuffs or braces; 'saving time' as it takes much less to put it on and take it off. The socio-cultural climate in which the whole story took place was marked by a few significant events: since 1912, Balla had been fighting the '*abito passatista epidermico scolorito funebre decadente noioso antigienico*'; Marinetti created the manifesto 'Against Female luxury'; Lydia de Liguoro, editor of *Lidel* and promoter of a campaign against the excesses of fashion, spread the message 'don't buy', following the suggestions of the Milan Women's Fasces.

The Dress as a Commodity

The creative process is the common element to artists, designers and industrialists, all of whom assume a context, choose a given design procedure and then select a way to spread it. Being mainly functional clothes, work clothes perform a number of different tasks, including communicating the idea of belonging and making it one's own in the best way possible. They reveal their function and therefore are style-free – free from fashion and styling. This might appear as a disadvantage at first, because they lack seasonal references and orientations. The deliberate detachment from fashion places this area of design under an unchallengeable aura, while granting it a close dialogue with styling, and offering itself as a counter-attraction for all those who, at work or in their free time, consciously choose to wear specialised clothing. Each sector tends to define a field of action in order to make its own commodity categories emerge. Freestyling mainly depends on considering clothes as elements to dress the body, replacing clothes in a wider context, as the communicative interface of a moving body in very diverse fields of action and interaction.

Clothes Types and Structure

The dress breaks down into layers and becomes a commodity, in the guise of a foreign body, of a structure made up of overlapping pieces, like a prosthesis or several patches. Commodity-garments make up protecting layers and interfaces for communication. Above all a technical dress, the garment features a degree of updating which makes it the champion of technological and formal innovation. The design process highlights the conception of the dress as a whole, each and every part of which has its own shape, technical content and performance; it adheres and adjusts to the body as much as possible and eases its movements, which change from one working context to the other. In a general conception, some flexible areas are highlighted, identified as **adaptive areas**, which are treated mainly with elastic materials. Thanks to their flexibility and adaptability, these materials follow the size variations of the moving body, expanding or shrinking accordingly. They mime and functionally follow the changing morphology of the muscles and tendons that contract, expand, stretch… especially at the knee and elbow, where the different densities of the materials used enhance adaptability. Alongside adaptive areas are **collaborative areas**, which aim at protecting the parts of the body that are most exposed to traumas or constant pressure, defending them from indoor pollution and chemical risk and protecting the parts of the dress which are most liable to wear and tear.

Materials and Technologies

The study of materials and technologies gives a crucial contribution, with the aim of optimising needs and achieving the best performance. Materials are chosen on the basis of the performance required; they are modified or adapted by affecting directly their composition or by combining them with other materials to compensate for any weaknesses, thus completing the list of essential requirements for use. A material is chosen for its ability to guarantee the best performances in terms of heat exchange: in the areas most exposed to wear and tear, thicknesses are calibrated and, if necessary, reinforced by combining them with special materials; pre-formed parts are designed to protect certain parts of the body, acting as a sort of body shell that guides the right posture and eases traumas.

Analysis of Life Contexts

the scenario has taken as an example the so-called 'Bloomers' that see life as a constant, difficult experimentation with products and services. Once the critical thresholds have been crossed, new dynamics and, most importantly, new psycho-physical balances appear which must be taken care of by means of specially designed, *ad hoc* products.

The sixth world economic summit, 'Europe and the Demographic Challenge', launched a serious warning. The European population is declining and as early as 2050 the mean age will go up to 49. Only a century ago the population of Europe accounted for 15 per cent of the whole world population – a ratio which will be reversed by three times in 2050.

Figure 1: Domestic activities – unloading the car

This translates into an 'older' society, requiring more care and more services in the health sector. The generational turnover will affect economic dynamism and the levels of innovation to achieve. The increased average longevity also entails a greater risk for psychic conditions leading to depression. According to the WHO, depression will have become one of the world's most widespread diseases by 2020, while the symposium of the American Psychiatric Association highlighted the need to identify new challenges and devise new trends to spur innovation in pharmacology.

The natural decay process taking place with ageing highlights a consumption, and consequent weakening, of the muscles. The reduced volume and functionality of the muscles is accompanied by a slow atrophy of the bone structure and the stiffening of joints. The result of this is a loss of strength which causes the stooped, uncertain walking typical of old age.

Analysis

The methodology of analysis included daily monitoring of a woman in pre-elderly age during her everyday activities.

Photographic analysis of the activities

The photo sequences collected show some of the most common activities including: unloading the car (Fig. 1); lifting and moving books whilst standing on a ladder (Fig. 2); lifting and placing weights (Fig. 3).

Photo analysis of the postures

Over the years, everyday activities, poor posture and disease produce irreversible changes in the body. Wrong postures compromise the muscle balance and gradually deform the bone structure which contracts the muscles, producing fragility, intense and frequent pain.

The following photo sequences show the most common postures adopted during rest due to body changes, including: amplification of sagittal curves and scoliosis at the spine level (Fig. 4); postures typical of the seating position (Fig. 5); posture during walking (Fig. 6).

Photographic observation made it possible to examine all the most stressed parts of the body, which need to be protected and helped in order to work safely without being hurt. The analysis of the body of a woman in her 60s highlighted its most fragile parts and, at the same time, the parts suffering the greatest stress and deriving pathologies.

Results

The main symptoms recorded are the following: cervical spine – cervical lordosis; shoulder joints – evident signs of 'closed shoulders'; winged scapula; wrist joint – persisting inflammation; lumbar area – lordosis; abdominal area – relaxed tissues stretching the lumbar rachis and causing flexing of the hip to compensate for the unbalance produced.

In addition to these evident symptoms – which cause major unbalances and alterations both in the posture and in the general balance of the exoskeleton, due to everyday actions whose effects are no longer controlled – there are alterations caused by traumas.

Even following a minor or underestimated trauma, the body will always try to adapt and find a new balance to be safe from pain. Body segments arrange themselves

Figure 2: Domestic activities – lifting and moving books whilst standing on a ladder

Figure 3: Domestic activities – lifting and placing weights

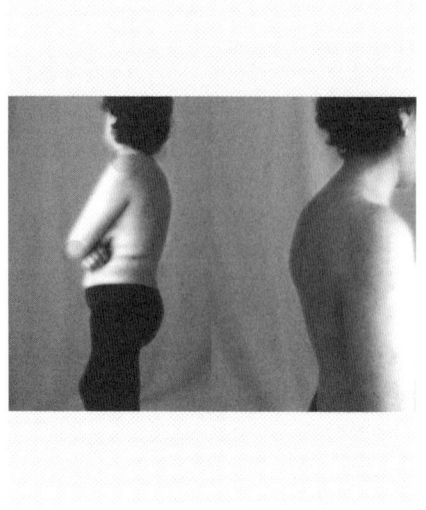

Figure 4: Common postures – amplification of sagittal curves and scoliosis at the spine level

Figure 5: Common posture typical of the seating position

breaking the static balance, recruiting muscles which are not normally used for certain movements and thus overloading certain joints. This is a defence reaction compensating for damage. The areas at highest risk of trauma and inflammation are those which are most exposed to stress and which suffer deformations; but it is possible to intervene with a contrasting action in order to achieve a re-balanced posture.

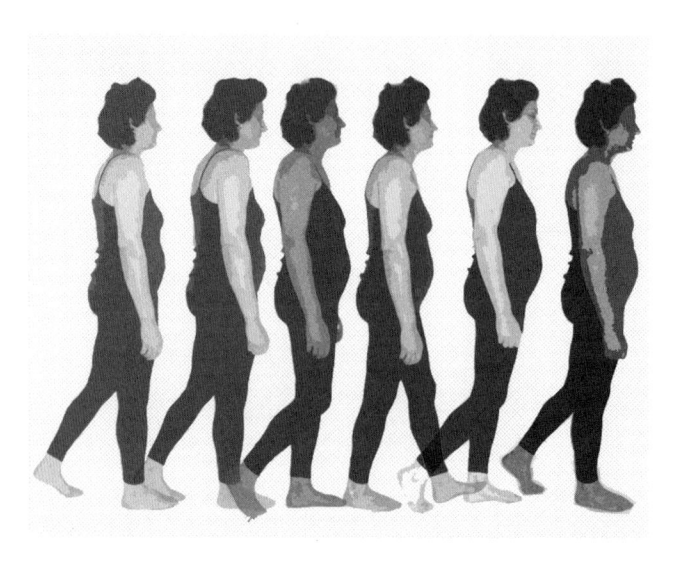

Figure 6: Common posture during walking

Treat, Support, Re-shape, Protect

The product's concept took into account a few materials of recent conception like Cognis, with its microencapsulated fabrics, and INDAS, which produces yarns using silver and ceramic to obtain antistatic and antibacterial fabrics.

The morphology of the human body and the careful observation of the movements involved in everyday actions have highlighted the most active – and hence most fragile – parts of the body. The resulting clothes follow the shape of the body and the location of muscles and their combinations during movements. It must be considered that movements are very slow which means the pressure due to weights is greater. For this reason weights must be well supported and must transit as quickly as possible.

The best type of clothes was based on the combination of several garments following the structure of the muscles and stressing the lines defining and separating one area from another. These areas define some strong lines which shape the garments generating a flexible frame which surrounds the body in an elastic net, easing and controlling movements at the same time.

Each garment is shaped following a number of elements: 'empowerment of critical areas' to respond better to efforts; 'protection' for protection against traumas; 'compression' to cope with an excessive relaxation of tissues; 'support' to keep a balanced structure and improve performance and comfort.

The use of a variety of textile materials contributed to the development of the garments, taking into account application rules suited to each garment such as the use of unperceivable shockproof supports in the most stressed parts; the use of compression fabrics able to reshape the silhouette and, most importantly, to produce a constant wellbeing.

Conclusions

The analysis on the field brought to light the causes – physical activities performed over long periods of time, diseases, traumas – whose effects transform the body which assumes wrong, degenerative postures. The aim of the project is to improve the life conditions of women in elderly and pre-elderly age, supporting them in their everyday activities. With reference to the risks and efforts the women may be subject to, the project wishes to provide a new 'shell' which may support, empower and compress the most sensitive areas.

Images of the Collection

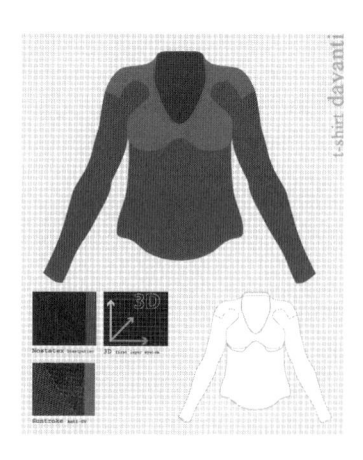

36 Articulating Design Thinking

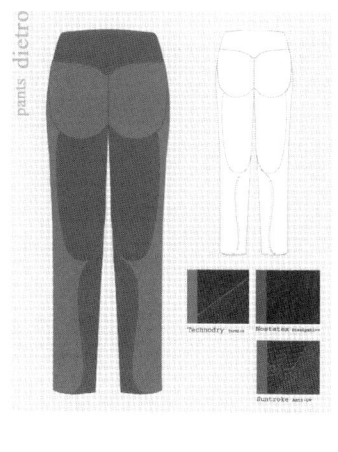

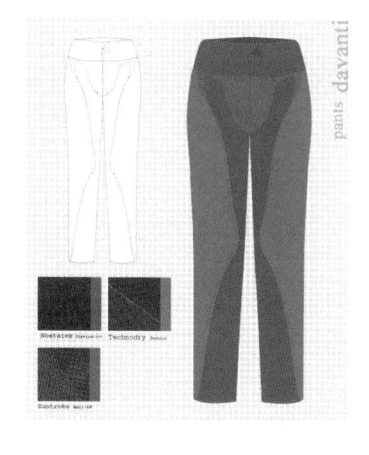

References

1. Fabris, G. (2003) Il nuovo consumatore: verso il postmoderno, Milano: Franco Angeli.
2. Fabris, G. and Minestroni, L. (2000) Valore e valori della marca, Milano: Franco Angeli.
3. Muniz, A. and O'Guinn, T. (2001) *Brand Community*, University of Chicago Press.
4. Norman, D.A. (2000) *Emotional design*, New York: Basic Books.
5. Pine, J. and Gilmore, J. (2000) L'economia delle esperienze, Milano: Etas.
6. Maalouf, A. (1998) Les identités meurtrières, Parigi: Grasset.
7. Maffesoli, M. (1998) Au creux des apparences. Pour une éthique de l'esthétique, Parigi: Plon.
8. Morin, E. (2003) L'identità umana e la sfida della convivenza, Varese: Scheiwiller.
9. Nancy, J.-L. (2001) Essere singolare plural, Paris: Galilée.
10. Appadurai, A. (2000) Modernità in polvere, Minneapolis-London.
11. Cavalli Sforza, L.L. (2006) L'evoluzione della cultura, Torino: Codice Edizioni.
12. Ceppi, G. and Gafforio, L. (2000) Neomerci trans cutanee, Milano: Modo.
13. Combi, M. (2000) Corpo e Tecnologie Rappresentazioni e Immaginari, Milano: Meltemi.
14. De Kerckhove (2000) La pelle della cultura, Milano: Editori associati.
15. Giachetti, M. (2001) Corpo e realtà virtuale, Milano: Modo.
16. Husserl, E. (2005) Libro dello spazio, Milano: Guerini e associate.
17. Mangiarotti, R. (2005) Design del corpo Brain technology, Milano: Modo.
18. Morace, F. (2000) Previsioni e presentimenti. Stili di pensiero per un futuro ormai presente, Milsano: Sperling & Kupfer.
19. Mulvey, L. (1998) Visual and Other Pleasures, Bloomington: Indiana University Press.

20. Rifkin, J. (2000) L'era dell'accesso, la rivoluzione della new economy, Milano: Mondadori.
21. Gorz, A. (2003) L'immatériel. Connaissance, valeur et capital, Paris: Galilèe.
22. Gorz, A. (2004) Métamorphoses du travali. Critique de la raison économique, Paris: Folio essias.
23. Antonacci, F. and Lapiccirella, D. (2004) Thayaht e Ram da Futurismo al Novecento, from Giacomo Balla 'Manifesto Futurista Il vestito antineutrale'.
24. Carmagnola, F. (2001) Vezzi insulsi e frammenti di storia universal, Roma: Luca Sossella.
25. Thachara, J. (2000) *Design after modernism*, London: Thames and Hudson.
26. Florida, R. (2003) *The Rise of the Creative Class*, Milano: Mondadori Editore.
27. Fortunati, L., Kats, J. and Riccini, R. (2002) Prospettive sul corpo. Il corpo umano tra tecnologie comunicazione e moda, Milano: Franco Angeli.
28. Lipovetsky, G. (2000) L'empire de l'éphémère, Paris: Folio essais Gallimard.
29. Lipovetsky, G. (1998) L'ère du vide, Paris: Folio essais Gallimard.
30. Marcellini, M. (2003) Lezione di comunicazione nuove prospettive di interpretazione e di ricerca, Gruppo Editoriale Esselibri.
31. Prece, J., Rogers, Y. and Sharp, H. (2002) *Interaction Design Beyond human-computer interaction*, John Wiley & Sons.
32. Zucchermaglio, C. and Alby, F. (2005) Gruppi e tecnologie a lavoro, Bari: Laterza.

Richard HERRIOTT

Department of Design, Aarhus School of Architecture

AND

Birgitte GEERT JENSEN

Department of Design, Aarhus School of Architecture

STUDENTS' RESPONSES TO INCLUSIVE DESIGN

Introduction

Students at the Aarhus School of Architecture carried out a project in the 7th semester which was intended to focus on health and welfare. For this semester, ending 24 May 2011, the theme for their assignment was to design an object or service for use in a domestic setting (either in a private residence or a managed care home). The goal of the exercise was to use inclusive design to give the students a range of tools and strategies to work within a complex, contemporary problem area. This was also a project to explore the design implications surrounding the sense of health and well-being. The assignment was designed to give the students experience of developing an object's aesthetic qualities and it was one in which the possibilities for interaction were given a high priority. In the case of industrial design students, users were placed at the centre of the exercise. Students with an architectural interest could approach the project from the viewpoint of the experience of space and its furnishings.

The completed projects included food packaging for delivered meals, a cooking service for elderly people, furniture, a cafe, a work station for the visually impaired, outdoor furniture, a sitting room, a lamp, a dining room table and chair set, a device for use in case of falls, a mobile communication device and a service design for elderly people. There were eight project diaries collected from this class (fewer than the total number of students). The data was collated and analysed for work patterns.

This chapter is structured as follows: a literature review is followed by a background section in which are explained inclusive design, design methodology and the students' course work. The section titled 'Theoretical Aspects' introduces the inclusive design model from the Cambridge Engineering Design Centre and puts it in the context of soft systems models. Then a section on methodology explains how the data was gathered and analysed. The results are then presented graphically. The conclusions are discussed in the final section.

Literature Review

The literature on inclusive design teaching tends to look at examples of students' work [1] and issues related to the sociology of introducing new material into the curriculum [2,3] or else it considers ID from a meta-level, as in Callanan et al. [4]. This latter study's aim was to research existing practices in universal design teaching both in Ireland and internationally. Stappers et al. [5] looked at how a specific user-centred approach was operationalised in a classroom setting but this paper did not go into detail concerning the application of the methods to particular projects. Instead, the project 'presents a review of five years' user-centred education in the mainstream industrial design engineering curriculum'. A more detailed examination is found in Kose et al. [6]. In this case, the report gets closer to the students' activities: 'The teaching basically comprised... lectures on disabilities and universal design concepts, simulation activities of changing abilities due to disability or ageing, then group or individual design survey and proposal followed.' There is some consideration given to the different responses of architecture compared to design students. The paper doesn't look into the design processes used within the project, rather at their outcomes. Similarly, Hewer [7] looked at how design competitions arranged by agencies and organisations outside educational institutions could affect students' chosen design methods. Among these competitions were some related to ageing and disability. Some individual cases were chosen for discussion. Primarily the outcomes were examined rather than the course of the design process itself. What was focused on was the changed way students related to users which was to view them as 'design advisors'. The main focus was on the teaching itself, rather than the results. Dong [8] discusses some of the problems teaching inclusive design over a three-year test period. These are to do with the practical matters of combining large class sizes with intensive user interaction, ethical problems, a lack of interdisciplinary co-operation and, finally, a lack of case studies of the 'appropriate level and depth'. In Dong's pilot studies, the classes all worked on the same problem. For example, in year one all the students worked on a project to redesign earplugs and in year three all the students redesigned a pill dispenser. For the first project, personas were the main study method and, for the third year, observations, focus groups and user-testing were carried out. The paper also considers students' own reactions to inclusive design methods.

What is indicated in this review of literature is that studies of inclusive design, in the context of teaching, do not focus on the design process itself. Rather, the interest is primarily in how to introduce the subject and how to structure teaching programmes.

Background

This chapter asks what work patterns emerge when students use inclusive design methods. 'Inclusive design, as one of the many user-centred design approaches... has the potential to help students appreciate user capabilities, needs and expectations: a first step towards user-led innovation' [8]. According to the British Standards Institution [9], inclusive design is the 'design of mainstream products and/or services that are accessible to, and usable by, as many people as reasonably possible on a global basis, in a wide variety of situations and to the greatest extent possible without the need for special adaptation or specialised design' [9]. Pattison and Stedmon phrase the matter this way: 'Inclusive design aims to cater for as many users as possible and therefore incorporate diverse user requirements – it is therefore more of a design philosophy than an end product' [10]. The Aarhus School of Architecture incorporates ergonomics, user-centred design and ID in its teaching activities. Its activities follow the strategy cited by Macdonald: students on the Glasgow Product Design Engineering (PDE) course are taught 'context, people models, inclusive and universal design principles and a typology of user research methods' [11]. At Aarhus this teaching involves courses in the use of ergonomic methods and inclusive design strategies. The latter course makes use of simulators to encourage students' empathy with the conditions of users who fall outside the ergonomic mainstream. These simulators include vision-altering glasses and devices to affect manual dexterity. Students are often profoundly surprised by the experience. Students are also taught how to locate and use a variety of ergonomic references and databases in order to reduce the tendency to assume that what works for them will work for others. Students can also receive individual tutoring in the ergonomics issues related to their own project.

The students' coursework prior to their assignment alternated between brief lectures, presentations, group work, knowledge collection in the field and production of mock-ups. The first phase started with theory on user involvement and fieldwork. Students were presented with information on interviews (qualitative and quantitative), focus groups, and observational methods where patterns of action, working procedure and 'silent knowledge' could be monitored. The purpose of the fieldwork was primarily to analyse the everyday life and needs of the elderly and to create an understanding of the complexities of problems the chosen target group may have.

Students were then asked to examine concepts around idea development. The purpose was, in other words, to find solutions to the problems observed through the analysis of results and the use of a number of creative methods. This was done by means of the following four idea development phases: (1) establishing a new mindset, (2) idea generation, (3) idea development and qualification and (4) idea evaluation and selection.

In Phase 1, in order to develop new ideas, a variety of methods were used to put the students in a new mindset. These methods used scenarios related to future conditions which thereby released the grip of preconceptions and unquestioned assumptions. Specifically, the students were to imagine that they were present in the future where, among other things, they had new technologies at their disposal along with having the potential for production. Using counterfactual thinking, the students were forced either to use or to disregard various solution perspectives and thereby to think along new lines. The value of getting away from the desk was stressed: by going into the field they could experience things at first hand, always a powerful way to create insight.

For Phase 2, idea generation, the following methods were presented:

- Thinking aloud: by thinking aloud and sharing one's thoughts, associations and ideas with others, it is possible to inspire each other and build on each other's ideas.
- Thinking in pictures: the students were given a number of picture cards that were to work as inspiration.
- Forced lateral thinking: the starting point here is to use ideas from a completely different area, ideas that have nothing to do with the subject. These ideas are then to be transferred to the chosen complexes of problems with the purpose of examining whether they can be directly used as solutions or serve as inspiration to new ideas.
- 'Speed thinking': idea generation was made with a time limit so that the students took turns having one minute to come up with as many ideas as possible. The speed exercises also functioned as changes of pace that injected new energy and dynamics into the idea generation.

In Phase 3, the following method was used for developing and qualifying the ideas:

- Synergy design: build on each other's ideas after swapping them.
- Idea discussion: the potential of each individual idea is discussed and everybody must find the advantages as well as disadvantages inherent in the ideas. The advantages must then be further developed whereas the disadvantages must, as far as possible, be eliminated.

Phase 4 was idea evaluation and selection. After all the ideas had been further developed and had thereby demonstrated their worth in principle, they were evaluated. This should as far as possible take place following a number of fixed criteria that are based on the user analysis and also on the purpose and focus of the assignment.

Theoretical Aspects

As part of their tutorials in inclusive design, students are introduced to models for design processes which are essentially normative: 'Most of the theories that are promoted in design areas can be described as normative. They are action prescribers such as manifestoes, design principles and standards based on ideological positions about what the world, good design, good architecture or good cities should be.' [12] Such models make the proposition that design is an activity made up of nominally separate

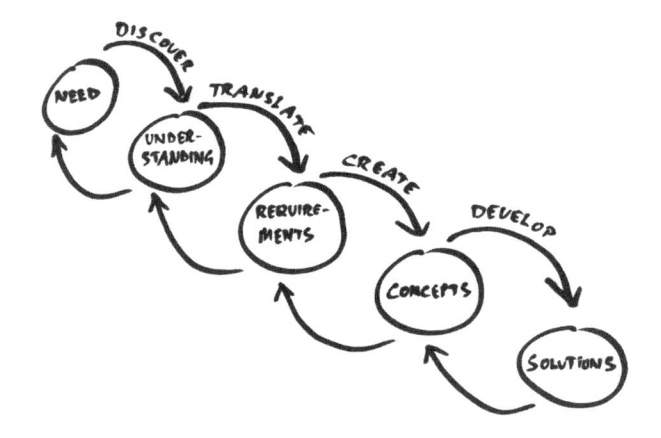

Figure 1: The Cambridge Engineering Design Centre model for inclusive design Clarkson et al. [20], reproduced with permission.

steps. There are a very large number of models for the design process and it is not possible to examine all of them for their advantages, disadvantages and aims. In this chapter we focus on one, chosen for its relevance to inclusive design. Below is shown an example of what one might call an authoritative inclusive design process, a waterfall model prepared by the Engineering Design Centre in Cambridge [13]. This shows a set of steps and these are presented in a particular order. Referring to a classification outlined by Broadbent [14], the EDC model is a soft-systems method (SSM). Broadbent notes that SSMs 'should find particular application in complex design projects in which diverse stakeholders are perceived to have varied but legitimate interests in the outcome.' Since the projects followed in this study are at a small scale, there are necessarily fewer actors involved but, in principle, an inclusive design process is scale independent. One could use the same process for one user as for three hundred.

It is recognised that actual design activities tend to be less well ordered than the models which are proposed. Hitchcock et al. [15] demonstrated this with regard to the integration of ergonomics into the design process for a new check-out desk. In that project, the designers, ergonomists and the customer were separate actors. As such 'a number of iterative loops were needed in the design process, requiring input from a number of sources.' For a project carried out by a single student, these loops will still exist as the student switches between being designer, engineer and ergonomist and on to internalising the critical role of a disinterested third party. Arising from this is quite how different steps in solving design problems are actually arranged and how small each meaningful step can be. In metaphorical terms, are the parts of a design process arranged as small but still discrete elements or is there in fact blending and blurring of activities? This is a point to which we return in the discussion section.

The demands of increased user-involvement are quite heavy for individual students, who may lack the resources to locate a relevant user-group and to keep them involved throughout the process. User-centred design (of which ID is a development) requires that there are users to be centred upon. ISO 13407:1999, 'Human-Centered Design Processes for Interactive Systems', specifies four principles, one of which is to: 'Ensure iteration of design solutions (by involving users in as many stages of the design process and implementation as is practical.)' [16]. The expectation was that the students would engage with users in a less extensive, more episodic way than if they were supported by the resources more commonly found in a commercial setting.

Methodology

The methodology presented here was developed for this study. To track the students' activities they were given a diary with which to record each part of their design process. Accompanying the diary were instructions for use: 'Please record your activities for each day of your project. Use the code provided below. You are welcome to add some notes if you wish. If you produce a concrete object as a result of your activities, please say what it is.' It was explained that a 'concrete object' referred to a model or sketch or CAD model. Students were free to write in Danish or English. The list of activities was presented in random order and with randomly assigned code numbers. For this exercise the activities listed are assumed to be the core of the design process.

21 – Develop (refining selected concept)

01 – Defining requirements (evaluating information)

06 – Ideation (sketch drawing or making sketch models)

09 – Other

34 – Research (find out the information you need)

45 – Solution (preparing presentation materials)

The list of activities was left unstructured and randomly numbered so as to avoid prescribing a particular order of steps. Three examples of a diary entry were provided to indicate how to use the journal. One of these was: '2 May. 45 – CAD modelling final design solution, 8 hours. Changed appearance of grab handle.' The resultant diary was designed to create a timesheet for the project so that the order of activities and the time spent on them could be examined and quantified. The possibility for students to add additional commentaries provided a further qualitative element.

One criticism that could be made is that using predefined categories introduces circularity into the research. However, the general subcategories of design activity are not unlimited; drawing student's attention to, say, 'ideation' or 'research' is not very likely to make them focus more on these than on the other unidentified possible activities they could otherwise have undertaken. It allows the journal to be a log of intention (the intention to create ideas or refine, for example) rather than the means employed which are more ambiguous (drawing can be used to ideate or refine or research). There also remained freedom for the students to determine which activity fell into each category. However, using predefined categories eliminates the need to interpret the students' journal entries and provides a standardisation to allow cross-comparison of the data sets. In the context of this study, a standardised data set could be collated and analysed reliably and also converted for graphical forms of representation.

During the final presentation of their work the students were asked: 'Is there a difference in the design process when designing for the elderly or disabled?' This question was asked and answered verbally and recorded. By asking this question verbally and at the end, rather than including it in the written diaries, it was hoped to avoid prejudicing the students' thought processes.

At the end of the project the diaries were gathered and the data coded and tabulated. The data captured the number of occasions students engaged with particular design steps ('work unit'). Each recorded activity was assigned one unit. Units could be overlapping. The data has been converted to a diagrammatic form where the area of each activity box is proportional to the number of consecutive days during which the activity was carried out. The arrow graphic signals the direction of flow of the activities as the student proceeded through the project. For example, Project 6: '24th March. 06 – Marker sketches and paper models. 34 – Research into existing cook tops. Mainly controls.' This data counts as two work units: one for category 06 and one for category 34. On the spreadsheet, two cells would be marked with a separate colour code.

The data was also subject to simple statistical analysis. The number of work units per student was totalled. Then the number of instances for each individual work unit was counted. From this it was possible to see what percentage of the work units belonged to each category. This is only intended to be an approximate guide. The diaries did not log precise hours in most cases but rather listed the activities on a given day.

Qualitative data was also logged. Students provided some notes (not extensive) on their activities and these notes help to distinguish between research at the desk and research with users or between ideation on paper and ideation using CAD programmes. This provides some extra insight into the process of how the projects developed.

Results
The following two sections present the quantitative and qualitative aspects of the data extracted from the project journals. It is important to note that as the sample size of the survey is small, the statistical treatments are presented only for the purpose of general indication.

Quantitative Elements
The structure of the activities of the eight projects was analysed and represented diagrammatically. The schematic breakdown of these projects is shown in figures 5 and 6. The area of each box is proportional to the number of work units allocated. This

Figure 2: Project 6, 'A cooktop for all generations'

shows where a designer spent more time during each step. Larger blocks mean more time was spent on the task. These diagrams show two things. One is that students alternated between work processes a great deal more than would be expected from a 'waterfall' design model. The other pattern is that some students worked in a highly non-linear way at the start before settling down to a more linear finishing phase. The alternation from activity to activity is quantified as the 'switch between' ratio which is described further below.

Project 3 has a highly non-linear start phase with four activities (research, definition of requirements, ideation and development) all occurring at the same time in the first phase. Then there is a node in the process where research and the definition of requirements are the main activities. After this the remaining seven steps are done in series, which is to say that the designer does not do more than one thing in a given day. The solution phase consists of 11 uninterrupted work units which bring the project to completion.

In Project 6, the non-linear, multi-activity phase began a little later, after an initial phase of ideation preceded by research which took place in two groups of work units. Then ideation, the definition of requirements and research were carried out in parallel and in small bursts: the student did some research which lead to ideation which led onto more research and back to ideation. Thereafter, the remaining time was divided between a longer phase of development followed by a concluding phase of finalising the desired solution. There is some ambiguity about what constitutes ideation and what constitutes project development. For Project 6, the student listed 3D model-making (CAD modelling) as ideation. Another interpretation is that this was project development where various small-scale design choices were made concerning what one could call craftsmanship problems. Such problems are to do with the arrangement of fillets at intersecting surfaces or the best way to resolve the graphics on the product. These are distinct from the kinds of principle design choices which affect the gross appearance of the object.

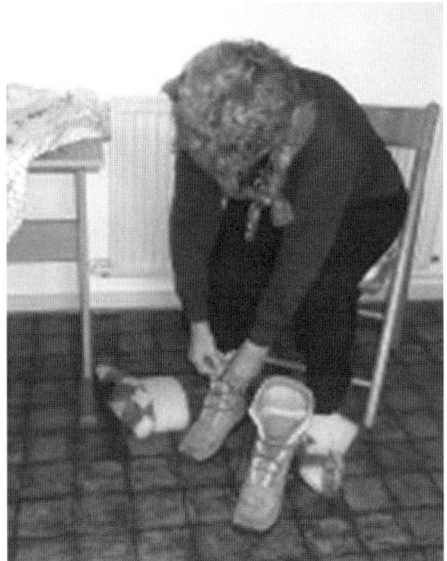

Figure 3: Project 7, 'Multi-purpose stool'

Project 4 also had a non-linear start. Research, ideation and the definition of requirements were carried out in discrete work units: 9 work units of research were done in 8 parts; 5 work units of requirement definition were done in 4 parts; and 8 units of ideation were done in 7 parts. This means that at the start the student alternated rapidly between the initial activities of the design process.

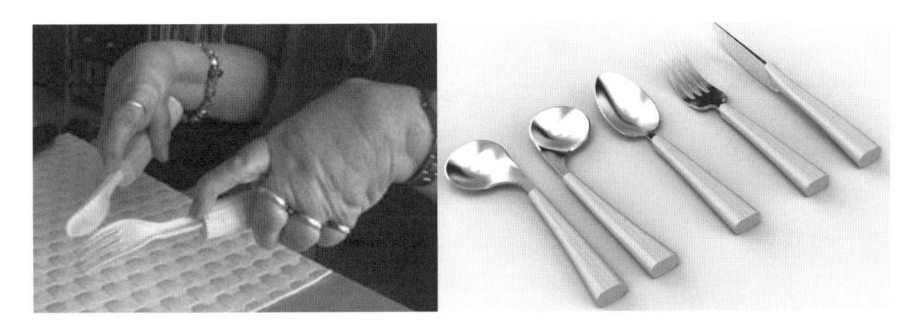

Figure 4: Project 4, 'Cutlery'

The most linear project was number 2, a table. In a sense it is two attempts at the same problem. In the first twenty days the student proceeded through the work cycle, with later activities corresponding to the later stages of the waterfall model. The first 20 days ended with a mid-project critique and what the student called a 'change in direction'. After a pause, the student resumed researching and then switched to ideation, development and then finalisation; this was mostly done in larger chunks of uninterrupted work units. That there is no reporting of defining requirements implies that this was carried over from the first half of the project unchanged, giving the project a clear direction in the second attempt at a resolution.

Figure 5: Projects 1 to 4

Figure 6: Project 5 to 8

Of the six phases into which the students could classify their activities, defining requirements was the least reported. Noting the small sample size, the average number of work units allocated to the definition of requirements is 3. Approximately 10.5 work units were allocated to research. In the case of ideation, an average of 11 work units was allocated, with quite little variation about the mean.

The 'switch-between' ratio (SB ratio) is the number of work units per day. The term was coined for this project. A larger SB number means the designer carried out more individual steps. A value of 1 would mean that the designer carried out one work unit per day. A larger value (e.g. 1.29) would mean that the designer carried out several steps during some work days. The maximum number of work units per day was four. The activity class 'other' was not included in this analysis as, according to the diaries, these were predominantly unrelated activities which did not further the project.

Table 1: Variation in activities

Project	Work days	Work nits	SB ratio
1: mobile phone	27	35	1.29
2: table	43	48	1.12
3: meal service	31	44	1.42
4: cutlery	30	35	1.16
5: lamp	27	32	1.19
6: cook-top	29	40	1.38
7: multipurpose stool	32	33	1.03
8: strategic design	18	29	1.61

The average SB ratio is 1.28 or, in other words, designers carried out 1.28 steps per working day, overall. If one looks at the SB ratio for the first half of the projects (up to the mid-review), the average value is 1.35. After this the SB ratio decreases to 1.22 (some discrepancies occur due to rounding). The project with the highest switch-between ratio was a strategic study for a web-site for elderly users. This project was shorter in duration than the others and featured less time spent on the resolution phases which in other assignments involved model building and graphic presentation. This project still had a higher switch-between ratio for the first phase than the second phase. The project with the lowest switch-between ratio was for a table for a café. This also turned out to be the most linear. That said, the individual steps were small, there being few large blocks of consecutive days where the same type of activity was carried out.

Qualitative Elements

This section examines some of the annotations and comments made alongside the notations of work activity. An example is from project 7: '21–25th of March. 06 – Ideation (sketch brainstorming, getting ideas on paper… "kill your darlings" to go on.' Another is from project 3: 'April 24. 21 – Develop (try to clarify what the project is about and with which methods.)'

The methods chosen for research divided into three categories. Product analysis was done by means of interviews with producers, Internet searches and fieldwork. This involved, as in the case of the café table, ethnographic observation. Most students reported preparing interviews and speaking with users though the journals did not go into detail as to how this was conducted or what the precise findings were. Where expert advice was sought it involved discussions with an ergotherapist and with a specialist engineer on plastics in the case of the meal packaging.

The designers used brainstorming and sketching for the ideation phases. Some of the brainstorming was done as part of group work where students exchanged ideas and commented on each other's work. In some cases 3D models were made using either workshop materials or CAD (Rhino).

Since definition of requirements constituted only a small part of the reported activities little information was gathered on how this was done. One exception is that one designer reported doing a product analysis and mapping.

The development phase again featured sketching but also the use of digital and material models. This area shows a kind of transitional phase where sketching segues into the finalisation of the concept on paper and as a Rhino model. Students did not provide any gloss on what was done during modelling, a point which is returned to in the following section.

Discussion

The projects showed a general tendency for rapid alteration of activities (or non-linear work patterns) in the first half, followed by a more methodical sequence of activities in the second half. As such, this pattern looks like a compromise between the methodical, sequential design process as described by waterfall models and the oft-cited observation that design is more like a disorderly sequence of activities concluded only due to a lack of time. Sanders and Stappers' diagram (Fig. 7) shows this chaotic interpretation visually: a random squiggle proceeding from left to right, described as the 'fuzzy front end' [17]. The switch-between ratios show that not all projects are equally disorderly. The relatively simple project for a table had the lowest SB value, while the paper-based strategic design for the website and the more classically designerly projects for a meal service and a stove showed higher levels of task-alternation. Yet these also settled down in the second half of the project's duration. The implication of asking students to design inclusively is that they are required to switch quickly between their different tasks as they adopt different roles. This quantification can also be used as a tool for self-analysis: how quickly they alternate tasks is indicative of the intensity and, indeed, complexity of their work.

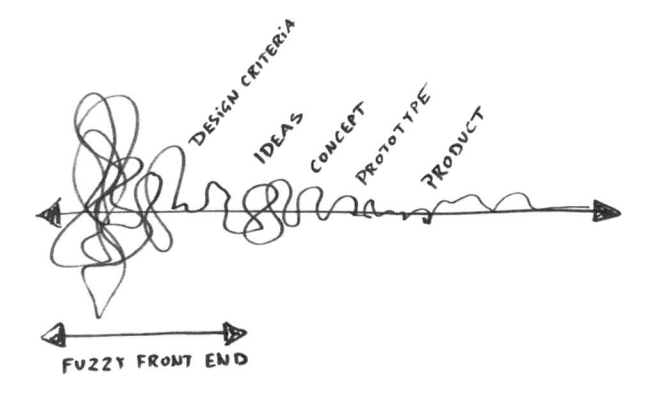

Figure 7: Sanders and Stappers' fuzzy front end

This analysis also points towards a compromise between the design-is-chaos school of thought (as per Fig. 7) and the flow-chart school of thought. The start phase of a design project features toggling between tasks and then settles down to a more focused, linear finish which resembles the waterfall diagram.

What is occurring in the first phase is the finding of information that raises questions, which in turn require ideation or further research: this could be conceived as small loops and partial loops and half-steps towards further knowledge. Seen from above, as it were, the activities of the students are not random and are not undirected although they seem so at 'drawing board level'. Perhaps the chaos and disorder of the design process is a matter of perception. It also seems chaotic because one would not have planned the process to take that form *in advance*. But in hindsight the diversions and explorations evolve into what another student referred to as 'a little path we had to follow'. So, the design process is complex and it is perceived as disorderly whilst not really being so when looked at in structural terms.

In the section 'Background', above, this question was posed: are the parts of a design process arranged as small but still discrete elements or is there, in fact, blending and blurring of activities? The answer is that the work activities showed a clear granularity in the early stages of the project. Students were either creating ideas or working on research as distinctly separate tasks. Later during refinement and resolution it seems there is a blending of tasks since ideation (at a detail level) and refinement become intermingled.

Those students better able to alternate between tasks or to multi-task are more likely to find that the demands of designing inclusively are less of a burden. Involving users requires checking and cross-checking which means toggling frequently between research (or referring to their users) and other tasks. It takes the uncertain, data-gathering activity further into the design process or, in other words, research continues longer and critical points are returned to for further examination. This is in contrast to the classic hard systems model where the data was gathered once (and therefore problematic issues were found only once), at the start. The designer could then proceed with no further 'interference' from the users. In a sense it is less satisfying to stop and start various activities but it is critical in an inclusive-design project to refer the state of the project and key problems back to the users for confirmation of ideas, criticism of proposals and validation of solutions.

One of the instructions to the students was 'If you produce a concrete object as a result of your activities, please say what it is.' More emphasis might have been placed on this point as the diaries did not yield much useful information on the particular results of logged activities. This would have been particularly relevant during the model-making stage where such descriptions would have produced more of an insight concerning what they were trying to achieve with each model and what the model was intended to show or test.

The paucity of information concerning what was achieved during the later stages of 3D modelling shows that more could have been learned about how designers use this stage to refine their ideas further. 3D models can be presented to users and can be more readily understood than sketch drawings or verbal explanations of requirements. They are also amenable to a certain level of testing using digital mannequins. Only one student (carrying out project 4, a design for cutlery suitable for arthritis patients) reported doing validation at this stage but they did not report whether the model was a hard model or a digital model. There were two phases of validation reported here, involving both an expert and a disabled person. Further research could usefully be done to investigate more intensively how 3D modelling is used to ideate on screen and used to present concepts to users. Clearer briefing of the students could have provided this information during this investigation. Follow-up studies will place more emphasis on this stage. Students tended to note the times spent but not what was done during this time. The brevity of their notes also reflects the time pressure they may have been under at this stage in their project.

Some of the methods and strategies outlined in the teaching that preceded this project were not cited in the diaries. Focus groups, in particular, were not a popular option. Practical reasons are the most likely explanation. Focus groups are costly in time and resources. For students, the expense is reason enough for them not to deploy this strategy. Compounding this is the difficulty of working with older and disabled users for whom health problems are a significant obstacle, a point discussed by Barrett and Herriotts [18].

Finally we turn to the follow-up question put to the students at the end of their project: 'Is there a difference in the design process when designing for the elderly or disabled?' The answers (in Danish) had two main themes, both of them showing a fuller understanding: 'The life of older people is very different from mine; it [the work] required a greater insight on my part' (Project 2). The other class of answer was to the effect that working with users required more time: 'When you design for people with disabilities, you have to spend more time on the user' (Project 6); spending time with the user requires being there with them to see how they live: 'You need to observe how the disabled live in their own home' (Project 5). Another response related to seeing that the user had their own realistic views of their condition: 'The mobility-impaired users are very clear about their needs and limitations' (Project 4). This kind of clarity about the user adjusts the way they are seen by the designer. It steers the designer away from the idea of the user as a delicate entity lacking self-awareness, someone who is passively 'being helped'. The teaching and design processes had shifted the students' understanding of ways of being. This is one of the aims of the coursework. Porter and Porter [19] discuss the fallacies concerning ergonomics, amongst which is the assumption of designers that what works for them will work for others. Another mistake is that the designer assumes that their likes and dislikes are the same as those of the user. The shift in preconceptions the students underwent is what is needed to avoid these classic designer's fallacies.

In conclusion, this project shows how students reacted to the challenges of designing inclusively. The observed behaviour patterns indicated the effects of checking and cross-checking information and the increased integration of users into the students' design process. It also provided some preliminary suggestions of how actual logged design activities differed from the opposing models of the systematic design process on one side and the un-ordered design process on the other. There is less order than the former and more order than the latter. A larger survey might provide clues on underlying patterns in designers' behaviour. This and the need to examine how designers use CAD modelling in the context of inclusive design are areas for further possible research.

References

1. Bencetić, B. (2011) 'Talking about it is a beginning: The first students' inclusive design projects', *Proceedings of Include 2011*, Helen Hamlyn Centre, RCA. London.
2. Danieli-Lahav, Y. (2009) 'Learning Center for Inclusive Environments: Breaking fresh ground by a "teach and learn" process', *Proceedings of Include 2009*, Helen Hamlyn Centre, RCA, London.
3. Afacan, Y. (2009) 'Universal Design as an Integral Part of Design Curriculum: A Case Study in Bilkent University', *Proceedings of Include 2009*, Helen Hamlyn Centre, RCA, London.
4. Callanan, M. et al. (2009) 'Universal Design in Third Level Design Teaching in Ireland', *Proceedings of Include 2009*, Helen Hamlyn Centre, RCA, London.
5. Stappers, P.J., Sleeswijk Visser, F. and van der Lugt, R. (2007) 'Teaching context-mapping to industrial design students', *Proceedings of Include 2007*, Helen Hamlyn Centre, RCA, London, p.1.
6. Kose, S., Sakamoto, T., Miyoshi, I. and Sako, H. (2007) 'Teaching universal design to undergraduate students at the Faculty of Design', *Proceedings of Include 2007*, Helen Hamlyn Centre, RCA, London.

7. Hewer, S. (2007) 'Using the User – encouraging design students in user-centered research: lessons from the field', *Proceedings of Include 2007*, Helen Hamlyn Centre, RCA, London, p.2.
8. Dong, H. (2010) 'Strategies for teaching Inclusive Design', *Journal of Engineering Design*, volume 21, issue 2–3, pp.237–51.
9. British Standards Institute (2005) British Standard – BS 7000-6:2005, Guide to managing inclusive design, London, p.4.
10. Pattison, M. and Stedmon, A. (2006) 'Inclusive Design and human factors: designing mobile 'phones for older users', *Psychology Journal*, vol. 4, no. 3, p.272.
11. Macdonald, A.S. (2006) 'The Inclusive Challenge: A Multidisciplinary Educational Approach', in Clarkson, J., Langdon, P. and Robinson, P. (eds), *Designing Accessible Technology*, London: Springer, p.5.
12. Downton, P. (2003) *Design Research*, Melbourne: RMIT University Press, p.79.
13. 'Inclusive Design Toolkit', retrieved 2 February 2011 from http://www.inclusivedesigntoolkit.com/betterdesign/misc/contentdesc.html (2006).
14. Broadbent, J. (2003) 'Generations in design methodology', *Design Journal*, 6 (1), pp.2–13.
15. Hitchcock, D., Haines, V. and Elton, E. (2004) 'Integrating ergonomics in the design process', *Design Journal*, 7 (3), pp.32–40.
16. ISO 13407:1999, 'Human-Centered Design Processes for Interactive Systems', International Standards Organisation, Geneva.
17. Sanders, E. and Stappers, P.J. (2008) 'Co-creation and the new landscapes of design', in *CoDesign: International Journal of CoCreation in Design and the Arts*, 4, 1, 2008, pp.5–18.
18. Barrett, J. and Herriotts, P. (2002) 'Focus Groups: Supporting Effective Product Development', in Langford, J. and McDonagh, D. (eds), *Focus Groups*, Boca Raton: CRC Press, pp.115–28.
19. Porter, J.M. and Porter, S. (2001) 'Occupant accommodation: an ergonomics approach', in Happian-Smith, J. (ed.), *Introduction to modern vehicle design*, Oxford: Butterworth-Heinemann, pp.233–76.
20. Clarkson, P.J., Coleman, R., Hosking, I. and Waller, S. (2007) 'Inclusive design toolkit', Engineering Design Centre, University of Cambridge, UK.

Gabriela GOLDSCHMIDT
*Faculty of Architecture and Town Planning, Technion,
Israel institute of Technology*

AND

Paul A. RODGERS
School of Design, Northumbria University, UK

THE DESIGN THINKING APPROACHES OF THREE DIFFERENT GROUPS OF DESIGNERS BASED ON SELF-REPORTS

Introduction

A lot of work has been published in recent years on the subject of design thinking and how designers think and work [6, 9, 15, 16]. A frequently held consensus across those publications is the notion that design thinking has a number of common features, typified and made manifest in a strong commitment and personal motivation of the individual. Moreover, it is widely suggested that designers possess the courage to take risks, that they are prepared to fail and that they work hard. Furthermore, during their design thinking activities, designers regularly (re)define and/or frame the problem, they adopt holistic thinking and they sketch, draw and model possible ideas throughout the design process. Cross [9] suggests there are three key strategic aspects of design thinking that appear to be common across a wide range of design disciplines, namely:

1. [Designers] take a broad 'systems approach' to the problem, rather than accepting narrow problem criteria;
2. [Designers] 'frame' the problem in a distinctive and sometimes rather personal way; and
3. Designers design from 'first principles'.

This chapter sets out to examine the claim that, despite individual and disciplinary differences, many aspects of design thinking are common across different design domains by comparing and contrasting the design thinking processes, methods and approaches of three different groups of designers – ID (Industrial Design students), ARCH (Architecture students) and DPHD (Design PhD candidates) – with each group comprising four individuals. Table 1 highlights relevant background information of the participant design students. This information includes the participants' age, gender, year of study and previous educational qualifications and experiences.

Table 1: Participants' background information

ID1	ID2	ID3	ID4
Male, 21 years of age, Industrial Design student, year 3 of 4	Male, 21 years of age, Industrial Design student, year 3 of 4	Male, 21 years of age, Industrial Design student, year 3 of 4	Male, 22 years of age, Industrial Design student, year 3 of 4

ARCH1	ARCH2	ARCH3	ARCH4
Male, 23 years of age, Architecture student, year 5 of 5	Male, 23 years of age, Architecture student, year 5 of 5	Male, 28 years of age, Architecture student, year 5 of 5	Male, 23 years of age, Architecture student, year 5 of 5

DPHD1	DPHD2	DPHD3	DPHD4
Female, 25 years of age, year 1 of 3-year PhD; bachelor's degree in Fashion Design and Technology; master's degree in Fashion Design	Male, 27 years of age, year 1 of 3-year PhD; bachelor's degree in Industrial Design; master's degree in Industrial Design	Male, 26 years of age, year 1 of 3-year PhD; bachelor's degree in Industrial Design; master's degree in Design Innovation	Male, 29 years of age, year 1 of 3-year PhD; bachelor's degree in Industrial Design; master's degree in Conceptual Design

All twelve designers were given a short design brief and worked, individually and in their habitual environment, on a design proposal which, when ready, was submitted in the form of one or two presentation boards. They were also debriefed about their processes. Using their self-reports, the chapter seeks to explore and examine any differences in the scope and nature of the designed 'solutions' proposed by the three groups. Moreover, the chapter examines the design processes of the three groups, studying how each individual designer planned his/her time, whether their design process was a linear activity or something else. The chapter also quantifies the amount of time that each participant spent on particular activities including studying the brief, planning the design process, collecting information, looking at examples, consulting with others, thinking about solutions and sketching them, analysing and comparing alternatives, evaluating interim and the final proposal(s), and preparing the final presentation.

We start by looking at the construal of the problem, which pertains to Cross's first and second aspects of design thinking. We then look at the design activities the participants pursued, which will illuminate the principles that guide them. We look at the sequence of activities and the time allotted to each. We conclude with questions regarding the status of design methods in practice and education in an era in which designers are called upon to lead innovation at all times. The study is based on the participants' submitted designs and their self-reported attitudes, main focus points and the sequence and duration of design activities. While, in the past, self-reporting methods have been criticised for collecting data that has been either exaggerated by the respondent or hampered by respondents who forget crucial details, self-report methods and techniques are a reliable, valid and applicable way of collecting information [25]. Methodologically similar to questionnaires and surveys, self-report methods are widely used in areas such as delinquent and criminal behaviour research [11], the usage of health care services [4] and organisational behaviour research [24], amongst many others.

Construing the Problem

The design brief posed to the three groups of students (ID, ARCH and DPHD) was very short and open-ended, and allowed for any number of problem definitions and possible design responses. It read:

> 11% of the world's 6.9 billion people are over 60. By the year 2050 that figure will have doubled to 22%. If we are to support a growing number of older people we need to produce products, spaces and services that allow them to stay healthy and well in and around their own home. You are asked to design a domestic product, living environment or service for older people that surpasses conventional expectations.

It was therefore necessary to focus on an issue within the wide range covered by 'domestic product, living environment or service for older people that surpasses conventional expectations.' Each of the participants did so, alone or in dialogue with others: peers, teachers or potential users. Once a need was identified, the designer could frame the problem; that is, demarcate the initial design space [23] within which the problem is being explored and a solution envisioned [29]. The term 'design space' pertains to a combination of a problem space and a solution space in the context of design or, in Schön's terms [23], the state space of possible designs. The task was construed within each designer's design space, thus emphasising aspects related very specifically to age symptoms (which, as we know, are similar to disability symptoms that are not necessarily related to age) at one end of the spectrum or, at the other end, having more to do with innovative products that may attract a range of users. On the average, all three groups rated the difficulty of the task as 3 on a scale of 1 to 5, which confirms that the brief was appropriate for this sample of designers.

Eight participants out of 12 who took part in this experiment chose to design products meant to support common daily activities and states of people with physical difficulties, discomfort or who cannot trust their memory (ID1, 2 & 4; ARCH1, 2, 3 & 4; DPHD1).

Two designs proposed new services (DPHD3 & 4); one was a promotion and marketing idea for inclusive design (DPHD2) and, finally, one project offered a simple interactive means to enhance safety by identifying knocks on the door as typical to specific visitors (ID3). Table 2 lists the various projects by the 12 participants.

Table 2: Choice of design task

ID1	ID2	ID3	ID4
Plate to make one confident when eating	Bathroom aids (e.g. grips) that double as regular features	Door knock records, to identify who is at the door	Day's activities planner as puzzle
ARCH1	**ARCH2**	**ARCH3**	**ARCH4**
Cane that doubles as device to pick up fallen objects	Umbrella-handle arm support	Tablet dispenser with clock	Stay-warm thermal under wear
DPHD1	**DPHD2**	**DPHD3**	**DPHD4**
Coats with built-in posture aiding memory foam to support sitting	IDC – accreditation mark to recognise inclusive design	Buddying correspondence scheme between elderly and orphans	Internet-based service offerings by the elderly

Legend

- Product
- Safety
- Promo
- Service

It is not surprising that most participants chose to design products but it is noteworthy that all architecture students, who could have been expected to concern themselves with 'living environments', designed consumer products; in fact, living environments were not tackled by any of the participants. Most designs were relatively original – some less so (the least original was the cane that doubles as a device to pick up objects; such pick-up devices exist, with a mechanism similar to the one proposed here).

When a problem is highly ill-defined, as in this case, deciding what the purpose of the design should be is an indispensable preliminary phase. In the case of this short exercise, this meant choosing a context the designer was at least somewhat familiar with and that fitted with his or her values. As DPHD1 put it: 'My main design goal was to fulfil the brief whilst incorporating aspects that were familiar to me'; and ARCH2 said he wanted 'to make something that is useful'. The availability of sufficient information within the short time frame of this assignment also played a role as it was not possible to research a subject matter thoroughly, build up knowledge and develop new competencies. This may explain the choice of products that were proposed as solutions to deficiencies in today's market (ARCH2 stated that his main design goal was 'to design something that fills a gap in the market'), all of which were related to known and well-understood activities (e.g. better grip of umbrella handle, pill dispenser with alarm clock) and states (e.g. discomfort due to cold environment, uncomfortable seating). All of the proposed products were conceived as realistic commodities (ARCH4's main design goals was 'to conceive of something that could work in reality') and, although most participants said they regretted not being able to test real prototypes and get feedback, their projects were presented as market-ready products requiring just a little further development.

The scope of design has been widened in recent years and is no longer confined to products. The literature on design thinking stresses that design concerns itself with products, services and systems and, in essence, it is a methodology to generate innovative ideas (e.g. Brown [6]). Leading corporations and business schools adopted this approach and now see design as a prime vehicle for economic success. It is therefore surprising that only three of the proposals in our experiment approached design from a service or system perspective. One proposal called for a universal accreditation mark to recognise inclusive design. The universal design approach claims that all products should be designed such that they would be appropriate for all users, including people with disabilities or difficulties due to advanced age (e.g. Covington and Hannah [7]). The rationale is that, first, what the elderly or disabled can handle is comfortable for the rest of the population and, second, that singling out the elderly and disabled by providing special and different products for them adds unnecessarily to their negative feelings of decline and isolation. For this reason, the design proposal by DPHD2 to tag products that have been tested for universality in terms of ease of use is a system design proposal that is most appropriate in the current context. There were two service proposals: one is Internet-based, geared at posting services that elderly people may offer, particularly in their communities; the other service suggests a correspondence scheme between the elderly and orphan children, for the benefit of both parties. Both services are in line with the predominant expanded view of design as expressed in the literature on design thinking. We shall return to the issue of design thinking later in this chapter.

Design Activities and Sequences

After completing their design projects, participants were presented with a list of nine design activities (in random order) and asked to indicate which of these activities they were engaged with and for how long. Table 3 shows the number of participants who reported being engaged in each design activity (in this table and in subsequent tables and figures, the sequence of activities follows standard prescribed design methods; however, this is not the order in which the activities were presented to the participants).

Obviously, all participants studied the brief and all of them prepared a final presentation (required). The only other activity that they all engaged in, according to the reports, was 'thinking about solutions and sketching them'. However, other activities were not as universally practised. Two participants did not look at examples; three participants did not consult with others. The same number of participants were not engaged in 'analysing/comparing alternatives'. Four participants reported not collecting information beyond the givens in the brief (which were quite scant). Five participants – almost half – did not evaluate their designs, either along the design process or at its conclusion. Less than half the participants reported having planned their design processes. The distribution of 'planners' was particularly interesting: none of the architecture students, and only one industrial design student, planned their process. One of the architecture students (ARCH2) explained: 'Because of the compressed nature of the task I didn't really plan the design process, all the stages tended to be compressed.' In contrast, all of the graduate design students found it necessary to plan their processes, which may mean that they used a conscious strategy in the design process. We shall comment about the differences among the various designer categories and their behaviours as reflected in this experiment later in the chapter.

Table 3: Number of designers engaged in activities
(max. 4 in each designer category and 12 in total)

	Studying the brief	Planning the design process	Collecting information	Looking at examples	Consulting with others	Thinking about solutions and sketching them	Analysing/comparing alternatives	Evaluating interim and the final proposal(s)	Preparing the final presentation
ID	4	1	1	2	3	4	3	2	4
ARCH	4	0	4	4	3	4	2	2	4
DPHD	4	4	3	4	3	4	4	3	4
Total	12	5	8	10	9	12	9	7	12

We held a structured debriefing interview with each participant after he or she completed the design. Regarding the design activities, participants were asked to indicate the order in which they undertook them as well as the amount of time dedicated to each activity. We shall discuss the time allocation in the next section; here we would like to review the activity sequences. Figures 1, 2 and 3 show this sequence for each participant within the relevant designer category. The straight diagonal line in each of the figures represents a theoretical linear process, in which activities are undertaken in the order in which they appear at the bottom of the figure, from left to right. This order is, as mentioned earlier, more or less a 'textbook sequence' as prescribed in various design methods handbooks (e.g. Roozenburg and Eekels [22]). As figures 1 to 3 show, the process followed by our participants did not mirror the recommended methods. We must qualify this assertion: when asked whether their process was linear, most participants said it was not. Moreover, many of them said they went back and forth between two or three activities, something we could not account for in the figures below.

The main deviation from the classic model concerns the stage at which participants chose to augment their knowledge or solicit other opinions. Thus collecting information, looking at examples or consulting with others occurred, at various points in time, usually after 'thinking about solutions and sketching them'. Those who reported undertaking analysis of alternatives did so after 'thinking and sketching'. In conventional design process models, analysis occurs before a solution is sketched. Here, however, analysis refers to proposals that have already been generated and therefore it is sensible to

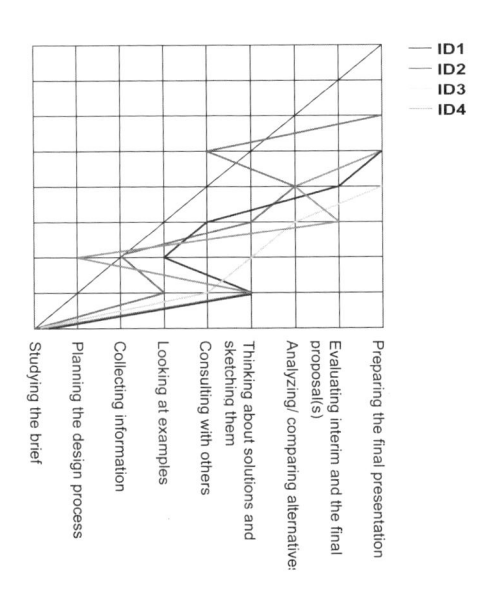

Figure 1: Activity sequence, industrial design students

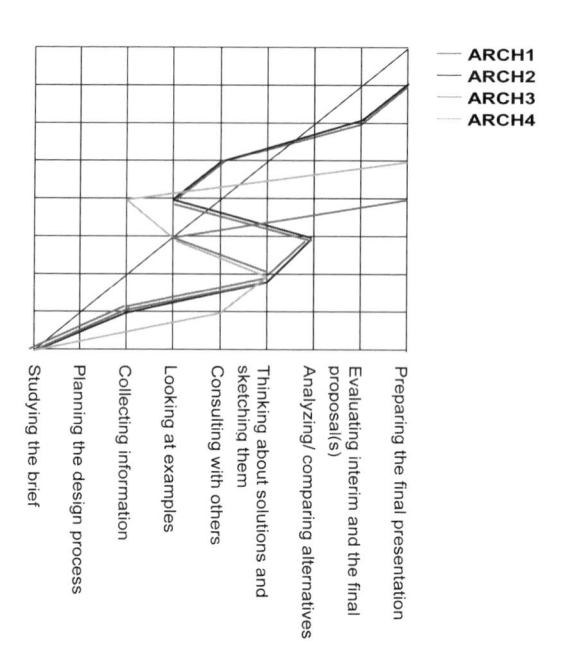

Figure 2: Activity sequence, architecture students

engage in it after having done at least some thinking about solutions and sketching them. Analysis that occurs late in the process may reflect a process dominated by trial and error.

It is particularly interesting to learn when planning of the process took place, when it did (as mentioned earlier, only five participants planned their processes). One would expect this to happen early in the process, but this was not always the case. In one case planning was undertaken only after thinking and sketching (ID4) and in two other cases it occurred rather late, and after intensive information handling (DPHD1, DPHD2). It is also interesting to notice that in two cases the design process did not commence with studying the brief; in one case the participant started thinking and sketching and only then went back to the brief to study it (DPHD4). In the other case the designer consulted with others first and only then resorted to the brief (DPHD2).

Clearly, in such a compressed process wherein the problem was critically ill-defined, we cannot expect 'textbook' processes. All the same, the diversity revealed in this experiment raises useful questions about the status of a prescribed design method and the consequences of not observing an orderly convention. There is plenty of evidence that designers consciously ignore methods they were taught at school (e.g. Goldschmidt [13]) and the question then is: what should be taught? We shall return to this issue later in the chapter.

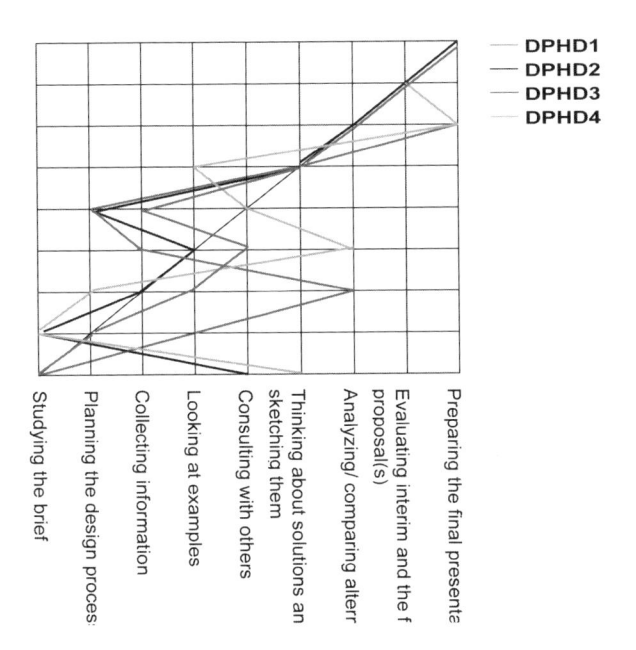

Figure 3: Activity sequence, design PhD students

Time Allocation

As in the sequence of activities, we notice considerable individual differences among participants in the time they devoted to the various activities. The overall design time ranged from a minimum of 153 minutes (DPHD4) to a maximum of 900 minutes (ID4) and the average was 603 minutes for the ID participants (or 503 minutes, if we ignore ID4 who devoted a lot of time to the production of a working prototype of his puzzle design), 326 minutes for the ARCH participants and 357 minutes for the DPHD participants. Figure 4 is an overview of the mean percentage of time devoted to activities, by design category.

The figure reveals a few interesting differences among the three constituencies of participants. First, we cannot fail to notice how much time was devoted to preparing a final presentation – 32.1% in the case of ARCH participants and 24.7% for both ID and DPHD participants. The undergraduate students devoted a lot of time to thinking about solutions and sketching them, 31.8% for IDs and 29.6% for the ARCH students. The graduate students, DPHD, allocated only 18.1% of their time to this activity. Another interesting observation is that whereas the DPHD participants devoted approximately 10% of their time to each of the three information summoning activities, the two other groups showed different patterns. The ID students devoted some 6% both to collecting information and to looking at examples, and spent more than double the time – 13.5% – consulting with others. The ARCH students spent very little time consulting with others,

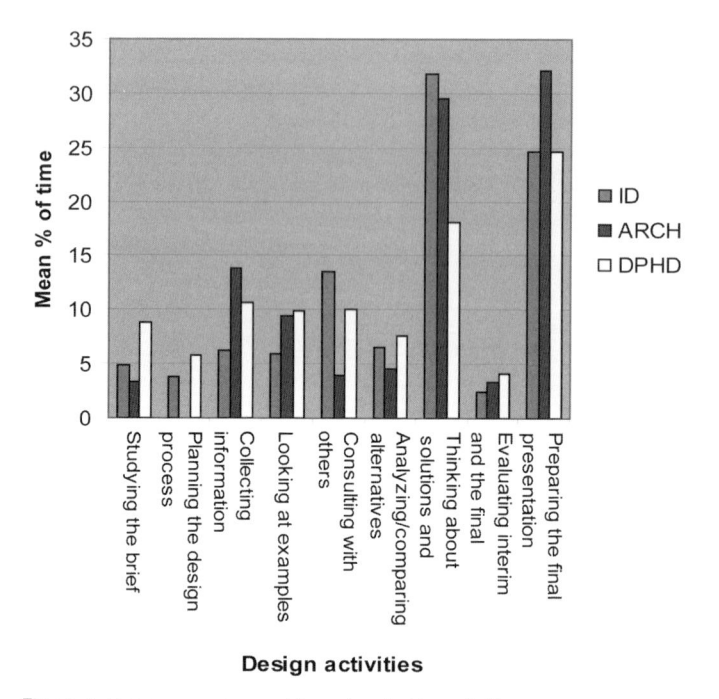

Figure 4: Mean percentage of time devoted to activities

only 3.9%, but in revenge they dedicated 9.4% and 13.8%, respectively, to looking at examples and collecting information. The overall percentage of time dedicated to the three activities is, however, quite similar for the three groups: 25.7% for ID participants, 27.1 for ARCH participants and 30.7% for DPHD participants.

Other interesting differences among the groups are that the DPHD students spent about twice the amount of time studying the brief than the other groups and, as mentioned earlier and evident here, the ARCH participants spent no time at all planning the design process. On the similarities side is the very minimal time devoted to evaluating interim and final designs by all groups, as already mentioned.

We must qualify these observations not only because of the small number of participants but also because of the significant individual differences among students in each of the groups. If we look at but a few examples in the activities that everyone undertook, we find, for instance, that the percentage of time devoted to preparing the final presentation among ID participants ranged from 4.5 to 46 per cent. Studying the brief ranged from 5 to 12.5 per cent among DPHD participants and, among the ARCH participants, thinking about solutions and sketching them ranged between 18.3 and 36.8 per cent. Despite these qualifications we believe that, with due caution, we may all the same conclude that some trends that distinguish among the groups do exist and we discuss these in the next section.

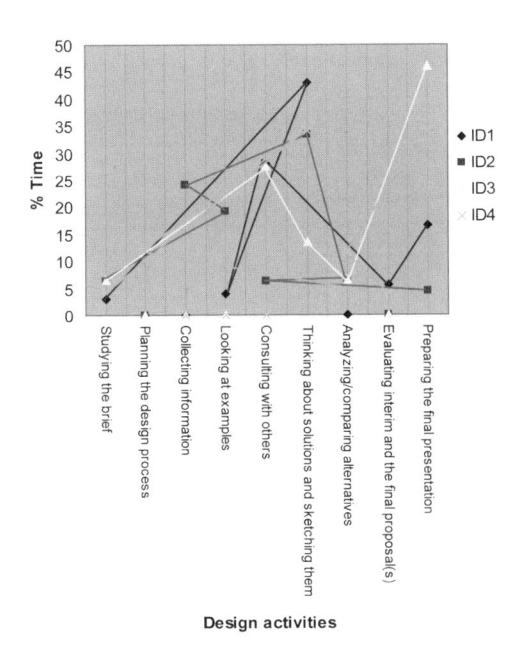

Figure 5: ID students – chronological sequence of activities and percentage of time spent

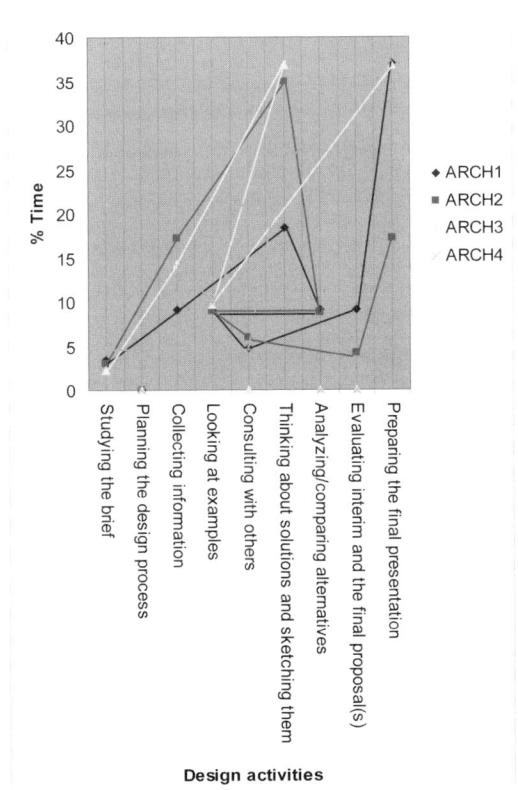

Figure 6: Arch students – chronological sequence of activities and percentage of time spent

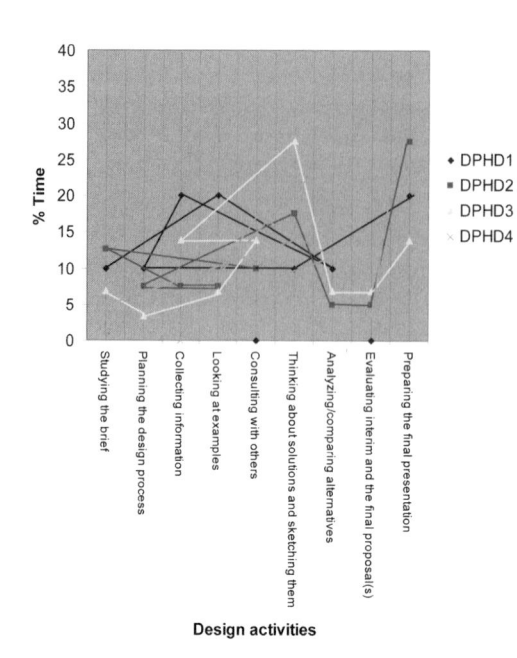

Figure 7: DPHD students – chronological sequence of activities and percentage of time spent

Figures 5, 6 and 7 combine the activity sequences and percentage of time spent for each participant within the three groups.

Undergraduate Versus Graduate Students

Despite the small size of the sample and the individual differences among members within the groups, it seems to us that some interesting distinctions among the groups suggest themselves. We already indicated some differences between the ID and ARCH participants and, most noticeably, divergence in their information sources, plus some more attention to the final presentation on the part of the ARCH participants. But we find that the more significant differences are between the two groups of undergraduate students, ID and ARCH, and the group of graduate students, DPHD. We pointed out the differences in subject matters – tangible objects for all undergraduate students and mostly services (and a system) in the case of the graduate students. In terms of design behaviour – in our case time allocation and activity sequences – we have already mentioned the fact that DPHD participants paid more attention to the brief and that all of them planned their processes, as opposed to only one undergraduate participant. Planning the process ahead may signify that a particular strategy was employed. This is in line with the finding by Ahmed et al. [2] that experienced designers use particular design strategies, as opposed to novices who tend to display a trial-and-error behaviour pattern. The graduate group tended to use all channels of information uniformly, in contrast to the undergraduate participants. In addition, the graduate participants engaged in more design activities (average of 8.25 out of 9) than the undergraduate participants (average of 6.0 and 6.75 for the ID and ARCH groups, respectively).

Undergraduate participants started the process with a short study of the brief; then most of them engaged in one information-soliciting activity, followed by thinking about solutions and sketching them. With one exception of a participant who started the process with the thinking and sketching activity (DPHD4), all graduate participants deferred it and preferred to summon information first in various ways, plan their processes and engage in a few other activities. Table 4 shows the chronological stage at which the thinking and sketching activity was undertaken (out of 9 possible activities). The difference in chronological order is, of course, related to the total number of activities which, as stated, is significantly higher for the DPHD group.

Table 4: Chronological order of the activity 'thinking about solutions and sketching them'

Undergraduate students (mean: 6.4 activities)									Graduate students (mean: 8.3 activities)			
Industrial Design				Architecture				PhD in Design			
ID1	ID2	ID3	ID4	ARCH1	ARCH2	ARCH3	ARCH4	DPHD1	DPHD2	DPHD3	DPHD4
2	4	3	2	3	3	3	3	6	6	6	1

This difference is most telling. The more experienced graduate students are probably also more research-minded and display a more systematic design behaviour. All of them engaged in analysis, whereas only a little over half the undergraduate students did so (see Table 3). Deferring decisions regarding solutions is in line with creative problem solving [e.g. 12, 26], although it would have made sense to generate candidate solutions or at least partial candidate solutions earlier in the process. Because of the reported iterations and the going back and forth that participants experienced, partial solutions may have been generated in fact, but it is interesting that these participants chose nonetheless to report that they engaged in this activity later on. Interestingly, DPHD4, who was the exception and started the process with thinking and sketching, reported that his process was 'quite linear' and added: 'I considered a few options then just went for one. I didn't reconsider my idea.'

Is this difference in design behaviour a result of the relative expertise of the DPHD participants, compared to the ID and ARCH participants who are still novices? Or does it have to do with the fact that, having chosen to pursue an advanced degree, the DPHD participants belong a priori to a self-selected category of research-oriented designers who naturally approach design problems more methodically? It is hard to tell and the answer may not be 'either or' but rather both: experience combined with a methodical disposition makes it possible for these participants to tackle an open-ended, ill-defined problem with routines they have already mastered earlier. Our results concur with several other researchers' work where studies have been made between 'novice' and 'expert' designers and the superior efficacy of the expert designers' design activities over their novice counterparts was demonstrated [1, 2, 3, 21].

The novices, in contrast, have fewer routines and probably work more intuitively, especially when the problem is unusually open-ended and compressed, something they are not used to. As ARCH2 confided: 'The design process that we follow in architecture [school] is usually set for us by weekly sheets that accompany tutorials and working towards stage reviews'. Therefore, it seems, novices need to sketch earlier. The fact that most DPHD participants proposed services or a system rather than a tangible object had seemingly no effect on the displayed design behaviour (although it may explain the significantly lower percentage of time devoted to thinking and sketching, as no details had to be worked out). Services and systems need thinking about, of course, if not necessarily sketching; and DPHD4, who started with 'thinking and sketching', was one of the service proposers. We definitely notice a different approach and pattern in the design behaviour of the two constituencies, novice and relative experts, which is very interesting and may have consequences for design education.

Design Thinking: The Designer–Entrepreneur

Our main findings in the limited experiment we have conducted are summarised as follows. Most students (two-thirds) responded to the brief by proposing a physical object (product) regardless of their course of study. Most participants did not plan their processes or did so to a very limited extent. Most of them did not follow a linear process: they went back and forth and iterated a lot between one activity and another. On average, between a quarter and a third of the participants' time was devoted to the preparation of a final presentation. Both sets of undergraduate design students (ID and ARCH) spent an average of close to one-third of their time on 'thinking about solutions and sketching them.' The DPHD students spent far less time – possibly because, for the most part, they did not design physical objects, which may have required fewer problem-solving cycles. Alternatively, the DPHD students' superior design experience and knowledge may have impacted on the time they spent on this activity, which was far less than the ID and ARCH students spent. Finally, and perhaps unsurprisingly, the most important source in collecting information for all students was the Internet. The ARCH students spent twice the amount of time as the ID students searching the web for information. However, the ID students consulted with others more than three times as much as the ARCH students.

These findings converge to show that methodological prescriptions should be eased in open-ended design tasks and under time constraints. The great variety in design behaviour parameters we have found leads us to some very general conclusions pertaining to design and design education, which we take to be fundamentally significant to the wider and more entrepreneurial scope of design in the era of design thinking.

The design time in this experiment was short – up to 15 hours (and as little as 2.5 hours, in one case) with an average a little over 7 hours – and most students saw the assignment as 'compressed' and atypical. ARCH4 said: 'One-off exercises like this are rare.' But should such exercises be rare? The boundaries of what is included in the term 'design' have expanded considerably in recent years to include a wide range of consultancies, organisations and companies that seek to innovate in many ways. Now design extends from the design of objects and spaces that we use on a daily basis to cities, landscapes, nations, cultures, bodies, genes, political systems, the way we produce food, to the way we travel and build cars [14]. Moreover, with accelerated design activity anticipated well into the twenty-first century, it is clear that an increasing number of practitioners across a diverse range of creative disciplines routinely regard their methods as rooted in design practice or are using methods that could be considered designerly [8]. It is also equally clear that design is expanding its disciplinary, conceptual, theoretical and methodological frameworks to encompass ever-wider activities and practice. The way designers think, it is claimed, is conducive to innovative solutions [6, 18, 19]. Certain design communities and quite a range of business communities are adopting the so-called design thinking method to enhance innovation in enterprises of various kinds, which consider it to be the most contributory factor to competitive advantage. The term 'design thinking' is in good currency in both academia and among practitioners, and has produced a host of recent publications [e.g. 6, 9, 17, 18, 28]. There is no agreed definition of 'design thinking' but the strongest common denominator is the centrality of the user or even, in the view of some, being 'empathic to the human condition'*. (Other features of design thinking such as iterative exploration, prototyping and teamwork are irrelevant to the current 'compressed' case.) Design thinkers are expected constantly to challenge the boundaries of known solutions and venture into uncharted territories. Their processes are expected to be systematic but not rigid, and flexibility of thought and exploration are key concepts. The designer, it seems, is expected to demonstrate an entrepreneurial approach, even when the task is initiated by someone else (a client). In addition, designers must work fast as competition in the marketplace drives short design cycles. 'One-off', compressed assignments are very realistic occurrences in practice. Does design education address these challenges?

If indeed we subscribe to the notion that design thinking is a key to innovation which, in turn, is the fuel that turns the wheels of the economy, then we must ask: how should we educate design thinkers? What methodologies should they learn, what design processes do we want to encourage? Textbook methods [e.g. 5, 20, 22, 27] are on the rigid side. They foresee a linear process, albeit with iterations. They are tacitly based on the assumption that, at the time the problem-solving or design process starts, the task has been sufficiently clarified and the problem is more or less well defined, even well structured. They have a hard time seeing a problem and a solution being co-developed [10], as we know is very often the case in design, particularly when innovation is the goal and the problem definition may be revised or at least negotiated at almost any stage.

---

*   Alison King, email to the DesignX community, Center for Design Research at Stanford University, 19 April 2011

Do the design methods we teach our students prepare them to handle ill-defined and ill-structured problems, even wicked problems, wherein innovation is a prime goal and the pace is very fast? Do we teach them adequately to take risks? Do we ask them to go to extremes and explore entirely new directions of thought, as is often required today? The modest task in this experiment called for a design that 'surpasses conventional expectations'. Did the student participants rise to the challenge and what in the processes they underwent supported or hindered success? Trying to follow a linear process was not necessarily advantageous. Interestingly, the two developers of new services, both DPHD students who were, appropriately, aware of the expanded scope of design, reported 'quite linear' and 'more or less linear' processes. So did some of the designers of the less-original designs in the ID and ARCH groups. Those who took the liberty to go back and forth had somewhat more opportunities to experiment and explore, and finally embarked upon somewhat more original design ideas. Extremely ill-defined problems and tight design schedules are excellent opportunities to think differently, to bypass or revise standard methods, and therefore it is highly recommended that they do not continue to be a rare exception in design education.

It seems that we should encourage our students to devote more time and effort to explorations and certainly not focus so much attention on preparing final presentations (especially in very compressed exercises). Should we teach methods? We definitely should – but it must be emphasised that normative methods are to serve as general guidelines, check lists perhaps, rather than rigid prescriptions and that the order in which activities are undertaken is often flexible and context related. It is reassuring that even a most limited experiment of the kind we have conducted allows us to reach a conclusion of such magnitude. If we want designers to merit the credit they are given today even outside of the world of design as strategic players in the forefront of innovative initiatives, we should prepare them accordingly. The world is ready to acknowledge the artistry of design, not just the 'science' of design, as advocated by Donald Schön decades ago [23]. But are designers and design educators ready to let go of an adherence to rigid 'methods'? Learning to do so is one of the challenges facing design education as well as practice.

References

1. Adams, R., Turns, J. and Atman, C. (2003) 'Educating Effective Engineering Designers: The Role of Reflective Practice', *Design Studies*, 24 (3), pp.275–94.
2. Ahmed, S., Wallace, K. and Blessing, L. (2003) 'Understanding the Differences between how Novice and Experienced Designers Approach Design Tasks', *Research in Engineering Design*, 14, pp.1–11.
3. Atman, C., Cardella, M. and Turns, J. (2005) 'Comparing Freshman and Senior Engineering Design Processes: An In-depth Follow-up Study', *Design Studies*, 26, pp.325–57.
4. Bhandari, A. and Wagner, T. (2006) 'Self-Reported Utilization of Health Care Services: Improving Measurement and Accuracy', *Medical Care Research and Review*, 63 (2), pp.217–35.

5. Birkenhofer, H. (ed.) (2011) *The Future of Design Methodology*, London: Springer Verlag.
6. Brown, T. (2009) *Change by Design: How Design Thinking Transforms Organizations and Inspires Innovation*, New York: HarperBusiness.
7. Covington, G.A. and Hannah, B. (1997) *Access by Design*, NYC: Van Nostrand Reindhold.
8. Cross, N. (2006) *Designerly Ways of Knowing*, London: Springer.
9. Cross, N. (2011) *Design Thinking: Understanding how Designers Think and Work*, Oxford: Berg.
10. Dorst, K. and Cross, N. (2001) 'Creativity in the Design Process: Co-evolution of Problem-Solution', *Design Studies*, 25 (5), pp.425–37.
11. Farrington, D.P., Loeber, R., Stouthamer-Loeber, M., Van Kammen, W.B. and Schmidt, L. (1996) 'Self-reported delinquency and a combined delinquency seriousness scale based on boys, mothers, and teachers: Concurrent and predictive validity for African-Americans and Caucasians', *Criminology*, 34, pp.493–517.
12. Goel, V. (1995) *Sketches of Thought*, Cambridge, MA: MIT Press.
13. Goldschmidt, G. (2008) 'Sketching is Alive and Well in this Digital Age', in W. Poelman and D. Keyson (eds), *Design Processes: What Architects and Industrial Designers can Teach each other about Managing the Design Process*, Amsterdam: IOS Press, pp.29–43.
14. Latour, B. (2008) 'A Cautious Prometheus? A Few Steps Toward a Philosophy of Design (With Special Attention to Peter Sloterdijk)', in F. Hackne, J. Glynne and V. Minto (eds), *Proceedings of the 2008 Annual International Conference of the Design History Society*, Universal Publishers, pp.2–10.
15. Lawson, B. (2006) *How Designers Think*, Oxford: Architectural Press/Elsevier.
16. Lawson, B. and Dorst, K. (2009) *Design Expertise*, Oxford: Architectural Press/Elsevier.
17. Lockwood, T. (ed.) (2009) *Design Thinking: Integrating Innovation, Customer Experience, and Brand Value*, New York: Design Management Institute/Allworth Press.
18. Martin, R.L. (2009) *The Design of Business: Why Design Thinking is the Next Competitive Advantage*, Cambridge, MA: Harvard Business School.
19. Nussbaum, B. (2009) 'Innovation is Dead. Herald The Birth of Transformation as the Key Concept for 2009', *Business Week Online*, accessed 25 August 2009.
20. Pahl, G. and Beitz, W. (1984) *Engineering Design: A Systematic Approach*, London: Design Council.
21. Popovic, V. (2003) 'General Strategic Knowledge Models Connections and Expertise Development in Product Design', in N. Cross and E. Edmonds (eds), *Expertise in Design: Proceedings of DTRS'6*, Sydney: Creativity and Cognition Studios, pp.251–70.
22. Roozenburg, N.F.M. and Eekels, J. (1995) *Product Design: Fundamentals and Methods*, Chichester: Wiley.
23. Schön, D.A. (1983) *The Reflective Practitioner*, New York: Basic Books.
24. Spector, P.E. (1994) 'Using self-report questionnaires in OB research: A comment on the use of a controversial method', *Journal of Organizational Behavior*, 15 (5), pp.385–92.
25. Thornberry, T.P. and Krohn, M.D. (2000) 'The Self-Report Method for Measuring Delinquency and Crime', *Criminal Justice 2000*, vol. 4, pp.33–83.

26. Treffinger, D.J., Isaksen, S.G. and Stead-Dorval, K.B. (2006) *Creative Problem Solving: An Introduction*, 4th edition, Waco, Texas: Prufrock Press Inc.
27. Ullman, D. (1992/2003) *The Mechanical Design Process*, New York: McGraw-Hill.
28. Verganti, R. (2009) *Design Driven Innovation: Changing the Rules of Competition by Radically Innovating What Things Mean*, Cambridge, MA: Harvard Business School.
29. Woodbury, R.F. and Burrow, A.L. (2006) 'Whither Design Space?' *Artificial Intelligence for Engineering Design, Analysis and Manufacturing*, 20, pp.63–82.

John S. GERO

Krasnow Institute for Advanced Studies, USA

Morteza POURMOHAMADI

University of Sydney, Australia

AND

Christopher B. WILLIAMS

Virginia Polytechnic Institute and State University, USA

THE EFFECT OF EMPLOYING DIFFERENT DESIGN METHODS ON THE DESIGN COGNITION OF SMALL DESIGN TEAMS

Introduction

The ninth Design Thinking Research Symposium set the following generic brief:

> 11% of the world's 6.9 billion people are over 60. By the year 2050 that figure will have doubled to 22%. If we are to support a growing number of older people we need to produce products, spaces, and services that allow them to stay healthy and well in and around their own home. You are asked to design a domestic product, living environment, or service for older people that surpasses conventional expectations.

Within that brief, two existing briefs for the design of assistive devices were used to study the effects of employing different design methods on the design cognition of small teams. The experiment described in this paper was used to test hypotheses about the effects of using two different design methods while designing. The two design methods were brainstorming and morphological analysis.

Brainstorming is an unstructured, freeform concept-generation technique targeted at stimulating the rapid production of ideas [1]. Aside from a few rules geared towards suspending one's judgment of the feasibility of concepts presented until after the exercise is completed, there is little other structured guidance. In brainstorming, groups of participants are encouraged to engage in rapid idea generation, by presenting all ideas (including those that may be infeasible) and by building off teammates' ideas

[2]. Different structures and communication techniques have been suggested for brainstorming sessions but the essence of all is to generate as many ideas as possible in a short period of time. The ideas are then to be classified and used as alternative solutions. It is claimed that the chances of potentially useful ideas showing up in a larger collection are higher than in a small collection of ideas. Brainstorming techniques rely on this claim to raise the quantity, as well as the quality, of the ideas generated by randomly exploring the solution space [1].

Morphological analysis, on the other hand, provides a much more structured framework for concept ideation. Morphological analysis is centred on the idea of decomposing a larger problem into a list of needed features or functions [3], known as sub-problems. Once the problem is decomposed, potential solutions for each sub-problem are ideated. These solutions are then organised in a morphological matrix [4] with a few potential solution concepts listed for each function. The overall solutions to the design task are generated by systematically combining concepts from each sub-problem. As opposed to brainstorming, morphological analysis is centred on ideation by first abstracting the core of a product's functionality.

Given the differences between the two techniques, the following four commonly held hypotheses, derived from the structure of the respective methods, regarding their impact on design behaviour were put forward and evidentiary support for them was sought:

1. As morphological analysis is focused in promoting concept generation through functional abstraction, designers will discuss design issues related to a product's expected behaviour more frequently than they would using brainstorming;

2. Similarly, designers using morphological analysis would spend less time relatively in a design session discussing issues related to the structure of a product than those designers using brainstorming;

3. As morphological analysis asks a designer to evaluate compatibility and feasibility amongst the functional concepts, we expect a higher frequency of an analysis design process than those using brainstorming; and

4. Because morphological analysis has a prescriptive means of capturing concept ideation in a matrix, we expect its users to display more of a description design process than those using brainstorming.

The remainder of this chapter outlines the experiment design, which uses the protocol analysis method and presents and discusses the results in terms of the four hypotheses along with some unexpected results.

Experiment design

The Participants

The experiment described in this paper is a within-subject study with students from the senior capstone design sequence in the mechanical engineering (ME) department of a large mid-Atlantic land-grant university. This two-semester sequence features teams of students working on large-scale design problems that culminate with a functional product. In class the design projects range from national design competitions (e.g. Formula SAE, ASEE Model Design) to faculty-sponsored projects (e.g. design of a small-scale wind turbine, design of a robotic humanoid hand).

In the first semester of the sequence, students attend a lecture series related to all aspects of the product realisation process. Relevant to the study described here, students attended lectures related to ideation techniques: specifically, brainstorming [2], morphological analysis [4], and TRIZ [5]. Following each lecture, 10 pairs of students attended an out-of-class design session to participate in the experiment. For each session, each group solved a speculative design brief using the ideation technique covered in the previous week's class. In this paper, the authors present the results from comparing students' use of two ideation techniques: brainstorming and morphological analysis.

The Briefs

Each group was assigned two different design briefs, one for each ideation technique. In the first experimental session, students were asked to use brainstorming to design a device that could assist the elderly tenants of the building with the force needed to adjust the window sliders without relying on electric power. The brief explained how changes in the humidity during the summer months cause the windows of a 65-years-old nursing building to 'stick', thus requiring a significant amount of force to raise and lower the windowpanes. It also included a brief introduction on the structure of double-hung windows and links to online resources.

The second session's design task challenged the students to use morphological analysis to design a device to help stroke patients, who are unable to perform bilateral tasks, with opening doors in a rehabilitation hospital (adapted from [6]). The brief included a short description about limitations of stroke patients and their difficulties in opening doors by turning the knob and pushing or pulling the door at the same time. The teams were asked to design a system that allows a stroke patient to unlock and open a door at the same time with only one hand.

The Experiment

The experiment covers two ideation techniques: brainstorming and morphological analysis. For the design sessions, each team had the use of a computer with access to the Internet and a whiteboard with colour markers that they could use for sketching or writing notes. The teams were allowed to continue until they came to a conclusion

Figure 1: Two screenshots from two of the recorded design sessions

on a satisfactory design. Sessions typically lasted between 45 and 75 minutes. Since the interest is in the design cognition of the teams of designers, the absolute length of a protocol plays no significant role. All of the design sessions were recorded on video to facilitate protocol analysis. Figure 1 shows screenshots from two of the recordings showing the setting of the experiments.

Analysis Method

the participants were asked to verbalise their thoughts while they designed; this verbalisation occurs naturally when participants are in teams. The sessions were audio and video recorded. The verbalisations by the participants were transcribed and then non-verbal behaviours such as writing and drawing were added to the text. Segmenting and coding of the protocols [7, 8, 9] was carried out by two separate coders and then arbitrated using the Delphi method [10]. The coders' agreement with the arbitrated version ranged from 83.3 to 97.1 per cent with a mean agreement of 91.7 per cent across the 20 protocols, which is considered a statistically reliable agreement percentage. The Function-Behaviour-Structure (FBS) design issues coding scheme [11, 12] was utilised to segment and code the 20 design protocols. An example from one of the protocols of the segmentation and coding of an excerpt from the utterances is given in Table 1. The design issues become the base data that represents the cognitive design activity in each session.

Table 1: An excerpt from the coded brainstorming protocol B-5

#	Subject	Utterance	Code
193	A	Because we don't necessarily need to open the window for the person we just need to assist it.	F
194	A	So, if we take half the load [...], they might have an easier time opening it. So...	Be
195	A	We could do something like that,	S
196	A	where it just takes a lot of the load off.	Bs
197	B	I think it's just some sort of a, um... you got a... like a damper system	S
198	B	I think is how they work, because you've just got like hydraulic fluid in there.	S
199	B	Because they are more for resisting.	Bs

Function-Behaviour-Structure Coding Scheme

The Function-Behaviour-Structure design issues coding scheme and its supporting ontology were used for coding the protocols. The FBS ontology of design uses the concept of design issue as the basic unit of its ontology and defines six foundational non-overlapping design issues [9]. The ontological variables that map onto design issues are: function, behaviour and structure plus a design description, Figure 2. Outside the direct control of the designer is the set of requirements, labelled R, provided by the client. The function (F) of a designed object is defined as its teleology; the behaviour (B) of that object is either derived (Bs) or expected (Be) from the structure, where structure (S) represents the components of an object and their relationships. Therefore, any design utterance or activity fits into one of these six categories, namely, functions (F), expected behaviours (Be), structure behaviours (Bs),

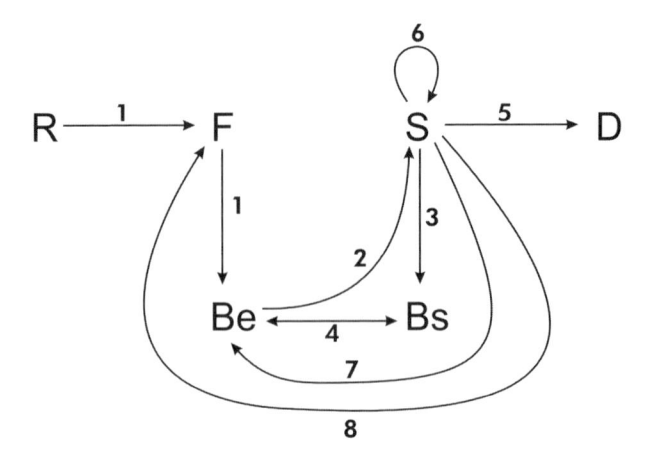

Figure 2: Design issues, labelled with symbols, and the resulting design processes, numbered 1 through 8, defined by the FBS ontology of design

structures (S), descriptions (D) and requirement (R) [13]. The aim of design activity is to transform a set of function issues into a set of structures and finally document them as a set of descriptions. However, there is no direct route from functions to structure. Instead, the designer goes through a series of transitional processes between different issues to reach a final design. The transition from one design issue to another is a design process. Figure 2 shows the relationships of the six design issues and resulting eight design processes.

In Figure 2, formulation (R→F, F→Be), labelled 1, is the design process of producing a set of expected behaviours from the requirement and function issues. The design process synthesis (Be→S), labelled 2, is the design process of generating structure issues from the expected behaviours. The analysis process (S→Bs), labelled 3, occurs when a set of behaviours are deduced from the structure issues. The evaluation process (Bs→Be, Be→Bs), labelled 4, of the ideated structures is produced when comparing the expected and structure behaviours. The documentation process (S→D), labelled 5, can be of the structure or the externalisation of any other design issue. In addition to these processes, the FBS ontology of design has three types of reformulations. These processes are aimed at capturing the actively changing state of the design and account for changes in structure, behaviour or function issues. The processes are respectively called reformulation-1 (S→S), labelled 6, reformulation-2 (S→Be), labelled 7, and reformulation-3 (S→F), labelled 8, in Figure 2.

Based on the FBS coding scheme, two types of transition processes can be generated from any coded protocol: semantic and syntactic design processes. In the semantic approach, the semantic connection between coded segments of the protocol generates a link between them and, depending on which design issue is at each end of the link, a particular design process is produced. This kind of linking generates a semantic linkograph. For example, if segment number 100 with code S is semantically linked to segment number 120 with code Bs, then the design process analysis (S→Bs) is produced between them. Despite its strong conceptual foundations, employing a semantic approach in protocol analysis depends on the generation of the semantic links between segments that needs a considerable amount of time and resources.

The syntactic approach is based on a weaker model of design activity and relies on the sequential order of the design issues to generate the links between and to produce the design process, which is called the syntactic design process. Here each segment is linked to its immediately preceding segment. We employ the syntactic approach in this paper to produce the syntactic design processes by the participants in each protocol.

Measuring Design Issues and Design Processes

Measures of design issues and design processes provide the foundation for the understanding of the design cognition of the participants. The occurrences of design issues and design processes are initially measured through the descriptive statistics of means and standard deviations. Any differences are indications of effects of educational interventions.

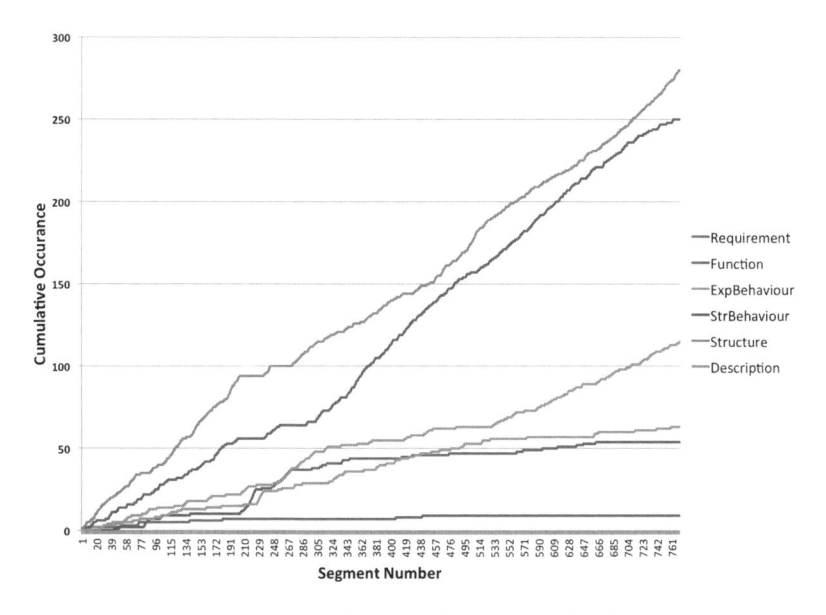

Figure 3: Cumulative occurrence of design issues for brainstorming design session of team B-3

The cumulative occurrences of design issues and design processes provide other measures. To calculate the cumulative occurrence of each design issue, the generation of that issue throughout the coded protocol is counted in an additive manner. In other words, if a segment number, n, is coded as x, then c, the cumulative occurrence of x at segment n, will be $c = \Sigma i-1\ ^x c$ where x_i equals 1 if segment i is coded as x and 0 if segment i is not coded as x. Plotting the results of this equation on a graph with segment numbers, n, as the horizontal axis and the cumulative occurrence values, c, as the vertical axis will illustrate the cumulative occurrence of the design issues. An example of the cumulative occurrence of design issues for the brainstorming protocol of team B-3 is shown in Figure 3. Juxtaposing the graph lines for all of the design issues provides a qualitative representation of how the design issues are occurring while the participants are designing.

The cumulative occurrence is an indicator for the amount of cognitive effort that that design team has put into each issue up to that point. Each design issue's cumulative occurrence graph is modelled by a linear regression. To assure that the linear regression is the best fit for modelling the results, we calculated the coefficient of determination, the R-square values, for each protocol. The average R-square value is 0.909 for brainstorming sessions (SD = 0.148) and 0.856 for morphological analysis sessions (SD = 0.236). This shows that a linear regression could be a proper representation for cumulative occurrence of the design issues. Table 2 shows the results for the exemplary design protocol B-3.

Table 2: Linear regressions of design issue occurrences and their R-squares for the brainstorming design protocol of team B-3

	Requirement	Function	Exp. Behaviour	Str. Behaviour	Structure	Description
Linear Regression (Slope)	0.008	0.080	0.091	0.344	0.337	0.140
Linear Regression R-Square	0.785	0.870	0.966	0.986	0.995	0.984

Measuring the linear regressions for the occurrence of the design issues also enables summarising and comparing different protocols. Such cross-case comparisons are usually not possible due to the different lengths of their design protocols. However, summarising the occurrence of the issues with a single value (i.e. the slope of the regression line) along with the general applicability of the FBS coding scheme enables comparisons across different protocols, regardless of their length. After measuring the best-fit regression line, the slope is used as a single-value indicator for the rate of occurrence of each design issue. The means of slopes are used to summarise the performance of brainstorming and morphological analysis groups. A paired t-test is used to assess any significant differences in the occurrence of design issues between the two groups. The results of these analyses are presented in the next section.

Results
Design Issues
Table 3 shows the means and standard deviations for distributions of design issues in the brainstorming and morphological analysis groups. Each result is the aggregation of the results of the 10 teams that form each group.

Table 3: The means and standard deviations for distributions of design issues in the brainstorming and morphological analysis groups

	Requirement	Function	Exp. Behaviour	Str. Behaviour	Structure	Description
Brainstorming						
Mean %	1.30	4.40	7.21	27.71	40.01	19.38
Standard Deviation	0.004	0.015	0.020	0.028	0.048	0.037
Morphological Analysis						
Mean %	0.66	6.65	11.80	22.98	37.40	20.51
Standard Deviation	0.003	0.018	0.026	0.034	0.040	0.053

LINKOgrapher [14], an open-source design protocol analysis tool, was used to calculate the statistical descriptors and the cumulative occurrence of design issues in each team. For each design team, the linear regression line was calculated and the slope of the regression line was taken as an indicator for the generation of design issues by each team. The performance of the teams in each group is summarised by calculating the mean slope for each group. Figure 4 shows the mean slopes of cumulative occurrence of design issues in each group. Table 4 presents the numerical values of the average slopes and their standard deviations for the cumulative occurrences of design issues for the brainstorming and morphological analysis groups.

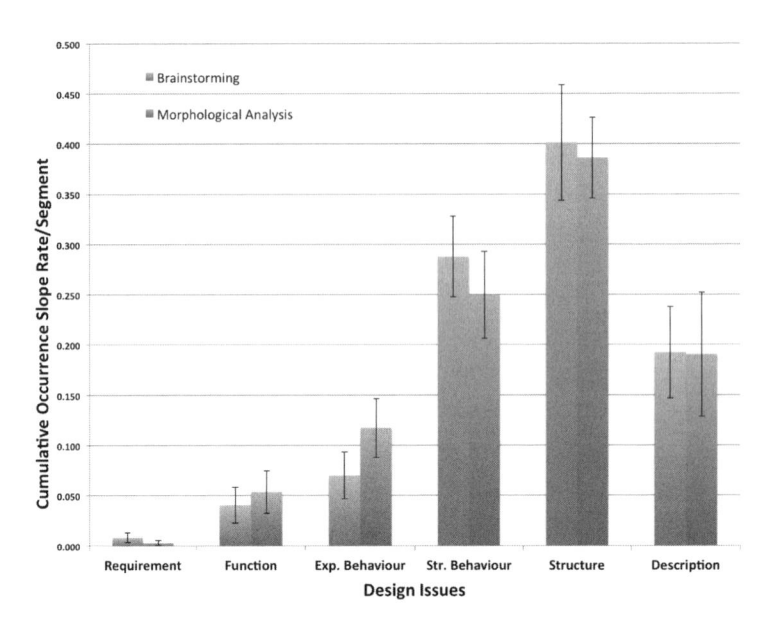

Figure 4: The means and standard deviations for the slopes of cumulative occurrence of design issues for the brainstorming and morphological analysis groups

Table 4: The average slope and standard deviations for cumulative occurrence of design issues in the brainstorming and morphological analysis groups

	Requirement	Function	Exp. Behaviour	Str. Behaviour	Structure	Description
	Brainstorming					
Average Slope	0.008	0.040	0.070	0.288	0.401	0.192
Standard Deviation	0.005	0.018	0.023	0.040	0.057	0.046
	Morphological Analysis					
Average Slope	0.003	0.053	0.117	0.250	0.386	0.190
Standard Deviation	0.002	0.021	0.029	0.043	0.040	0.062

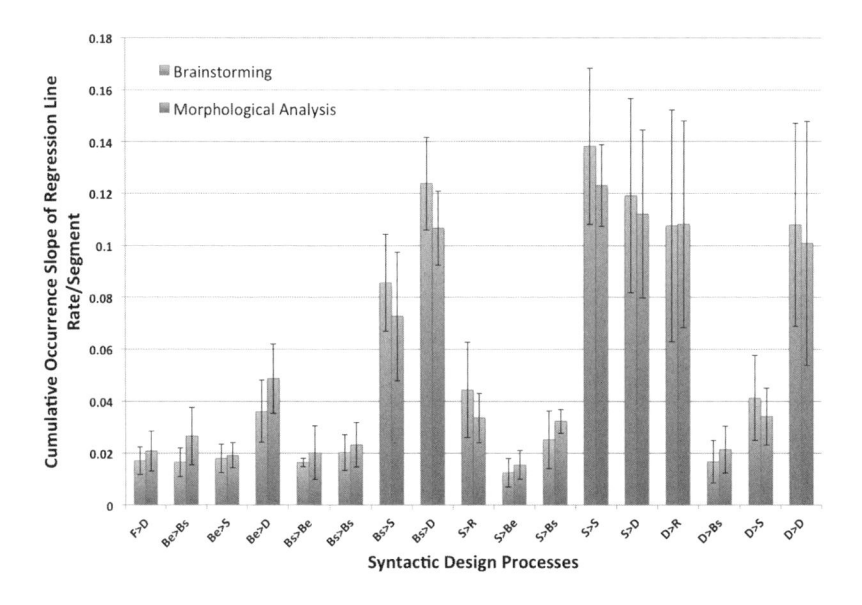

Figure 5: The average slopes of the regression lines for the cumulative occurrence of syntactic design processes in the brainstorming sessions and the morphological sessions

Syntactic Design Processes

A syntactic model of design processes was produced for each design session following the FBS coding scheme. The cumulative generation of design processes by each team was calculated. Figure 5 shows the slopes of the regression lines for the generation of those syntactic design processes that map onto the FBS ontology.

Discussion

Four hypotheses were presented in the Introduction for which evidentiary support is sought through this experiment. The four hypotheses were:

1. Designers using morphological analysis would discuss issues related to expected behaviour more frequently than those using brainstorming;
2. Designers using morphological analysis would discuss structure design issues less frequently than those using brainstorming;
3. Designers employing morphological analysis would conduct the analysis design process more than those using brainstorming; and
4. Designers employing morphological analysis will conduct the description design process more than those using brainstorming.

After generating the statistical models for the cumulative occurrence of the design issues and processes in each group, the hypotheses could be tested using paired t-test between the results from the brainstorming sessions and the morphological analysis sessions. The following sections discuss each hypothesis based on the results of these tests.

Higher Structure Design Issues in Brainstorming

Hypothesis 1 is that brainstorming produces more structure design issues than morphological analysis. Running a paired t-test (t(18) = 0.859) between the slopes of the regression lines for occurrence of structure issues in brainstorming group (M = 0.401, SD = 0.057) and the morphological analysis group (M = 0.386, SD = 0.040) shows no significant difference in the generation of structure design issues (p = 0.2). Therefore, hypothesis 1 is not supported by the data from this experiment. The basis of this hypothesis was that designers using morphological analysis would expend less of their cognitive effort on discussing a product's embodiment and structure due to the focus on functional abstraction. This does not appear to be case.

Lower Expected Behaviour Issues in Brainstorming

Hypothesis 2 is that brainstorming has less expected behaviour design issues than morphological analysis. In the Mechanical Engineering senior design course, morphological analysis is presented in the context of the systematic design methodology proposed by Pahl et al. [15]. Specifically, students are taught to decompose a design problem by a product's various functionalities; i.e. the actions, or 'expected behaviours', that the product must perform in order to satisfy the design requirements. To complete this part of this mental exercise, designers must frequently revisit the overall purpose of the design. Thus, as the discussion of a product's function and expected behaviour drives the problem decomposition in morphological analysis, it is hypothesised that the occurrences of expected behaviour issues are significantly (t (18) = 3.895, p = 0.0005) lower for student designers using the brainstorming technique (M = 0.070, SD = 0.023) compared to the same student designers using the morphological analysis technique (M = 0.117, SD = 0.029). Hence, hypothesis 2 is supported by the data from this experiment.

Lower Analysis Processes in Brainstorming

Hypothesis 3 is that designers involved in brainstorming conduct less analysis design processes than when performing morphological analysis. Running a t-test (t(18) = 2.854) on the results from two sets of design protocols shows that the rate of occurrence of structure behaviour issues in brainstorming group (M = 0.288, SD = 0.040) is significantly (p = 0.005) higher than in morphological analysis group (M = 0.250, SD = 0.043). The initial expectation is the opposite given that brainstorming focuses on the production of ideas rather than analysing them. To confirm these results, we use the syntactical model of design processes and produce the cumulative occurrence charts in the same way (see Figure 5). By definition, the structure behaviour issues are a result of analysing the structure issues. In other words, higher occurrence of structural behaviour issues should be accompanied by higher occurrence of analysis in the process level. As mentioned earlier, the syntactic model of design processes is a weak model. However, it is useful as a quick and easy way of looking at the occurrence of design processes during the design sessions.

A paired t-test (df = 18) was conducted on the results from brainstorming versus the results from morphological analysis. The test highlighted a statistically significant (p<0.5) difference in the average slopes of the syntactic analysis process (S→Bs), with the average slope across brainstorming sessions (M = 0.138, SD = 0.030) being higher than the average slope of morphological analysis sessions (M = 0.123, SD = 0.016). This is in line with our findings about the occurrence of the structural behaviour issues but contrary to our expectations as stated in Hypothesis 3.

One possible explanation for this may be that the protocols capture a length of the design session past the brainstorming period. Brainstorming is considered to be an unstructured, free-form ideation technique. Thus, during the concept ideation stage, ideas are presented without an analysis of the product behaviour. However, as the design process progresses past the ideation stage and potential solutions are evaluated, the designer must perform a significant amount of analysis to select amongst the numerous potential solutions. Thus one might expect a high rate for discussion of structure behaviour issues after using this technique.

Lower Description Processes in Brainstorming

Hypothesis 4 is that fewer description design processes (S→D) occur during the brainstorming sessions than during the morphological analysis sessions. The data from these protocol studies did not support this hypothesis. This result suggests that, although brainstorming lacks the prescribed instruction to document ideas as in morphological analysis, the frequency of a designer's description of concepts is not significantly reduced.

Conclusion

This paper has taken the generic brief of the ninth Design Thinking Research Symposium (DTRS9) and has utilised two briefs for designing assistive technology devices to study the effects on students' design cognition of utilising different design methods while designing. Four different hypotheses based on the literature about brainstorming and morphological analysis design methods [1, 2, 3, 4] were tested. Twenty design protocols were recorded from teams of two designers who used different design methodologies to ideate solutions for their given briefs. The hypotheses were tested using a cumulative approach to the occurrence of FBS design issues across the coded protocols, which enabled the comparison of protocols independent of their lengths.

The hypothesis that brainstorming produces more structure design issues than morphological analysis was not supported (t(18) = 0.859, p = 0.2) by the data from this study. The hypothesis that brainstorming has less expected behaviour design issues than morphological analysis was supported by the data from this study (t (18) = 3.895, p = 0.0005).

The hypothesis that brainstorming has less analysis design process than morphological analysis was rejected. The results of this study confirm the opposite of hypothesis 3 (t(18) = 2.854, p = 0.005), which means there are more analysis processes occurring across the brainstorming sessions. A possible explanation for this could be the need to analyse more ideas in the later phases of a brainstorming design process since more ideas are generated in the early stages of brainstorming. However, further experiments are needed to track the causes of this difference between brainstorming and morphological analysis sessions.

The fourth hypothesis, that brainstorming has less description design process than morphological analysis, was not supported, which suggests that designers' documentation practice is not impacted by prescriptive rules of ideation techniques related to visual organisation of ideas.

A novel analytical technique for protocol analysis was applied in this study: the use of cumulative issue and process graphs, exemplified in Figure 3. This produced the unexpected result that structure design issues are generated at a near-linear rate across the design session, independently of the two methods used. Such a result requires further investigation. If it is observed to occur more generally then this result has particular significance for education, which will be elucidated after further study.

Acknowledgements

This research is supported by the National Science Foundation under Grant No. CMMI-1015627. Any opinions, findings and conclusions or recommendations expressed in this material are those of the authors and do not necessarily reflect the views of the National Science Foundation. The assistance of Jacob Moore in collecting the source data and of Sergey Chernyak and Matt Dworsky in producing the coded protocols is gratefully acknowledged.

References

1. Jones, J.C. (1970) *Design Methods: seeds of human futures*, Wiley-Interscience, p.407.
2. Osborn, A.F. (1963) *Applied imagination: Principles and procedures of creative problem-solving*, Charles Scribner's Sons, 1963.
3. Dym, C.L. and Little, P. (2004) *Engineering Design: A Project-based Introduction*, MIT Press.
4. Zwicky, F. (1967) 'The morphological approach to discovery, invention, research and construction', in F. Zwicky and A. Wilson (eds), *New Methods of Thought and Procedure*, New York: Springer-Verlag, pp.273–97.
5. Altshuller, G. (1973) *The innovation algorithm: TRIZ, systematic innovation and technical creativity*, Worcester, MA: Technological Innovation Center.

6. Atman, C., Kilgore, D. and McKenna, A. (2008) 'Characterizing design learning through the use of language: a mixed-methods study of engineering designers', *Journal of Engineering Education*, vol. 97, no. 3, pp.309–26.
7. Ericsson, K. and Simon, H. (1993) *Protocol Analysis; Verbal Reports as Data*, MIT Press.
8. Van Someren, M.W., Barnard, Y.F. and Sandberg, J.A.C. (1994) *The Think Aloud Method: A Practical Guide to Modelling Cognitive Processes*, Academic Press.
9. Gero, J.S. and McNeill, T. (1998) 'An approach to the analysis of design protocols', *Design Studies*, vol. 19, no. 1, pp.21–61.
10. Linstone, H. and Turoff, M. (1976) *The Delphi method: Techniques and applications*, Reading, MA: Addison-Wesley.
11. Kan, J.W.T. and Gero, J.S. (2009) 'Using the FBS ontology to capture semantic design information in design protocol studies', in J. McDonnell and P. Lloyd (eds), *About designing: Analysing design meetings*, CRC Press, pp.213–29.
12. Gero, J.S. (1990) 'Design prototypes: a knowledge representation schema for design', *AI magazine*, vol. 11, no. 4, pp.26–36.
13. Gero, J.S., Kan, J.W.T. and Pourmohamadi, M. (2011) 'Analysing design protocols: Development of methods and tools', in A. Chakrabarti (ed.), *Research into Design*, Research Publishing, pp.3–10.
14. Pourmohamadi, M. and Gero, J.S. (2011) 'LINKOgrapher: An analysis tool to study design protocols based on FBS coding scheme', in S. Culley, B. Hicks, T. McAloone, T. Howard and Y. Reich (eds), *Design Theory and Methodology*, Design Society, Glasgow, pp.294–303.
15. Pahl, G., Beitz, W., Feldhusen, J. and Grote, K.-H. (2007) *Engineering design: a systematic approach*, 3rd edition, Springer Verlag.

Rachael LUCK

School of Construction Management and Engineering, University of Reading, UK

AND

Ian EWART

School of Construction Management and Engineering, University of Reading, UK

TOWARDS A LIVING FUTURE OF CALM

Introduction

There is difficulty in using the present to predict the future [1]. Yet the use of the present to characterise a 'problem', in response to which something may be made, is a persistent feature of design activities. This is what we do and engage with in various ways as designers all the time. How we do this provides a focus for this article, reflecting on what ordinary folk, 'future users' who happen to be 'older', do as they go about their daily lives and the field methods and approaches used within a design process. Through older people's reflection on their day-to-day activities, we learn some of the things they consider routine or important, as well as more difficult or problematic. These lived accounts constitute 'data' which can be further translated in a design realm. The emphasis in this article is on the formative stage of this process: what people say, how they narrate their perceptions of their home environment, the routine activities and events in their lives. These accounts are regarded as the articulation work for the older people engaged in this research, as they describe how the designed environment they encounter features in their day-to-day lived experience.

The article has three aims that are interlinked:

    i. To reflect upon user engagement practices and how 'information' from encounters formulates the 'problems' to which designers attend;

    ii. To compare what participants said with what is already known about universal design, lifetime homes and neighbourhood design guidance;

iii. Then to consider how these significant features of the lives of this group of older people might inform the vision of a calm future.

When Does Design Start?

Using the present to identify a problem, in order to design a solution, is more apparent in some situations than others. Indeed, acknowledging designing as an on-going course of action, we are familiar with the re-framing of design activity as an emergent problem-solution space [2] where the design co-evolves in design interactions. In user-engaged participatory approaches, users become part of, and written into, a design process in various ways. Whether the users are themselves acknowledged as designers in this process is contentious [3] and more frequently users are engaged in usability, prototype-testing phases in product development [4], or are characterised in use-cases and by personas [5] instead of more active design participation. Users sometimes feature in the problem-identification phase of a design process, as part of a requirements elicitation exercise and in requirements engineering, where use cases act as scenarios making assumptions about people and tasks, or as informational categories with scripts. To varying degrees, users routinely feature in the identification of 'problems' for designers to provide 'solutions' to; but for this to be considered as co-evolution, the methods and processes for engagement must be more nuanced.

The notion of makeshift users [6, p.95], where the world is constantly brought into being through the reciprocal relation between people and things, is the socio-cultural perspective from which this research is approached. Approaching the field, older people as they go about their daily lives, provides a different kind of lived insight into what might be a situation that designers can attempt to improve or fix. It is this personal, lived experience that this research begins to examine. It is an unmotivated examination, in the sense that the design 'problems' have not been anticipated in advance. It is the subjects and topics that these older 'users' bring into conversation that are an indication of what is important in their lives. The topics raised in conversation inform the design of the future for older people's lives to run more smoothly. In a similar way to architectural briefing, which questions whether a building is needed, this research acts as a sensitising exercise rather than assuming that there is a design problem. From this perspective, design is understood as 'changing an existing situation in a preferred one', whilst also acknowledging that 'everyone designs who devises courses of action towards changing an existing situation' [7, p.111]. The participants in this probe exercise are part of a course of action that co-evolves, and importantly design is considered to start with talking to these older people.

Design Age: 60 to End of Life

In many countries, the demographic of the population is getting older and this has been viewed as heading towards a 'crisis' that is going to happen in the near future. Planning for an older population is considered to require transformational change [8]. 'Older people' as a demographic category needs further consideration.

The category 'older people' spans the chronological age from sixty to end of life. The abilities and capabilities of someone who is 60 years old will be different from someone in their 70s or older, as well as their outlook on life and understanding of the world around them. While the term 'third age' for people aged between sixty and eighty is well known, increasingly advanced old age, people over eighty years old, is referred to as the 'fourth age' [9]. Chronological age is considered useful for making statements and predictions about anatomy, physiology and psychology [10, p.8] but the limitations of solely using chronological age to categorise older people is also acknowledged [11, p.460]. By engaging design for 'older people', age is both helpful and too glossed a term to be meaningful. A person who happens to be older will have individual capabilities and it is the specifics of each person's preference and experience that are foregrounded through this research.

A deliberate orientation has been to understand older people's lived experiences better through their accounts of personal capabilities; to assess things that are difficult and could be better for them as these arise in conversation rather than problematising ageing in the framing of the research. As with pregnancy, which is not an illness yet features in healthcare provision, getting older leads to a reduction in capabilities but not necessarily to a person's becoming a healthcare-service or care-home consumer. Approaching the problem of designing the future for older people's lives to run more smoothly, this formative design sensitisation exercise begins with talking to older people. How, methodologically, this was undertaken is next considered, starting with an introduction to the cultural probe approach.

Subverting the Probe Approach

The cultural probe approach is an interaction technique developed at the Helen Hamlyn research centre [12], designed originally for use with a group of older people. It is a novel technique to engage people in reporting aspects of their lives which are relevant in their eyes, self-selecting the topics of conversation with a researcher [12]. The cultural probe is a means of gaining sociological insight into people's lives. 'We wanted to lead a discussion with the groups toward unexpected ideas, but we didn't want to dominate it' [12, p.22]. Key to this approach was the intention to provide inspiration, rather than information. It is unlikely to be the most effective method for tackling explicit design problems or validating a design process but it is the potential of this approach for opening up the uncertainties of a design space that is appealing.

The cultural probe was never intended as a determinate methodology with a prescriptive way of being applied; rather it was developed with the understanding that a similar approach could be used in a variety of situations. The approach has been applied to the study of smart homes [13, 14] and the acceptance and rejection of assistive technologies, in situations where user-insights into the use of technology feature significantly. Yet the ethnographic element in technology research has been criticised as often misguided [15]. Indeed, there is a fieldwork problem. The home environment is difficult to investigate, since the private nature of many activities means they are likely to be influenced by the very act of investigation [14].

This research applies a probe approach deliberately to avoid interfering with peoples' lives and to prompt the self-selection of things that are important. Without a specific research agenda (for example, providing technological solutions to the 'problem' of ageing in place) this approach is attentive to what these older people wanted to discuss, acknowledging that what is important in someone's life may or may not constitute a design problem. This application returns the probe to its original demographic group, older people. The older people contacted to become part of the research were nominated by personal recommendation, knowing that, although 'older people' are potentially a vulnerable group, those involved in this exercise were individually able to give their informed consent. The six people that were part of this exercise spanned the age range of 69 to 88, as shown in Table 1. Two men and four women, including one married couple were part of this research. All the participants live in their own home.

Table 1: Age and gender of the participants

	Chronological Age			
	Third Age			Fourth Age (advanced old age)	
Female	69	72	79		88
Male				82	83

An initial meeting took place at the homes of the participants at which the background to the research was explained and the probe prompts were described. Each participant was left with a written copy of the prompts and a disposable camera to take photos to 'answer' each prompt. The participants were asked to take photographs of four things in response to each of these prompts:

1. What have you seen that you would like in your home?
2. What would an older person need in this house?
3. What would you like to be able to do that you can't?
4. How does this neighbourhood fit with your lifestyle?
5. What part does technology play in your life?
6. What is important for the future?

Interwoven in the original use of the probe approach was the use of a disposable camera to gather photographs, which would then act as prompts for a conversation with the research team. This visual method has resonances with an anthropological approach known as photo-elicitation [16]. Similarly, photographs formed part of the data for this research. The camera was collected in person when the exercise with the probe prompts was complete. This was followed by a conversation with each participant, using the photos as prompts for the participants to describe things that featured in their daily lives that they considered noteworthy. In this way the original motivation for the probe approach was upheld – for the participants to steer and self-select topics, to bring their own lived experience into conversation. Seemingly it was an appropriate, non-intrusive way to provoke self-reflection on what is important in their lives and as a means to encourage a participant-led conversation, in contrast with a researcher's agenda-driven semi-structured interview.

Engagement with the Probes

With this approach comes a welcome uncertainty over how the participants will respond and engage with the exercise. There are two issues associated with this: whether the participants will use the camera (or more generally provide responses to each prompt); and how to cluster the responses analytically under thematic headings. In part this is a generalisation issue, given that the number of participants involved is too small a sample to be viewed as representing a broader population of 'older people' – acknowledging, however, that the subjects discussed may affect other people. The thematic groupings of some photographs are presented. Reflection on the participants' engagement with the method is especially noteworthy.

In the application of the approach one participant questioned the relevance of taking photographs and another found it difficult to photograph some of their responses: 'how do you photograph "privacy"?' These responses illustrate that there were some difficulties engaging with this approach. However, other participants were able to represent abstract concepts photographically, such as the 'time wasted' on housework. One participant represented 'security' by photographing an icon from an image on the Internet. These actions are inferred to be subversions of the probe and took several forms. The participants' volition is acknowledged by not taking photographs for each prompt and by responding in different ways, for example, writing notes in preparation for the conversation with a researcher. The subversion of the probe by using the Internet to find images of things in response and taking photos of a computer screen was another. There were several shots of a computer terminal where the content on the screen was not visible. Attempting to use the Internet, with varying degrees of success, was in itself was noteworthy as creative engagement with this exercise and with the use of technology (a separate probe prompt). It was an indication of the extent that a computer and Internet access have become routine resources in the lives of some of these older people.

The photographs taken acted as visual prompts for a conversation; however, the sometimes-minimal engagement with this aspect of the exercise meant that the notion of the fieldwork as a form of photo-elicitation was more relevant to some responses than others. There was no content analysis of the photographs as such and instead the insight into these people's lives was through what was said in conversation. The conversations were recorded and transcribed. Some participants found the disposable camera difficult to use, claiming this was because of their dexterity, and several people admitted that family members had helped them take photographs. These observations problematise aspects of the research design: the choice of camera (ease of use, with/without a flash, speed of film) and more generally the appropriateness of this approach for some older people. The use of the probe form, designed to help people keep track of how many photographs they had been taken, was found to be difficult for the oldest participant to use. A seemingly simple approach, the taking of photographs to respond to questions and, at a later stage, remembering why each photograph was taken, was a cognitive task that tested the capabilities of some participants. Given the sample size, it is difficult to generalise; however, for this group it was seen that in advanced old age some assistance with this task and the taking of photos may be preferred.

Future Awareness

the participants in this research project were highly attuned to their future needs and, although they were not knowingly stating universal design principles or criteria embedded in lifetime homes design guidance, in many of their responses this is what they were doing. This is encouraging in two respects. Firstly, as an endorsement for the design guidance we currently use to design homes and neighbourhood environments, with the implication that new-build environments will likely fit older peoples' lifestyles better. Secondly, that the lifestyle preferences of these older people are seemingly reflected in current lifetime design guides, at least to some degree. However, new build is not always an option and the suggestion that this is always the answer has a modernist tone of technocratic determinacy: that is, if we simply demolished and re-built homes and communities to this script, older people's lives would be easier. Another view acknowledges that the retrofit, appropriation and improvisation within existing domestic environments and the provision of more accommodating service encounters may be part of the way forward.

Had our participants learned the received script about what an older person needs? By examining how these older people described their experiences, how they brought into conversation things they routinely do which could be improved, we can be attentive to what they consider important in their later lives. This sensitisation exercise raises our awareness of how these people's lives could be improved and is an indication of how well the design guidance we currently use reflects these older people's preferences.

What You Need

The notion of need was framed directly in this exercise by asking participants 'what would an older person need in this house?' This was intended to prompt reflection on their future capabilities as they got older. For several participants, routine domestic chores seemingly took too much of their time. If there were ways for cleaning and basic gardening maintenance to take less time and effort, perhaps with a robot or someone's assistance, this would improve their life. Time was acknowledged as a limited resource: especially while they are currently active and mobile, why waste time on cleaning? The effort involved in some tasks, bending and the physical force needed was acknowledged, even when getting into cars. Design for low physical effort is written into universal design principle number six: in situations of sustained physical effort, consider operating forces and maintaining a neutral body position [17]. The conservation of personal energy undertaking domestic chores has previously been noted [18].

Many responses to this prompt were similar to 'what would you like to be able to do but you can't?' which frequently led to conversations describing activities in their younger lives that they no longer do because of reduced mobility and dexterity, for example walking in the countryside, horse riding and sewing. The physical characteristics of ageing to some degree were acknowledged as changing the routine in their lives. Ease of access to a doctor and seeing a doctor rather than other healthcare staff featured in conversations with several people in advanced old age, 'like to be able to see a doctor… it's not too much to ask'. Without specifically prompting reflection on healthcare services, or ageing as a health issue, this featured in some conversations, and indicated an expectation from a service encounter that is not currently met.

Ageing in Place?

Do we want to move home as we reach an older age? This was problematised by the participants with varying views and opinions on this prospect. Ageing in place is interwoven in community development, pensions and healthcare planning [8]. Some people were adamant that they did not want to move. Others accepted that moving home might be something they would need to do in later life (already in advanced old age), acknowledging that the configuration of their current home might not adequately meet their future needs. The understanding of their likely future needs, and the resemblance of the responses with lifetime home design guidance, was most remarkable. It is because of this that the Lifetime Homes [19, 20] sixteen design criteria are used as categories to illustrate these older peoples' awareness of design criteria for homes.

Lifetime Home Design Criteria

1. Parking width and widening capability: photographed and mentioned twice, also the need for garage doors to be wider to use a garage more easily

2. Approach to dwelling: the width and gradients of footpaths for manoeuvring rubbish bins was photographed

3. Approach to entrance: a covered entrance was considered an advantage

4. Entrances: door widths, front and rear and a level threshold were considered important and if there is a step, for the size of step to be large enough to use

5. Communal stairs and lifts: the width of stairways to accommodate a stair lift was discussed and photographed

6. Internal doorways and hallways: photographed and acknowledged as a constraint that may limit the use of a wheel chair in a dwelling
7. Circulation space: the widths of corridors were discussed
8. Entrance-level living space: not specifically mentioned
9. Potential for entrance-level bed space: not discussed
10. Entrance-level WC and shower drainage: need for a ground floor WC and shower facilities were often mentioned
11. WC and bathroom walls: ability to add grab rails was discussed
12. Stairs and potential through-floor lift in dwelling: stairs with handrails and tread that does not taper were mentioned and photographed
13. Potential for lifting hoists in bedroom/bathroom: not mentioned
14. Bathrooms: walk-in baths, showers and wet rooms often discussed as a likely future modification, images from the web
15. Glazing and window-handle heights: discussed as well as the heights of electric sockets, switches, thermostats and energy meters

Figure 1: Future proofing and awareness of future needs

The phrasing of the prompt 'what an older person would need in this dwelling' is acknowledged to be more likely to lead to a discussion of features that are currently missing, under-sized or specified within their home, rather than those already present, e.g. an entrance-level living space. Many of the participants were not only aware of what they might need in the future in their home environment but were also considering how feasible it would be to modify their house. One person was aware of a research project investigating the retrofit of dwellings, adding a modular toilet as an extension to an existing building. Staying in place might be feasible if they had a downstairs toilet. Often stair lifts and walk-in baths and showers and modified bathing arrangements were mentioned. It was less clear whether it was known that commensurate with ageing in place is re-configuring domestic layouts, to live on a single storey, which involves using ground-floor space as a bedroom. Surprisingly, none of these participants commented on the aesthetics of potential modifications to their home, although others have [18].

Your Future Our Clutter

The prompt 'what have you seen that you would like in your home' was also an opportunity for the participants to reflect on their needs as well as their personal preferences. Discussions often led to an acknowledgement that they already had what they needed in their lives and the notion of aspirational consumption was rarely engaged. The economics and pay-back period for alterations to their home and new product consumption was a consideration. Thomas [21] has previously acknowledged that owner occupiers are subject to different levels of assistance than people in other situations. Retrofit upgrades of these properties would be at the owner's cost, so initial cost and pay-back periods were economic concerns and it was often acknowledged that the pay back would not be to the current occupier. One participant was surprised that this exercise did not include a prompt on personal finance in older age.

A prompt on consumption was often linked with waste, for those who remembered times of scarce resource. A ground-source heat pump was something one person would like in their home. By citing James Lovelock's views and Gaia as things that are 'important for the future', the future in a bigger sense than this person's lifespan was being engaged. In this conversation, the introduction of smart metering to ease building users' monitoring of domestic energy use was viewed favourably, although it was acknowledged that service providers already have technologies to read meters without entering people's homes, by scanning meter readings 'driving down the street'. Security and privacy, not having to hear, answer the door to 'strangers' and intrude on an older person's life, were important for some, as well as monitoring heating bills and more broad sustainability concerns.

Waste in another sense, waste management services, came under criticism for ease of use, cross-contamination of rubbish and convenience with daily life: restricting when people go out and the effort involved moving rubbish bins. Although there was no criticism of re-cycling in principle, knowing which bins to put out and when seemingly became a disproportionate concern for some in later life.

Figure 2: Your future our clutter

In My Area

Venturing outside the home into the neighbourhood, a 'free' bus pass, which reduces the frequency of car use, was viewed favourably as was the introduction of low-rise buses. The positioning of bus stops and bus shelters so these actually shelter could be improved (in specific cases). While the design of bus shelters is standardised, having fixed rather than tipping seats, and at a height appropriate for shorter people, was mentioned. A general public lack of consideration for others was an irritation, for example, parking on the pavement. The effect this has on access for all has previously been noted [22], in part attributed to the absence of a legislative minimum width for footpaths [23].

To support independent living in later life, distances of travel become a consideration when venturing outside the home, for example, walking, travelling and shopping. '[B]eing able to sit down when you need to' and knowing where public seating is located become part of a routine. A local shopping precinct was commended for its convenience and banking outlets. Banking services were not always viewed favourably. Online banking was viewed with suspicion, although there was recognition that some online services do have advantages.

Augmenting Design Guidance

Nested in these observations are lessons for designers applying design guidance, as well as evidence of daily-life irritations from lack of awareness of, adherence to or the enforcement of legislation. Lifetime homes and neighbourhoods design guidance [8] is more prescriptive than the universal design principles [17] and the guidance is specific, for example, in defining the minimum width for car parking spaces. When we consider design for the retrofit of existing dwellings there are also criteria used to determine whether home improvements and modifications are feasible, some conditions being: i. flat floor, no change in floor level, ii. handrail in critical places stairs and bathroom and iii. wider corridors and doors [24]. Not all dwellings will be suitable for future proofing and a retrofit upgrade.

Some observations made by this group of older people are not currently part of lifetime home design guidance. Several participants highlighted height and access concerns for elemental services in the home: to a mains water tap and energy meters. Lifetime homes guidance on services within homes at present only acknowledges the accessibility of electric sockets and light switches. Even in advanced old age, the basic maintenance of their homes featured in their responses and the occupants' ease of access to services in rare but event-critical times. These observations from lived experience are arguably the strength of this approach and exercise, tapping into the routine and pragmatic inconveniences of home life. Several universal design principles are relevant to these concerns: principle six, low physical effort, use maintaining a neutral body position; principle four, perceptible information to maximise 'legibility' of essential information [17]. While designers may know these principles, currently design concerns such as these are attended to in the detailed design of dwellings and the inspection of installations on-site, to check that components are positioned as specified. However, the availability of universal, inclusive and lifetime home design guidance does not mean that current environments conform to these standards, even for new build. Imrie's [25] programme of research acknowledges that it is through a network of actors, designers, house builders, building and planning control, design guidance, codes and governance procedures that the built environment gets built, to produce a built environment that underperforms in meeting everyone's needs.

A Future of CALM?

The vision of a future of calm has predominantly focused on experiences of the built environment that could be improved, yet universal design principles apply to products and services too. The technology-specific responses to the probe exercise are reported next, to illustrate the participants' understanding of, and engagements with, technology (in response to several prompts). First, a vision of ubiquitous computing is introduced, as this builds on the ways that some technologies and services are already embedded in our lives.

Reference to Mark Weiser's vision of ubiquitous computing (ubicomp UC) has become ubiquitous in articles in many fields of study. The vision of a ubiquitous computing world, where computers are all around us whilst we don't realise they are there, is well known. Less often acknowledged is the emphasis within this vision on calm [26], as Weiser saw the future:

> The most potentially interesting, challenging, and profound change implied by the ubiquitous computing era is a focus on *calm*. If computers are everywhere they better stay out of the way [27].

Technologies are already embedded in people's lives. Weiser was attuned to this: 'electricity… surges invisibly through the walls of every home, office, and car. Writing and electricity become so commonplace, so unremarkable, that we forget their huge impact on everyday life. So it will be with UC' [27]. However, the imbedded microprocessors in homes today 'do not yet qualify as UC for two reasons: they are mostly used one at a time, and they are still masquerading as old-style devices like toasters and clocks. But network them together and they are an enabling technology for UC. Tie them to the Internet and now you have connected together millions of information sources with hundreds of information delivery systems in your house' [27]. A vision of an Internet-driven smart home is being described that is attuned to an understanding that technology, in various forms, already surrounds us.

Embedded Technologies

Responses to the prompt 'what part does technology play in your life?' often started a discussion of what 'technology' is: 'well, it depends how you define technology doesn't it' and 'does it start with the motor car? …I have a cat's whisker radio'. Often there was an understanding that technologies are not only 'hi-tech' and digital technologies with an embedded computer chip, but that technologies have been interwoven in lives since the use of tools, through a reciprocal relationship between people and things.

The response 'as little as possible!' with the explanation, outside the recorded conversation, that this was because 'they break things', illustrated that even embedded, routine appliances such as kettles and washing machines break and the repair of these is beyond the capabilities of many people. Several people framed their partner as what can be viewed as a techno hero [28], when one person in the partnership was more actively engaged with the technical stuff, its on-going maintenance and sometimes repair. This person was more likely to be the primary adopter, engaging first with newly introduced gadgets in the household. This arrangement can work when both in a partnership are alive and well but it does introduce a power/control imbalance and dependency in the relationship.

With the use of some products and technologies there was an acknowledgement that understanding how something works was not always feasible or necessary. 'I don't mind how high the tech is, as long as I have an understanding of what it's supposed to do and how I can work it' – for example, watching television programmes on BBC

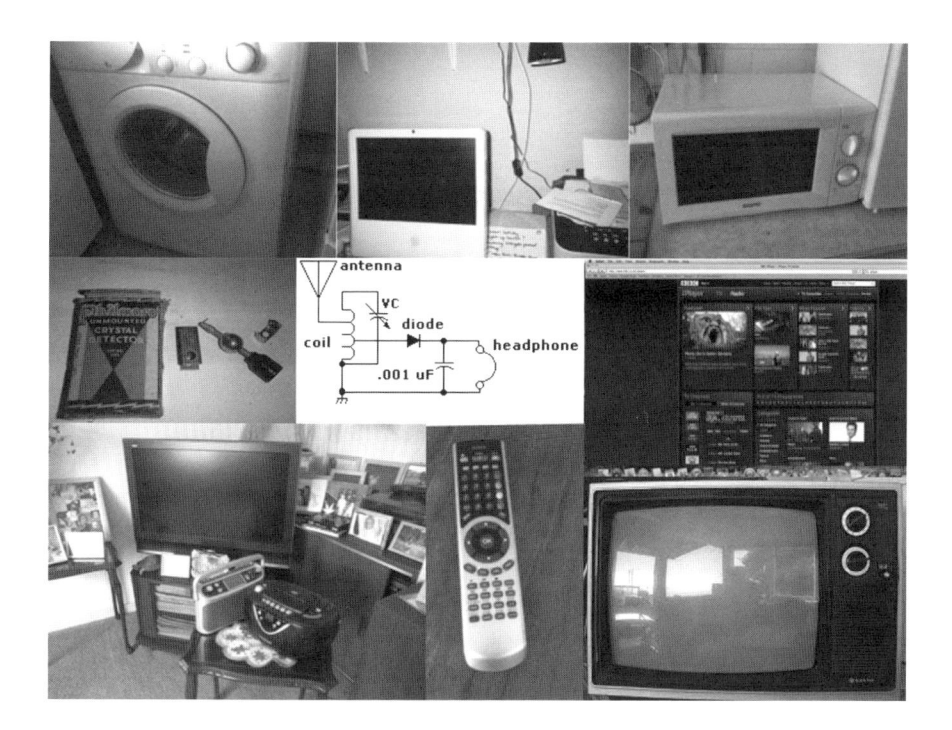

Figure 3: Embedded technologies

iPlayer. This person was not interested in knowing how it worked, only how to work it, accepting that an understanding of the mechanics of things is less helpful since the advent of electronics. Having a sufficiently developed understanding of how to use something, know-how, was seen to be important. Clark's [1] third law, where 'any sufficiently advanced technology is indistinguishable from magic', is seemingly becoming a reality as new products and technologies filter into the lives for this group of older people. Something happening 'as if by magic' was not framed as a problem, as long as it works and is reliable.

One person responded to this prompt listing an array of products, including Wii-fit and Nintendo DS, that have become part of their lifestyle to keep both body and mind active – enough product consumption to rival a Western teenager's acquisitions. In response to another prompt, an ipad2 and Bose wave sound system were listed as aspirational products, as objects of desire.

The discussion of technologies was not limited to the overt 'technology' prompt but featured in responses to several others. Delightfully, this group of older people often subverted the stereotype of this age group as less engaged or adept at using digital technologies. Indeed, studies of IT awareness in middle age [29] (age range 55–65) highlight that the old people of the future will already be adept at using computers in various forms before they reach old age. This exercise has illustrated that some older people have developed these skills to a workable degree. However, this observation does not hold universally amongst this group. The use of a microwave to heat prepared meals was part of a service provided for one person. This person also had difficulty adjusting the wall-mounted thermostat and using the tv remote (which way does it face, the buttons are too small). This illustrates that there is scope for the re-design of routine products, to make some everyday things in life easier. Some older people have no access to, or engagement with, the Internet.

Communication Technologies

The observation that older people assign special status to communication has been made [30, p.230] and this was evident in the conversations during this research. Landline phones and mobiles were often the first example of a technology people gave. Phones were used to maintain regular contact with family and friends, as well as for other purposes. Phones with large buttons and amplified ringers were sometimes used, illustrating that modifications to this product and service were sometimes needed; but this was not viewed as problematic. Routine contact with family members not living locally, by Skype and e-mail, was practised by some and was viewed favourably, especially as this is 'free' once the household has a computer and access to the Internet. Only one person said they had joined the Facebook social network, and admitted they did not use this often. Similarly, only one person mentioned using the Flickr online photo management and sharing application with family in other parts of the globe. To some degree there was engagement with the social affordances of the Internet, amongst an already-known network of contacts, as well as its use as an information source.

To illustrate that routine communication includes technologies as mundane and lo-tech as paper and writing, the oldest participant took a photo of the prompt sheet form to show that the presentation of information affects its comprehension. This form was too complicated for this person to use and they had assistance with the task. One person discussed communication in another form, through music and playing the violin.

A hearing aid is not conventionally considered to be a communication technology – it is an assistive device that is woven into a medical care experience – but it is an elemental technological means through which some people were dependent on hearing, even if they are 'a bit iffy' at amplifying all sounds. Being able to hear when sometime is talking to you is communication at its most basic. Indeed, many preferred communication in person, when people visit their home, and used communication technologies to make arrangements to meet.

Being able to contact a doctor has already been mentioned. Another method of assistance written into telecare services involves wearing a personal sensor, designed to detect when people fall and as an alarm in an emergency. Several people discussed personal sensors, with reservations: who has access to your information, who and what is behind the technology? Reservations with wearable sensors and ubiquitous monitoring have previously been noted [31] and whether this is perceived as Big

Figure 4: Communication technologies

Brother or Big Mother at work. The provision of personal alarms for older people is a means-tested service with many service providers. With the merger of Age Concern and Help the Aged to form Age UK, it is unsettling that the responsibilities for personal alarm service contracts are yet to be resolved.

'Good' Technology

While smart home technologies, it is considered, will feature in people's lives [13], how much do we need to be aware of the 'smart' and distributed intelligences? From these accounts, it is clear that computers are embedded in people's lives in various forms, often in the background, hidden within routine devices, and more overtly as a means of entertainment, to communicate with others and to access information beyond the home. The acceptance of Internet-based services was varied. Although it was explicitly stated that knowing how to use a device was important and how it works less so, the security of personal information was a concern. Seemingly some knowledge of what is going on behind the scenes is important in a migration to the digital. It is equally important to acknowledge the people who are marginalised through the complexity of devices and in the trend to shift many services online.

How aware are we of technology? Can it ever be unobtrusive, ambient and benign (as opposed to malignant)? There is a difference between a tool that can be laid aside, becoming inert, and a ubiquitous world, where ambient technologies are silently at work in the background. Even the telephone, a now routine piece of equipment, is not a benign technology. When it rings there is an injunction to answer – but we don't necessarily see the phone as making us respond; more probably, the person making the call is viewed as having this agency. Nevertheless, the equipment mediating this interaction provides a medium for the interruption of people's lives, which is often welcomed. Indeed, it is acknowledged that our lives are shaped by technologies and that 'technologies of communication are the means whereby we invigorate, shape and alter the very experience of what it means to be human' [30, p.8].

Science and technology studies provide a counterpoint to technological determinism by examining the shaping of society and environments by technology. The politics and social marginalisation that can occur through technology were illustrated in this exercise. In the design and re-configuration of products and services for older people, technological somnambulism [32] and Internet dependency creep are highlighted as designer's concerns. Indeed, questioning whether a technological solution is necessary is integral with the design of things [33]. Stirling Moss's experience is testament both to the advantages (in older age) of living in a 'smart home' and that even established technologies, such as lifts, fail. Designing for failure and attempting to predict the unintended consequences of design are routine. This probe exercise has illustrated the routine as well as the appropriation in-use of designed things and suggests a designerly orientation that marshals the good, the reliable and truly accessible for the design of our future lives to be calm.

Conclusions

This probe task acted as a sensitisation exercise, where the routine in these older people's lives was foreground, with the potential for these observations to be taken forward to inform the design of future living environments. The re-design of some service encounters were written into these accounts as well as the use of products and the configuration of people's homes to fit their lifestyles. Retrofit transformations of domestic environments will likely feature alongside new forms of technologically enhanced environments and re-location in the lives of older people. Many of the inconveniences noted were informative to ease everyday life for all and not only for older people as a special group. These observations of the mundane, where many difficulties were possibly predictable in advance, underplay the significance of engagement with users' lived-experience and talking to people when planning and designing the future. This exercise has highlighted some routine, domestic features that are not currently acknowledged in lifetime design guidance. The cultural probe, as applied in a simplified form for this project, was useful for articulating socio-cultural experience and preference, and the approach was engaged creatively. However, as an interaction technique designed for use with older people, the task was too complex for some people in advanced old age and was applied with assistance. This was not problematic for this exercise but does highlight that in advanced old age further simplification to the probe as a design method may be appropriate.

Computing and other technologies have crept into these people's lives in various forms, some even becoming objects of desire. For the future to become calm through technology, political, security, reliability, accessibility and marginalisation considerations are written into our relationship with technologies, not a techno-utopianism script.

Acknowledgements

This research would not have been possible without the conversations with the 'older people', who willingly gave their time and patience to work with a disposable camera and discuss their daily lives with the research team, and the people who suggested who to meet and talk to. Apologies for ripping The Fall, who provide an apt commentary on consumption, the routine and the mundane in daily life in the modern world.

References

1. Clarke, A.C. (1961/1999) 'Hazards of prophecy: the failure of imagination', in *Profiles of the future: an inquiry into the limts of the possible*, London: Indigo.
2. Dorst, K. and Cross, N. (2001) 'Creativity in the design process: co-evolution of problem-solution', *Design Studies*, 22 (5), pp.425–37.
3. Lindsay, C. (2005) 'From the shadows: users as designers, producers, marketers, distribtors and technical support', in N. Oudshoorn and T. Pinch (eds), *How users matter: the co-construction of users and technology*, London: MIT Press, pp.29–50.
4. Pagulayan, R. et al. (2003) 'Desiging for fun: user-testing case studies', in M. Blythe et al. (eds), *Funology: from useability to enjoyment*, Amsterdam: Kluwer Academic Publishers.
5. Turner, P. and Turner, S. (2010) 'Is stereotyping inevitable when designing with personas?' *Design Studies*, 32 (2), pp.30–44.
6. McHardy, J. et al. (2010) 'Makeshift users', in J. Simonsen et al. (eds), *Design research: synergies from interdisciplinary perspectives*, Oxford: Routledge, pp.95–108.
7. Simon, H.A. (1969/2008) *The sciences of the artificial*, Cambridge, MA: Massachusetts Institute of Technology.
8. Department for Communities and Local Government, Department of Health and Department of Work and Pensions, *Liftetime homes lifetime neighbourhoods: a national strategy for housing in an ageing society*, London.
9. Baltes, P. and Smith, J. (2008) 'Multi-level and systematic analyses of old age: theortical and empicial evidence for a fourth age', in V. Bengstron et al. (eds), *Handbook of theories of aging*, New York: Springer Publishing Company, pp.153–73.
10. Birren, J. (1959) 'Principles of research on aging', in J. Birren (ed.), *Handbook on aging and the individual: psychological and biological aspects*, Chicago: University of Chicago Press, pp.2–41.
11. Birren, J. (1999) *Theories of aging: a personal persepctive*, in V. Bengstron and K. Schaie (eds), *Handbook of theories of aging*, New York: Springer Publishing Company, pp.459–71.
12. Gaver, B., Dunne, T. and Pacenti, E. (1999) 'Cultural probes', *Interactions*, January–February, pp.21–9.

13. Haines, V. et al. (2007) 'Probing user values in the home environment within a technology driven Smart Home project', *Personal and Ubiquitous Computing*, 11 (5), pp.349–59.
14. Dewsbury, G. et al. (2004) 'Depending on digital design: extending inclusivity', *Housing Studies*, 19 (5), pp.811–25.
15. Dourish, P. (2006) 'Implications for design', in *CHI 2006*, Montreal: ACM.
16. Harper, D. (2002) 'Talking about pictures: a case of photo elicitation', *Visual Studies*, 17 (1), pp.13–26.
17. Valenziano, S. and Joines, S. (2011) 'Principles of universal design poster', *Design Research and Methods Journal*, 1 (1), http://design-dev.ncsu.edu/openjournal/index.php/redlab/issue/view/5.
18. Imrie, R. (2004) 'Disability, embodiment and the meaning of the home', *Housing Studies*, 19 (5), pp.745–63.
19. The Foundation for Lifetime Homes and Neighbourhoods (2010) *Lifetime Home Standard: 16 design criteria*.
20. The Department of Communities and Local Government (2011) *Code for Sustainable Homes: Technical Guide*, Crown Copyright.
21. Thomas, P. (2004) 'The experience of disabled people as customers in the owner occupation market', *Housing Studies*, 19 (5), pp.701–94.
22. Newton, R. and Ormerod, M.(2007) 'Inclusive design for getting outdoors', http://www.idgo.ac.uk/design_guidance/streets.htm, SURFACE.
23. Department for Transport (2007) *Manual for streets*, London.
24. Kose, S. (2008) 'Housing for an ageing society: adapting housing design towards universality is the design minimum requirement for inclusion', in W. Mann (ed.), *Ageing disability and independence*, IOS Press, pp.19–40.
25. Imrie, R. (2006) *Accessible housing: quality, disability, and design*, London: Routledge.
26. Rogers, Y. (2006) 'Moving on from Mark Weiser's vision of calm computing: engaging ubicomp experiences', in P. Dourish and A. Friday (eds), *Ubicomp 2006*, Berlin: Springer-Verlag, pp.404–21.
27. Weiser, M. and Brown, J.S. (1996) *The coming age of calm technology*.
28. Underwood, K. (2011) 'Facework as self-heroicisation: a case study of three elderly women', *Journal of Pragmatics*, 43 (8), pp.2,215–42.
29. Salovaara, A. et al. (2010) 'Information technologies and transitions in the lives of 55–65-year-olds: the case of colliding life interests', *International Journal of Human-Computer Studies*, 68 (11), pp.803–21.
30. Harper, R.H.R. (2010) *Texture: human expression in the age of communications overload*, London: MIT Press.
31. Moran, S., Luck, R. and Nakata, K. (under review) 'Determining user intention to wear ubiquitous monitoring devices: a decomposition of behavioural change theories in information systems', *International Journal of Human-Computer Studies*.
32. Winner, L. (1997) 'How technomania is overtaking the millenium', *Culture Watch*, p.B06.
33. Baumer, E. and Tomlinson, B. (2007) 'Questionning the technological panacea: three reflective questions for designers', in *CHI 2007*, San Jose.

Katja FLEISCHMANN
James Cook University, Australia

Gemma VISINI
James Cook University, Australia

AND

Ryan DANIEL
James Cook University, Australia

'WE WANT TO ADD TO THEIR LIVES, NOT TAKE AWAY…'

Introduction

Design thinking is described as a 'human-centred innovation process that emphasizes observation, collaboration, fast learning, visualization of ideas, rapid concept prototyping, and concurrent business analysis, which ultimately influences innovation and business strategy' [1]*. This process, best known in the academic environment from the d.school of the Hasso Plattner Institute of Design at Stanford University and the University of Potsdam, has become increasingly popular in higher education. In addition to increasing attention at the higher education level, the *Design Thinking Toolkit for Educators* [3], released by the design and innovation consulting firm IDEO, intends to involve primary and secondary teachers and their students in this process towards creating a more desirable future. Design thinking is, however, mostly applied in universities at the postgraduate level, in order to foster innovative thinking and collaborative interdisciplinarity to 'effectively meet the demands of an increasingly complex world within which design is practiced' [4]. This could be due to the fact that undergraduate design programs typically focus on creating employable 'problem solvers' rather than 'solution finders'.

Given the benefits and outcomes that the design thinking process provides, be this as an innovation strategy or through its power to impact on society [18], the researchers

---

* The term 'design thinking' has become ambiguous in its use referring either to 'traditional' research on design thinking or a 'new movement called design thinking' [2]. For a discussion on this issue refer to Badke-Schaub et al. [2].

felt it timely to consider how this process might be introduced at the undergraduate level rather than wait until students reach postgraduate study. This is particularly the case when most designers at the researchers' institution enter the industry as soon as they have obtained their undergraduate qualification. The move into this area was also considered appropriate given that, to date, the design students had experienced an innovative learning and teaching approach, referred to as the POOL model [7, 8, 9], in order to help them become a T-shaped person [10, 11, 12], otherwise described as a specialist with an interdisciplinary mindset. Through the POOL model process they had become accustomed to complex teamwork projects and how to respond to a brief or problem using multiple inputs and ideas, with expertise exchange across university, industry and community sectors. Hence, students had experienced approaching a problem within the context of the use or system to which it belonged [54]. Within this approach, however, the traditional design problem-solving method was not always entirely successful, with some projects lacking focus on the end user.

Generation 'ME' – A Rationale for Introducing the Design Thinking Process

As part of their undergraduate degree training, design students at the School of Creative Arts at James Cook University participate in a POOL model learning process, which includes projects such as a second-year collaboration between design students and others from IT, journalism and photomedia to create complex websites. These collaborations within and beyond the creative arts have generated positive learning outcomes for students, such as the development of enhanced interpersonal skills (e.g. teamwork, communication) as well as an understanding of other disciplines, in that they learn that their contributions are inextricably linked and necessary as a whole when approaching problems. While these benefits are in evidence, it has emerged that there has been a relative lack of deep consideration of the end user through this process, arguably due to the fact that there is a significant investment of time in the POOL model process in helping students to work together effectively and efficiently to achieve the end result. Indeed much of their time is spent on 'making the team work', especially as '[p]hilosophies underlying their respective disciplines regarding modes of creativity are often at odds with one another' [13].

There could be other reasons. Indeed, a recently published article, 'The Rise of "Me" and the Fall of "Us"', at the Education Insider News Blog suggests that 'today's college students are lacking in empathy' [14]. When testing empathy levels, investigators [15] found that the score had dropped by nearly 40 per cent over three decades. Indeed the current 'Me' generation is argued as showing rising rates of individualism, self-esteem, narcissism and positive self-views; in fact, according to some psychologists, 'the youth today is so intrinsically self-absorbed, rude, exhibiting selfish qualities that it comes as no surprise that they are fast losing the ability to empathize with other people' [16].

Hence the question: would design thinking engage these students more in connecting with the user and imagining the world from a customer or user perspective [1]? Would they 'pay close attention to what is visible and articulated, while sensing what is below the surface and unarticulated' [17]? While even design thinking advocates express concern that this process and looking at a few individual stakeholders in depth does not necessarily ensure that the bigger picture is considered (it may impede systems-thinking) [55], it was the intrinsically human-centred nature of design thinking [18] that was considered relevant to a comprehensive undergraduate design education. Therefore, while other tools to increase the understanding of the user were reviewed and considered (e.g. universal or inclusive design tools), the decision was made to test the design thinking process with a third-year group of design students in response to the DTRS brief.

Facilitating the Design of a Mobile Device Product that Surpasses Conventional Expectations for the Elderly

This six-week project was conducted with a cohort of 19 final-year design students and their design educator, representing a team of 20 designers. The DTRS brief was introduced to students as follows:

The Brief

How can the design of products, spaces, and services make growing old seem more attractive and inviting?

11% of the world's 6.9 billion people are over 60. By the year 2050 that figure will have doubled to 22%. If we are to support a growing number of older people we need to produce products, spaces, and services that allow them to stay healthy and well in and around their own home. You are asked to design a product or service for older people that surpasses conventional expectations. Your product or service will run on an iPad in the form of an application (app).

Steps Involved in this Assignment:

1. Introduction to design thinking process
2. Research in a group of two designers and creation of a persona
3. Workshop: learn how to prototype with Flash Catalyst
4. Brainstorming in teams: outcome product or service
5. Design product or service
6. Prototype, user test and change if required
7. Document
8. Present and submit

The project was structured around the six steps of the design thinking process: understand, observe, synthesise, ideate, prototype, iterate. Figure 1 outlines the project structure and process, with key points of the process aligned to required student

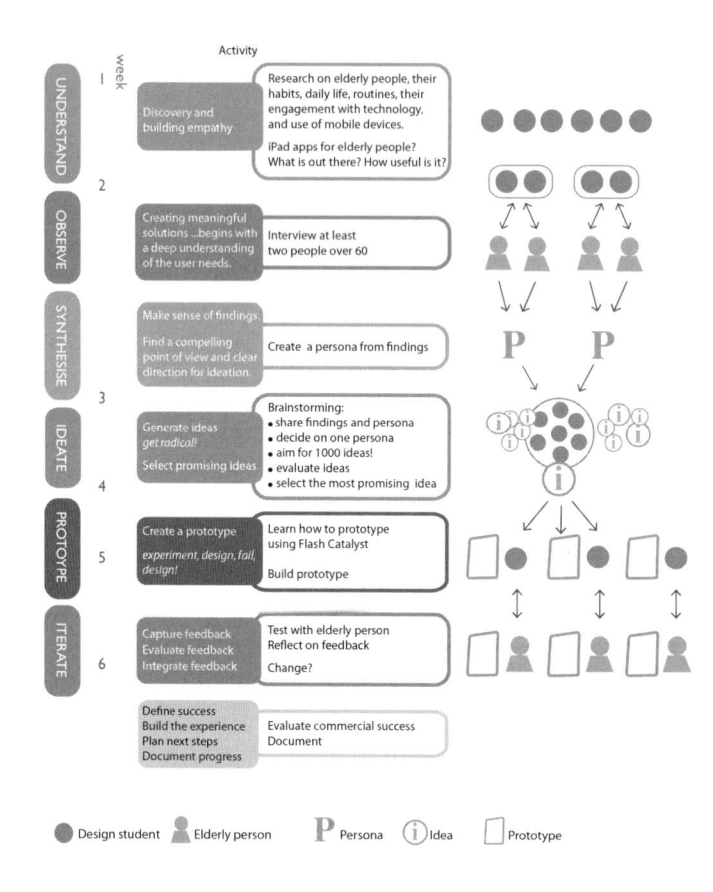

Figure 1: The design thinking process and project steps: apps for the elderly

activities, including whether the students worked in groups of two, in teams of six to seven designers or as an individual at different stages. While there is the potential for the design process to be organic and/or reactionary, and students were encouraged to move forwards and backwards between stages, in this case it was allocated across the first six weeks of the 13-week teaching semester and hence had inbuilt milestone points that kept the process moving in sequence.

Understand: When 'WE' Become the Elderly in 2050

After introducing the brief, the design team launched instantly into a discussion about what 'older people' means in terms of age and definition. A brief Internet query confirmed the students' thinking that most 'developed world countries have accepted the chronological age of 65 years as a definition of "elderly" or older person' [19]. In the end, the design team decided to use the term 'elderly', feeling more comfortable with this than 'older people'. It was also discussed in the early phases to look for

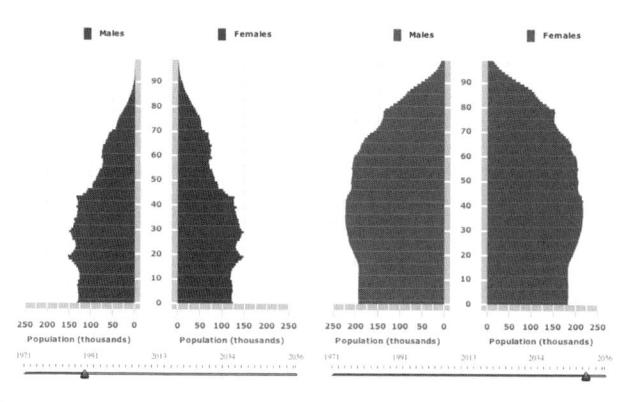

Figure 2: Estimated age structure in 1990 and 2050 in Australia [41]

data on the elderly in general, then more specifically on the elderly in Australia. This included looking for the extent of iPad use amongst this demographic as well as the identification of existing iPad apps for this group.

What was interesting is the fact that during initial discussions it became apparent that the 'elderly' seemed very old and distant to the majority of the design team and therefore the topic was not greeted with enthusiasm at first. An interesting twist was presented by one designer who raised the issue of how old each member of the design team would be in 2050. The result, startling for many, was that most team members would be between 59 and 65 years old at that time. This immediately led to a greater level of interest, in that the design team felt that they were potentially developing this app for themselves. Equipped with this adjusted attitude, each member of the team subsequently set out to conduct background research, with the results summarised in the following sections: an ageing population; the elderly and technology; existing apps for the elderly; and designing for the elderly.

An Ageing Population

Globally, an increase in life expectancy and a decrease in fertility have led to a rise in the median age of the population; in fact, the proportion of people over the age of 60 is increasing more rapidly than any other age group. According to the World Health Organization there will be 1.2 billion people over the age of 60 by 2025 and 2 billion people over the age of 60 by 2050 [20]. In most countries, life expectancy for females is greater than that for males and this is reflected in 'the higher ratio of women versus men in older age groups' [20]. In terms of the Australian context specifically, longevity continues to increase with 'life expectancy at birth being 75.9 years for males and 81.5 years for females during 1996–98' [21]. The shift in the median age of the population is also becoming noticeable in Australia, with this forecast shift between 1990 and 2050 outlined in Figure 2 below.

While an increase in life expectancy represents, on the one hand, a major achievement for the twenty-first century in terms of science and medicine, an ageing population presents a number of other social and economic implications for the future. Caring for an ageing population places a strain on social support systems and health care systems. In order to support this ageing population it is therefore necessary to design products, spaces and services that allow them to stay healthy and well. It is also important that the interface design of such products, spaces and services for the older population are designed appropriately, to suit their needs and interests, but also to cater to their physical limitations or access to technology.

The literature provides insights into the issues of relevance to a designer aiming to respond to the needs of an ageing population. For example, the World Health Organization argues that quality of life for the elderly is dependent on physical, social and mental well being [20]. Griffin and McKenna add that leisure activities are important after retirement from the workforce because they are closely linked to life satisfaction [22]. In relation to post-work activities, elderly men are more likely to pursue 'more instrumental solitary interests' whereas elderly women are more likely to engage in 'social and interactive interests' [23]. Research by the Intel Corporation into the attitudes of the elderly population across the United States and Europe has revealed four consistent needs and values: the desire to stay engaged and have a sense of purpose, the need to stay socially connected, the importance of maintaining independence and a denial of the challenges associated with ageing [24].

In the Australian context, the over-55 bracket has '25% of the country's disposable income and nearly 40% of its total wealth' [25]. Further, this is even predicted to increase over time [26]. Given the relative wealth and prosperity of this age group, many older Australians have the opportunity and flexibility to engage in more enjoyable and fulfilling experiences such as travel, hence becoming members of the 'grey nomad' sector [27]. The 'grey nomads' are retirees who typically travel without a particular schedule or date to return to their normal place of residence. No longer remaining in their homes, 'grey nomads' are challenging the conventions of retirement, given their transient lifestyle and interest in meeting people [28].

The Elderly and Technology

In the literature, there are frequent references to a generation (born 1946–1965) known as 'baby boomers' [29], who to a large extent are considered to be 'technically savvy with high spending power' [30]. With a number of baby boomers beginning to retire and enter the over-60s market today, new marketing opportunities are beginning to unfold. For example, Turner found that baby boomers in the USA are as likely to own a mobile phone or to use the Internet as are members of generations X and Y [29]. In addition, as more and more baby boomers reach retirement, their use of technology is expected to rise; for example, in Australia the number of adults over the age of 65 who access the Internet for email, chat sites and general browsing has more than doubled since 1999 [31]. According to Brandon [32], in reference to a study by the Pew Research Centre [53], the fastest growing number of social networking site users are baby boomers and seniors (i.e. the elderly). And while young adults still remain the greatest users of social media, 'almost half (47 per cent) of adults aged 50 to 64 now use social networking sites' [32].

Jaquette endorses the view that many baby boomers and seniors have embraced technology in order to engage in communications and stay connected with family and friends, through sites such as MySpace, Facebook and EONS, the latter where they can 'learn about and discuss topics such as retirement plans, dating or even the post-retirement job market' [33]. While new technologies therefore offer a number of opportunities in terms of access to information, communication and social networking, there are also challenges associated with this access, with a number of elderly people reluctant to engage with technology. While this may be due to a lack of experience with computers, Milne argues that problems with motor control and poor vision can also create difficulty for older technology users [34]. Desktop computers, for example, lack portability, laptops are heavy and may be difficult to use, while the small format of the iPhone is likely to present challenges for the elderly particularly in terms of vision. However, the recently released iPad is one new technology that may be highly suited to the older population and even the disabled [35].

The size and weight of the iPad potentially make this device highly suitable for the elderly, in addition to the simplicity of a touchscreen and user functionalities. Senior Technology News argues that the capacity of the iPad to provide white-on-black display, full-screen zoom magnification, voice-over screen reader, mono audio and support for playback of closed-caption content make it more accessible for elderly users [36], a view endorsed by both Dodge and Barangan [37, 38]. Cohen even suggests that the iPad's potential to create common ground between the elderly, their children and grandchildren 'cannot be understated' [39]. The iPad has life-changing potential; indeed, Reisinger provides an interesting example of a 99 year old who found it extremely difficult to engage in her favourite pastimes of reading and writing as a result of suffering from glaucoma. With the ability to enhance the brightness of the iPad display as well as customise the size of the text, this elderly lady is now able to read books and she is even 'writing poetry on the tablet' [40].

Existing Apps for the Elderly

While there are more apps available for the younger demographic than for the elderly, there are a number of existing apps for the elderly, ranging across the areas of health, memory enhancement and entertainment. Flavell cites a number of health and well-being apps – for example, self-check health apps and those that support memory and learning [42], the latter particularly useful because '[i]ntellectual skills which may have declined in old age, can be revived with coaching and practice' [43]. Other existing apps for the elderly that can be found in the entertainment area include brainteasers, scrabble, Sudoku and Tetris games. Table 1 overviews a sample of apps specifically targeted at the elderly, with the broad area defined in column one, indicative apps described in column two, and then positives and negatives presented in column three, these identified by the design team during the 'understand' phase.

Table 1: iPad apps specifically designed for the elderly

iPad Apps for the Elderly	Name and Description	Positives/Negatives
Health Self-Check Health Applications	**MedsLog by Modesitt Software** Helps the user to remember which medications to take and when; maintains a log of previous consumption; data can be emailed to doctor	+ Simple, easy to read layout + Easy to follow design - Lacks some functionality - Some small-button features
	iPharmacy by SigmaPhone LLC Medication guide; includes valuable information such as usage, dosage, warnings and precautions	+ Good source of information - Some small-button features
	HeartWise by SwEng LLC Records and calculates systolic and diastolic blood pressure, etc.; the export feature allows data to be sent directly to a doctor for review	+ Easy and reliable to use - Complex visualisation features may be problematic for elderly users
Memory Alzheimer's and Dementia Applications	**Alzheimer's Cards by Tracey Valleau** Stimulate memory and help more advanced sufferers to recognise their surroundings	+ Easy to use - No zoom option
	iKnowYou by Posit Science Assists the user to make better associations with names and faces	+ Easy to use - Only designed for iPhone screen dimensions resulting in smaller button features
Aging at Home	iDown by NMA, LLC Especially useful for the elderly who are at risk of falling. If a fall occurs the app sends an instant email or text message to designated recipients	+ Excellent idea - More development of the accelerometer is required to make the app more reliable
Productivity Aids	Chronolite – Timer by Treeness, LLC Especially useful for older users allowing them to set labelled timers and reminders	+ Simple to use - No repeat timer function

Entertainment	Epicurious Recipes & Shopping List by Conde Nast Digital Search more than 30,000 recipes, create shopping lists and follow step-by-step recipe instructions	+ Good source of information - Intrusive pop-up advertising
	iBooks by Apple Download and read books; useful for the elderly is the ability to customise the screen brightness, font size, type face to make for easier reading	+ Ability to customise screen brightness, font size and typeface for easier reading
	ScrapPad by Album tArt LLC Scrapbooking app; allows the user to place pictures on a page, add embellishments and text; share your work via email or Facebook	+ Easy-to-follow design + Lots of variety for personal creativity - Rotation and resize options are difficult to use - Some small-button features

The design team found it somewhat surprising that there is a variety of apps specifically targeted at the elderly available, with some being quite innovative in that they assist the elderly in making use of specific technological features of the mobile device, such as using the accelerometer of the iPad as a fall detector. What the team also found, however, were a number of issues that would affect the usability of these apps, including complicated visuals and small-button features that would make these challenging for the user.

Designing for the Elderly

Designing iPad apps for the elderly offers particular challenges for interface designers (e.g. vision, hearing, orientation matter); however, recent research has been undertaken which offers insights into how to manage these issues (e.g. Zajicek [44], Hawthorn [45], Leckie [46]). In previous research on speech systems for older people, Zajicek developed a system that enables elderly people to access web-based data using speech input and output. As part of this research, Zajicek developed four guidelines for designers:

1. Keep output messages brief, in order that elderly people are not confused or given difficulty in remembering complex information;
2. Reduce choice wherever possible, again due to confusion that can arise from attempting to retain all possible options;
3. Use mnemonic letters to indicate key press menu selections; and
4. Use confirmatory statements where possible to increase user confidence.

Zajicek also recommends the use of memory-supporting patterns to overcome the difficulties of remembering aspects of computer interaction [47].

Similarly, Hawthorn [45] identifies a range of recommendations when designing any form of computer interface for the elderly:

- Simple layouts that focus on clarity and consistency with simple, relevant graphics;
- Use lower-frequency tones for sounds to cater for hearing impairments;
- Use speech-recognition software to cope with slower speech; and
- Allow double-click speeds to be slower to cater for poor motor control.

Hawthorn also recognises that delays or distractions are problematic for elderly users with short-term memory problems. Consistent with Zajicek's first guideline [44], Hawthorn suggests the use of short texts or lists rather than paragraphs of text [45]. Finally, Leckie also provides guidance in relation to text, recommending particular fonts (e.g. Helvetica, Arial, size 12–14pt) and increased line spacing [46].

Observe: Elderly People, Their Habits and Daily Life Routines…

The background research gave the design team initial insights and a broad understanding into key issues of relevance to the elderly. The next step was to inquire directly about elderly people in the local area, in terms of their habits, daily routines and their engagement with technology and mobile devices. The design team was coached on how to achieve this through the design thinking process, with the design leader's approach reflecting Krieger's view that 'you need to understand your audience even better than they understand themselves, but the only way you'll get there is to develop a deep empathy for their habits, beliefs, quirks, workarounds… by asking as often as you can "WHY?"' [48] With this in mind, the design team split into pairs, with each pair required to interview at least two people over the age of 60. Interviewees were often friendly neighbours, grandparents and friends of the family, with a total of 33 elderly people (age 60 to 80 years old) interviewed.

The design pairs were subsequently required to prepare summaries of the interviews, with two examples of these provided below in Table 2, where pseudonyms are used to protect the anonymity of the interviewees.

Table 2: Example summaries of interviews with the elderly

	Couple One	Couple Two
	Sue (60) + James (62)	Mary (60) + Henry (65)
Relationship	Husband and wife	Husband and wife
Employed or Retired	James is a self-employed entrepreneur; Sue is not employed as such but is quite involved in her husband's work	Mary is employed full time by Queensland (QLD) Health; Henry is recently retired from QLD rail, but occasionally engages in temporary work – renovation/station work etc.
Daily Activities	Both travel extensively for work and pleasure (sometimes up to a couple of times a week). This travel is both domestic and international. Their domestic travel is often undertaken in a caravan. Sue and James often entertain guests from both Australia and overseas. These can be related to their business or just friends. They also try to see their children and grandchildren as often as they can for the weekend. Sue is involved in theatre and other cultural events. James takes daily walks and Sue participates in swimming.	Mary is the only full time maternity matron at her hospital. She also is a diabetic specialist for her ward. She is usually always on call and bases a lot of her free time around work. She often goes to conferences or tours at other hospitals as part of work. When she's not working she likes to shop for herself, her home and her grandchildren. Henry spends a lot of time fishing, building and renovating now that he has retired. Soon he will embark on a three-month stint at a station outside his town.
Attitude towards Technological Products	This couple is very tech savvy. Both own mobile phones, GPS, computers, laptops, plasma TV, pay TV. Sue has an iPod and even owns an iPad which she uses regularly to check weather and news. The couple uses the Internet to pay bills, write emails and book flights for example, however they prefer using alternative payment options (e.g. BPay) over credit card as they don't feel comfortable providing the details to the 'Internet'.	This couple also has a lot of gadgets, however Mary takes more interest in technological products than Henry does. Henry has a phone, utilises the Internet, television and GPS (for fishing). Mary also has a phone – it is touch screen and is able to download apps similar to an iPhone. She engages with the Internet (incl. chat and msn), television.

Synthesise: Who are These People?

Personas are fabricated models or archetypes of end users and they are often used in the design and development process of interactive work [49]. Personas 'help guide the design process by shifting the focus directly to the user... [which combined] with other tools, such as user testing and marketing analysis, can give the designer valuable insight into the user's needs' [49]. The design team by now had a wealth of information via research and personal interviews. Accordingly, it was decided to synthesise those findings through a creation of a persona, or 'a singular icon representative of an entire group' [49]. Using information from the background research and the example of 'Sue and James' in Table 2 above, where Sue provided the majority of the information, it was decided to create a persona named 'Gladys' which can be seen in Figure 3 below.

Another persona created was 'Ted', a retired 72-year-old male who is mildly familiar with the use of mobile phones and desktop computers, who is seen in Figure 4.

Figure 3: GLADYS – a female persona created through synthesising research findings and conducted interviews with elderly people

Persona: GLADYS

- Lives in North Queensland
- Enjoys an active lifestyle, walks half an hour each day to buy the local paper and swims regularly.
- Enjoys socialising and spending time with family.
- Moderately web savvy, occasionally accessing the Internet for emails, to book flights and pay bills using BPay rather than her credit card.
- Enjoys scrabble, crosswords and Sudoku.
- Currently retired, enjoys travelling with her husband in their caravan.
- Uses an iPod for audio use only, has no experience with online apps on a mobile device other than writing SMS.

Figure 4: TED – example of a male persona created by the design team

Persona: TED

Is a retired, 72 year old, who lives with his wife in an apartment in North Ward, Townsville

Wakes up at a leisurely 8 o'clock and walks down to shops to buy local paper each day

Visit's the doctor/physio on a weekly basis to get his weak knee looked at

Volunteers at the local op-shop, where he mainly tinkers and fixes equipment, as well as other miscellaneous shop tasks

Play bowls regularly at his local bowls club

Owns and uses an old-style Nokia mobile phone, knows how to SMS. Also owns a desktop computer which he uses fairly competently for email and Internet

Is reluctant about online shopping and putting personal information on the Internet, such as credit card details.

Image Source: http://www.thinkstockphotos.com.au/image/75676173/
(Used with permission - Royalty Free)

Ideate: Think 'Wild' First; 'Making It Real' Will Come Later

In the ideation session, the design team was split into three smaller teams of six to seven designers. The session was divided into two parts: sharing and brainstorming. During the sharing session, designers talked about their findings and introduced the personas. Each team then selected one persona that they felt was most suitable to brainstorm ideas for. The brainstorming process followed a number of general rules such as: defer judgment, encourage 'wild' ideas, stay focused on the topic, one conversation at a time and build on the ideas of others [48, 50]. All ideas generated by the groups were recorded on a whiteboard. One designer in each team was elected as facilitator to keep the discussion flowing in order to encourage the creation of as many ideas as possible. In order to give insights into the ideation stage, the following section provides an overview of how Design Team 1 approached this aspect of the design thinking process.

Ideation – Design Team 1

This group spent most of the time discussing how the elderly live. They initially focused on whacky and unique ideas for apps, which included Health Check, Social Networking for Grey Nomads and Virtual Pet apps. After the initial 'brain dump', they moved into the next stage of the brainstorming process which was to prioritise the good ideas, separating them from the not-so-good ideas. To achieve this, each member placed green post-it notes next to the ideas they liked and orange post-it notes next to those they disliked. Figure 5 provides a visual of the brainstorming process undertaken by Design Team 1.

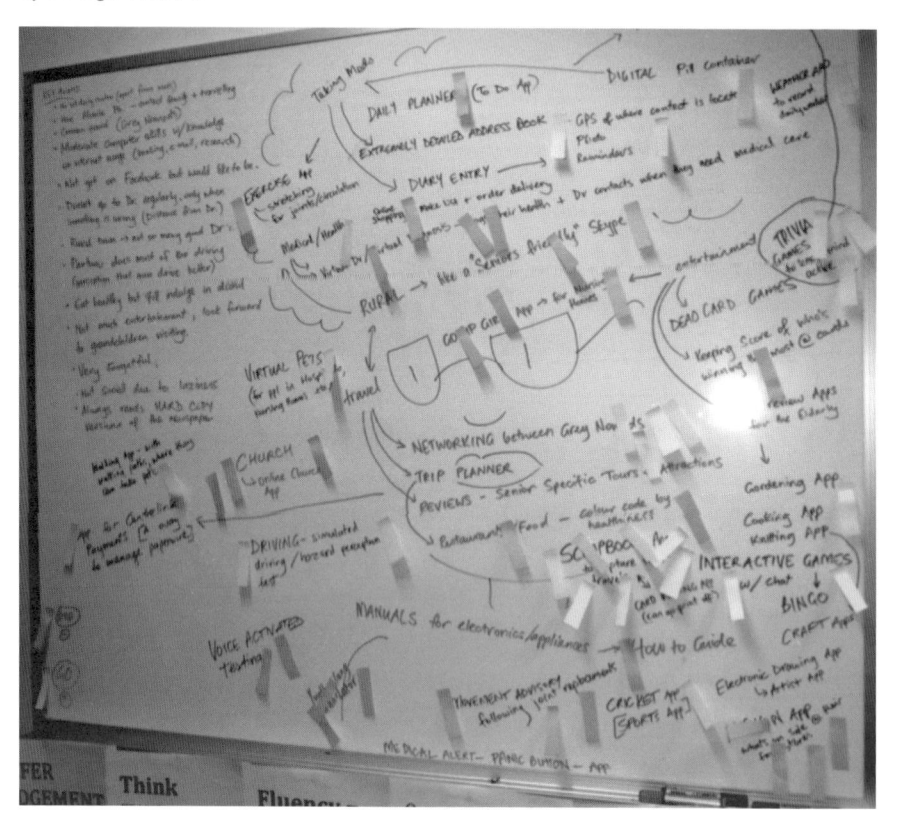

Figure 5: Example of a brainstorming session – Design Team 1

Design Team 1 then proceeded to transform this brainstorm into a mind map, as presented below in Figure 6.

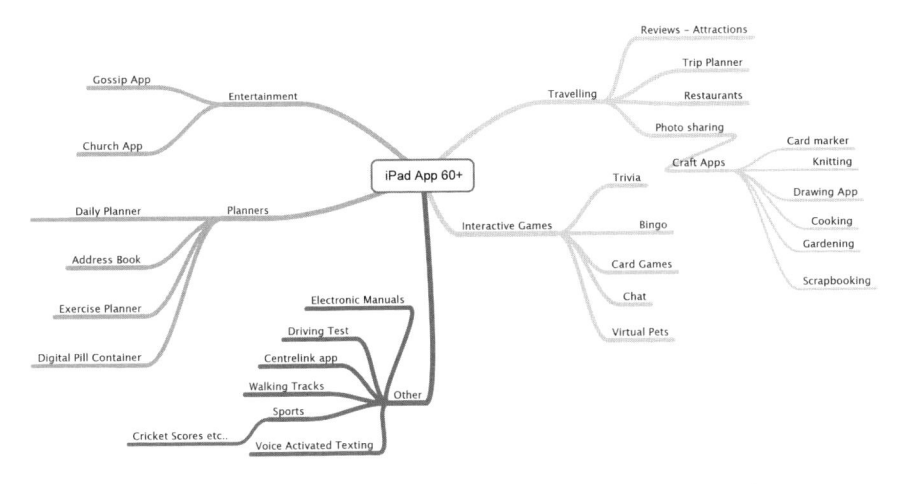

Figure 6: Brainstorming session translated to mind map by Design Team 1 (detail)

After this, Design Team 1 produced a list of 'good ideas' and 'not so good ideas' as seen in Table 3 below.

Good Ideas	Not-so-good Ideas
• Scrapbooking/card making app • Social networking app for caravan travellers/grey nomads • Gaming apps specifically to keep their mind active [Trivia] • Daily organiser app for when to take medications etc. • Virtual pet • App to organise paperwork/pension payments • Weather app • Digital pill container • Exercise app with maps of safe walking areas	• Youth translator • Voice activated text messaging app • Electronic manuals/how-to app • Sports apps • Church app • Fashion app • Seniors-friendly version of Skype • Daily planner • Restaurant/food app

Table 3: Outcome of prioritising process of Design Team 1

The next stage of the brainstorming process was to elect an idea the team wished to develop. The final decision process was guided by shared findings, for example, that elderly people tend to do a lot of travelling and they love to take photos of their trips. As a team it was decided that the most popular and most appropriate idea was the scrapbooking/card-making app. It was argued that introducing an online scrapbooking application with a capture option (for iPad2) would allow the elderly easily to take snaps out on the road and scrapbook them, in order to share them with family and friends via an easy Internet sharing option, for example email or Facebook. Design Team 1 also discussed the need to create the option for end users to be able to print their creations and for it to be easy to use.

Sharing Results and Summary

After finalising their idea, each team reported their findings to the rest of the design team. For example, Design Team 1 decided on a scrapbooking/card-making app, Design Team 2 on a virtual gardening app and Design Team 3 on a medication reminder that would include an innovative reminder option for the user's friends and family. During this session it became clear that in all three teams many ideas focused on connectivity and health issues. What is interesting is the view expressed by one designer which represented a consensus reached by all teams at the end of this part of the process: 'We don't want to remove any aspects of their routine, and replace them with an app (e.g. getting the paper – this is daily exercise). We want to add to their lives, not take away'.

Prototype: An iPad App for the Elderly

After each team had decided on a direction worth pursuing, designers were asked to work individually through the remaining stages of the design thinking process: the prototyping and iteration stage. Although prototyping is a rough and rapid portion of the design process in which the prototype can be a sketch, model or a cardboard box [51], the designers were nevertheless introduced to interaction design software that allowed them to create a fully interactive prototype without writing code (Adobe Flash Catalyst). The designers however were also advised to be wary of Krieger's experience: 'Users look at a lo-fi prototype and see potential; they look at a hi-fi prototype and see problems' [48]. In the end, several of the 19 designers created thoughtful and well-designed apps, with three of these provided in Table 4 below as brief examples.

Table 4: Examples of design and prototype ideas from Design Teams 1–3

Design Team 1 brainstorming outcome: scrapbooking/card-making	
	GreyNo
	Easy-to-use scrapbooking and card-marking app for grey nomads
	app includes:
	Scrapbooking and greeting-card feature with layout templates; a library of backgrounds and borders, template greetings
	User can upload photos
	Scrapbook and cards can be shared with family and friends via the GreyNomads network or by email
Design Team 2 brainstorming outcome: virtual gardening	
	iEARTHBOX
	Easy-to-use app for elderly people who enjoy gardening but due to their ageing bodies find it difficult to access a regular garden
	app includes:
	Step-by-step guide to creating a raised garden bed, or 'earthbox' which would allow the elderly to enjoy the therapeutics associated with gardening without straining their bodies
	Images of and information on plants (e.g. need for water, sunlight, what type of soil, etc.)
Design Team 3 brainstorming outcome: medication reminder	
	PillR
	Pill timer designed for the user to set up reminders easily to take their daily medication
	app includes:
	Conventional reminder functions (e.g. frequency selection)
	3D view of medication package and content helping elderly remember what to take (especially useful when prescription changes); this feature is also helpful for people assisting elderly people in taking medication
	Sync feature allows sharing a medication schedule with family or friends; they will be notified if a dosage is missed by the user

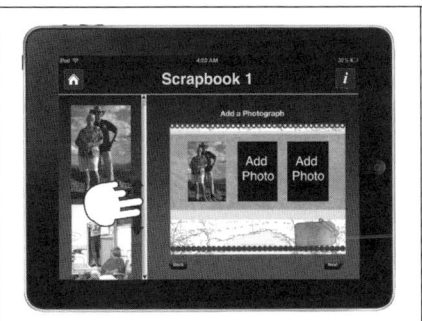

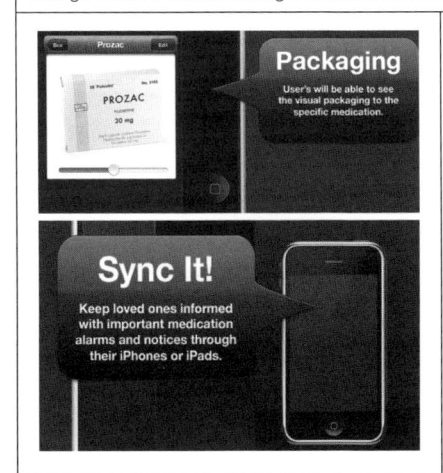

While Table 4 above gives brief insights into the type and functionality of the apps created by the design team, the following sections outline in detail the remaining stages of the design thinking process for the GreyNo app, in order to provide more in-depth insights into the process and outcome.

Design Idea and Prototype Development for GreyNo App

Considering the outcome of the brainstorming session of Design Team 1 – an app that would be an easy-to-use digital scrapbooking application for the elderly while travelling – it was decided that such an app would be particularly useful for grey nomads. The colours and font (Helvetica) used in the design were selected for their high contrast and legibility respectively, these also designed to cater to any vision impairments the user may suffer from. The scrapbooking and greeting-card features of the application were designed with the same pattern or sequence of steps. This was to address any issues the user may have with memory.

The use of pre-designed templates for the scrapbooking and greeting-card features of the application would also assist the user by limiting the number of options available. Zajicek suggests that limiting choice where possible will assist the user since the elderly may become confused with longer lists of options or have difficulty in remembering all information [44]. The networking feature of the application links to an existing website for grey nomads [52] where the user can participate in online forums. This networking aspect of the application was included because research suggests that a high number of baby boomers use Facebook, for example, and older women in particular engage in 'social and interactive interests' [23].

In order to give visual insights into this app, which the student named 'GreyNo', Figure 7 below provides parts of the storyboards and figures 8a and 8b show screen designs and indications for how the user would move and interact.

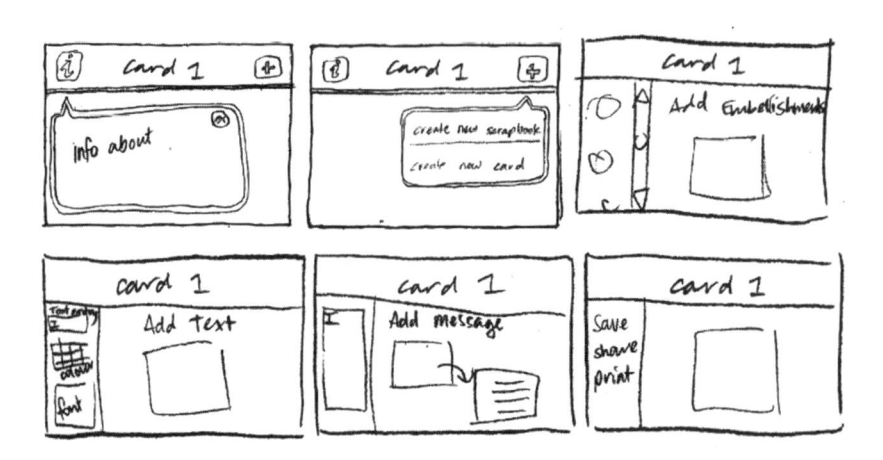

Figure 7: Storyboard for designing and developing the flow of the GreyNo app (extract only)

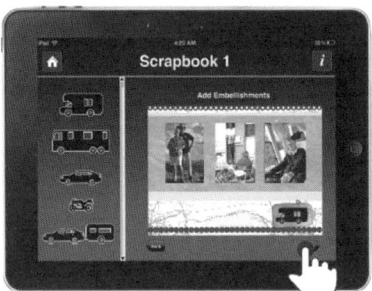

The fourth stage of the Scrapbooking feature is to Add Text. To add text the user will click in the text box.

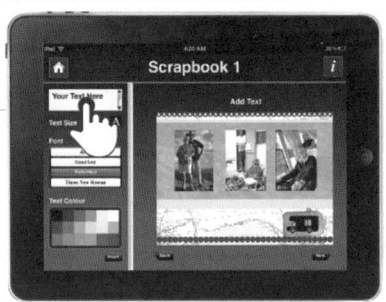

Once the embellishments are positioned in the desired location, the user will click the "Next" button.

The user will then edit their text size, font and colour.

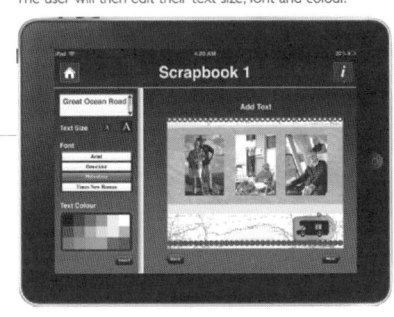

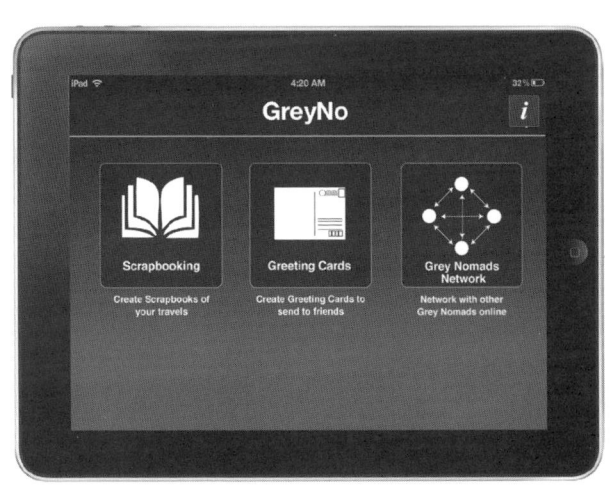

Figure 8a: GreyNo app icon and start screen

Figure 8b: Screen design indicating interaction of user and flow of GreyNo app (extract only)

'We want to add to their lives, not take away...' 125

Iterate: I like, I wish

Testing is part of an iterative process that provides designers with feedback, to learn what works and what doesn't, and then iterate. This means going back to the prototype and modifying it based on feedback. Krieger recommends an 'I like… I wish' approach to testing during which users point out things they like about the prototype and things they wish were different [48]. This approach was applied by many of the designers during their testing phase while the prototypes at this point were in various forms, ranging from sketches and printed screens to interactive devices. The following section overviews the iteration process for the GreyNo app.

Testing the GreyNo App

User testing was conducted with a 60-year-old elderly lady, with screen designs presented for feedback. At this stage the user was asked where she would want to 'click' or touch the iPad to test how intuitive the application would be. The layout of the application proved to be reasonably successful and the user found the overall design to be appealing. However, during the testing the user presented some criticisms (e.g. some buttons were too small) and this feedback was used to modify the final design. Table 5 provides examples of the GreyNo app designs before testing, the user feedback and resulting changes to the design.

As is indicated above in Table 5, the user testing stage proved to be a valuable opportunity to measure the success and failure of the application's interface and interaction design and to improve the app's design and functionality.

Reflections on Commercial Success

Although this project did not require designers to develop the app to the point of becoming fully functional, part of the reflection process entailed that they evaluate the potential commercial success of the iPad apps. This step was considered important in order to contextualise once more the design process within research findings as well as potential market realities.

Commercial Success of GreyNo App

The proportion of people over the age of 60 is increasing more rapidly than any other age group. An application such as GreyNo, which is specifically designed for the elderly, could be in high demand in the future. Most notably, the networking capabilities of the app would arguably appeal to both men and women because, according to Brandon, the fastest-growing numbers of social networking site users are baby boomers and seniors [32]. On the other hand, the networking capabilities may be more relevant to elderly women because they are more likely to engage in 'social and interactive interests' [23]. Regardless, Jaquette explains that staying connected, sourcing information, communicating with friends and having an alternative form of communication are among the reasons why seniors have embraced this new social media [33]. Hence, it was felt that the networking aspect of this app would be a positive

Table 5: Iteration of the GreyNo app

Before	Feedback	After
	The user identified that the titles for each stage of the application were too small. This issue was resolved by increasing the font size of each title.	
	The user commented that the 'Next', 'Back' and 'Insert' buttons were too small and might be difficult for older people to see. This issue was resolved by increasing the button size.	
	At times the user became somewhat confused with the sequential operations of the app. To overcome this problem, one step in the sequencing was deemed to be unnecessary and thus removed from the app. Markers at the top right of each screen were added to show how far the users had progressed in each sequential operation.	

indicator of success. While it would most likely be popular within a niche market, with further development, the designer felt that GreyNo had the potential to be a commercial success. However, the application would need to offer more features to make it more relevant to the grey nomads, such as maps, caravan park or camping guides as well as tourist information.

Outcome: Enhancing the Development of Empathy in Undergraduate Design Students

The DTRS brief was presented to students in order to test if the intrinsically human-centred nature of the design thinking process might be of value in general but also enhance empathy and help students to focus their design considerations on the customer or user. In order to explore this, students presented a final written reflection which required that they specifically respond to this issue. Although one student did not submit this final reflection, the other eighteen provided insights into the ways in which the process encouraged a greater focus on the end user, with the following five examples indicative of this.

Student 1

I obtained much more of an understanding about my user by undergoing the interviewing in comparison to if we were just given a topic and told to design for it.

Student 2

I did not think the elderly needed an application let alone an iPad to use. But through the researching process, I began to further understand the appeal and use it would bring to a new technological savvy generation in the future.

Student 3

I believe that meeting with a potential application target group (elderly person) was a good idea. It was good to find out the things that they needed and to try and brainstorm ideas to actually deliver that assistance. I found the project was engaging in the sense that you get out and interview potential clients/customers of your design/application and get the real truth about what they think of the product.

Student 4

Interviewing individuals from the target market group allowed me to fully understand the attitudes and typical activities of a population that is so different to my own.

Student 5

Talking to the elderly also captivated me. I never realised how they lived their lives and how little freedom and mobility they had. It was hard to realise where they were coming from and how life really was for them.

It is clear from the above five examples that exposing students to the end user requires that they develop both knowledge of the process as well as the development of a greater sense of empathy. Further evidence of the value of both the approach as well as the development of empathy within the designer was identified in the findings of a short final survey presented to this same group of students at the end of their semester after which they had completed a different multimedia project. In addition to 88.9% confirming that they enjoyed the initial design thinking approach, 72.2% of the participants also indicated that they were more readily applying the concept of empathy for the end user in their second multimedia design project. This is clear evidence that the project involving the design of an app for the elderly led the majority of students to change the way they approach the design process. While some students did not indicate that it was of influence in their next project, the fact that the majority indicated it was influential is a pleasing result for the researchers and a positive answer to the research question.

Conclusion

Overall, the introduction of the design thinking process for a group of third-year undergraduate design students was considered successful for two main reasons. Firstly, students developed and displayed enhanced empathy when designing an iPad app for the elderly. Indeed, whilst initially challenged by the brief and the process, the students increasingly enjoyed the process the more they learned about the elderly. Over time, assumptions about the user turned into understanding. Understanding created empathy which translated into app designs that showed considerations for the elderly; hence this became a positive new experience for the students as a consequence of participating in the design thinking process. Secondly, the design thinking process has encouraged a group of young designers to conceptualise the future, to understand a problem before attempting to design a solution and to undertake a more considered approach to the creation of products and services. While this process was challenging for all involved, the real benefits are likely to emerge in the future, once the students in the design team apply the learning they have obtained through this initial process to their future actions and activities.

Note from Author (K.F.)

Being an educator for quite some time, reading students' positive reflections on the design thinking process was very rewarding. I would like to thank all third-year students who participated in the design thinking process and in this project.

References

1. Lockwood, T. (2010) 'Foreword: The Importance of Integrated Thinking', in T. Lockwood (ed.), *Design Thinking: integrating innovation, customer experience and brand value*, New York: Allworth Press, pp.vii–xvii.
2. Badke-Schaub, P., Roozenburg, N. and Cardoso, C. (2010) 'Design Thinking: A paradigm on its way from dilution to meaninglessness?', *Proceedings of the 8th Design Thinking Research Symposium (DTRS8)*, Sydney, Australia, pp.39–49.
3. IDEO, Riverdale Country School (2011) *Design Thinking Toolkit for Educators*.
4. Ligon, J.E. and Fong, M.W.K. (2009) 'Transforming Design Thinking into Collaborative Innovation: Meeting the Emerging Needs and Demands of a Complex World Through Design Thinking and Collaborative Innovation', paper presented at the Icograda Education Network Conference, Beijing.
5. Design Council and Creative & Cultural Skills (2007) *High-level skills for higher value*.
6. Vining, P.F. (2007) 'Dr. Frankenstein Was a Designer: Methods for Educating Gen H— The Hybrid Design Student', Thesis, Master of Fine Arts, Louisiana State University.
7. Fleischmann, K. (2008) 'Overcoming disciplinary boundaries in undergraduate design education: Preparing digital media design students for collaborative multidisciplinary research practice', *Proceedings of the 2008 ACUADS conference* (online), Adelaide, Australia.
8. Fleischmann, K. (2009) 'Managing the increasing complexity of technology: A new learning and teaching model for digital media design in higher education', *Proceedings of the 2009 International Conference of Education Research and Innovation* (CD), Madrid, Spain.
9. Fleischmann, K. (2010) 'The POOL Model: Foregrounding an alternative learning and teaching approach for digital media design in higher education', *Art, Design and Communication in Higher Education*, 9 (1), pp.57–73.
10. Kelly, T. (2005) *The ten faces of innovation: IDEO's strategies for beating the devil's advocate & driving creativity throughout your organization*, New York: Currency/Doubleday.
11. Galloway, T. (2007) 'Creating the Strategic Generalist', paper presented at the School of Thoughts 3 conference, Art Center College of Design, Pasadena, CA.
12. Bailey, M. (2010) 'Working at the edges', *Networks*, no. 11, pp.42–5.
13. Fry, R. (2006) 'Defining the Obvious: Explaining Creativity and Design Thinking to Nondesigners', paper presented at the NEC 2006 conference.
14. Education Insider News Blog (June 2010) 'Generation Me: Study Finds College Students Lack Empathy', http://education-portal.com/articles/Generation_Me_Study_Finds_College_Students_Lack_Empathy.html, accessed 15 May 2011.
15. O'Brien, E., Hsing, C. and Konrath, S. (2010) 'Changes in Dispositional Empathy over Time in American College Students: A Meta-Analysis', http://sitemaker.umich.edu/skonrath/files/empathy_decline.pdf, accessed 15 May 2011.
16. Sehgal, N. (2010) 'College kids lack empathy-study', *The Money Times* (online), http://www.themoneytimes.com/featured/20100529/college-kids-lack-empathystudy-id-10115367.html, accessed 15 May 2011.

17. Fraser, H.M.A. (2010) 'Designing Business: New Models for Success', Chapter 4 in T. Lockwood (ed.), *Design Thinking: integrating innovation, customer experience and brand value*, New York: Allworth Press, pp.35–46.
18. Brown, T. (2009) *Change by Design: How Design Thinking Transforms Organizations and Inspires Innovation*, New York: Harper Collins Publisher.
19. World Health Organisation (2011) Definition of an older or elderly person, Proposed Working Definition of an Older Person in Africa for the MDS Project, http://www.who.int/healthinfo/survey/ageingdefnolder/en/index.html, accessed 15 May 2011.
20. World Health Organization (2002) *Active Aging: A Policy Framework*, World Health Organisation, Geneva, http://whqlibdoc.who.int/hq/2002/who_nmh_nph_02.8.pdf, accessed 31 March 2011.
21. Australian Bureau of Statistics (1999) 'Life expectancy continues to increase – ABS', http://www.abs.gov.au/ausstats/abs@.nsf/mediareleasesbytitle/543C8451189FA8EBCA2568A90013636B?OpenDocument, accessed 31 March 2011.
22. Griffin, J. and McKenna, K. (1998) 'Influences on Leisure and Life Satisfaction of Elderly People', *Physical and Occupational Therapy in Geriatrics*, vol. 15, no. 4, pp.1–16.
23. Keith, P.M. (1980) cited in Griffin and McKenna [22].
24. Intel Corporation (2008) 'Technology for an Aging Population: Intel's Global Research Initiative', http://www.intel.com/Assets/PDF/general/health318883001.pdf, accessed 12 May 2011.
25. Commonwealth Department of Health and Aged Care (2001) cited in Higgs, P.F.D. and Quirk, F. (2007) 'Grey Nomads in Australia: Are They a Good Model for Successful Ageing and Health?' *Annals of the New York Academy of Sciences*, vol. 1, 114, pp.251–7.
26. Prideaux, B., Ruys, H. and Wei, S. (2001) 'The Senior Drive Tour Market in Australia', *Journal of Vacation Marketing*, 7 (3), pp.209–19.
27. Oxford University Press (2011) 'Word of the Month: Grey Nomad', http://www.oup.com.au/dictionaries/wotm/grey_nomad, accessed 1 May 2011.
28. Leonard, R. and Onyx, J. (2005) 'Australian Grey Nomads and American Snowbirds: Similarities and Differences', *Journal of Tourism Studies*, 16 (1), pp.61–8.
29. Turner, K. (2009) 'Does the Tech-savvy Baby Boomer Exist?' Tech H2O, http://www.techh2o.com/does-the-tech-savvy-baby-boomer-exist, accessed 12 May 2011.
30. Keegan, V. (2008) 'Connecting older people to the world', *Guardian*, http://www.guardian.co.uk/technology/2008/oct/09/mobilephones.computing, accessed 12 May 2011.
31. Australian Bureau of Statistics (2004) cited in Barnett, K., Boulton-Lewis, G.M., Buys, L., David, N. and Lovie-Kitchin, J. (2007) 'Ageing, Learning and Computer Technology in Australia', *Educational Gerontology*, 33 (3), pp.253–70.
32. Brandon, E. (2010) 'Senior Citizens Expand Their Social Networking Online', US News, http://money.usnews.com/money/blogs/planning-to-retire/2010/08/31/senior-citizens-expand-their-social-network-online, accessed 2 April 2011.
33. Jaquette, L. (2011) 'Seniors Use Online Social Networking Sites for Communication and Information', 50 plus Northwest, http://swwashington.50plusnorthwest.com/archives/235, accessed 3 April 2011.
34. Milne, S. (2003) 'Taking Back the Interface for Older People', *ACM SIGCAPH Computers and the Physically Handicapped*, issue 75, January 2003.

35. Mellhuish, K. and Falloon, G. (2010) 'Looking to the future: M-learning with the iPad', *Computers in New Zealand Schools*, 22 (3), pp.1–16.
36. Senior Technology News (2009) 'A Little More About the iPad for Senior Citizens: It's Not Quite a Laptop but it's Close and it's Cool', Senior Technology News, http://senior-technology.com/wordpress/2010/04/09/a-little-more-about-the-ipad-for-senior-citizens-its-not-quite-a-laptop-but-its-close-and-its-cool/, accessed 12 May 2011.
37. Dodge, J. (2010) 'iPad opens digital doors for the elderly', Smart Planet, http://www.smartplanet.com/blog/thinking-tech/ipad-opens-digital-doors-for-the-elderly/3674, accessed 12 May 2011.
38. Barangan, Z. (2010) 'The First Look at the iPad', Elder Gadget, http://www.eldergadget.com/reviews/the-first-look-at-the-ipad, accessed 12 May 2011.
39. Cohen cited in Moeller, P. (2010) '10 Must-Have iPad Apps for Seniors', Money, http://money.usnews.com/money/blogs/the-best-life/2010/11/08/10-must-have-ipad-apps-for-seniors, accessed 12 May 2011.
40. Reisinger, D. (2010) 'iPad has "changed" 99-year-old woman's life', *The Digital Home*, http://news.cnet.com/8301-13506_3-20003192-17.html, accessed 12 May 2011.
41. Australian Bureau of Statistics, 'Estimated Age Structure in 1990 and 2050 in Australia', http://www.abs.gov.au/websitedbs/d3310114.nsf/home/Population%20Pyramid%20%20Australia, accessed 12 May 2011.
42. Flavell, W. (2010) 'iPad for Seniors', Right at Home: In Home Care and Assistance, http://www.rightathome.net/blog/ipad-for-seniors, accessed 31 March 2011.
43. Adkin, B., Barnett, K. and Buys, L. (2000) 'Information and Communication Practices: the Joint Concerns of Age and Gender in the Information Age', *Australasian Journal on Ageing*, 19 (2), pp.69–74.
44. Zajicek, M. (2004a) 'Successful and available: interface design exemplars for older users', *Interacting with Computers*, 16 (3), pp.411–30.
45. Hawthorn, D. (2000) 'Possible implications for interface designers', *Interacting with Computers*, 12 (5), pp.507–28.
46. Leckie, J. (2008) 'Accessibility – Designing for older people: 7 tips', A Noteblock on Interaction Design, http://jurgenleckie.wordpress.com/category/accessibility-designing-for-older-people-7-tips/, accessed 11 May 2011.
47. Zajicek, M. (2004b) 'A Special Design Approach for Special People', in Miesenberger et al. (eds), ICCHP 2004, *LNCS 3118*, Berlin, Heidelberg: Springer-Verlag, pp.88–95.
48. Krieger, M. (2010) 'Introduction into Design Thinking', Slideshare Network, http://www.slideshare.net/mikeyk/intro-to-design-thinking, accessed 15 May 2011.
49. Visocky O'Grady, J. and Visocky O'Grady, K. (2009) *A designer's Research Manual*, Beverly, MA: Rockport Publishers Inc.
50. d.school of the Hasso Plattner Institute of Design at Stanford University (2011) 'Rules for Brainstorming, http://dschool.typepad.com/news/2009/10/rules-for-brainstorming.html, accessed 15 May 2011.
51. Taking Design thinking to Schools d.school of the Hasso Plattner Institute of Design at Stanford University (2011) http://www.stanford.edu/dept/SUSE/taking-design/presentations/Taking-design-to-school.pdf, accessed 20 May 2011.
52. Grey Nomads, www.GreyNomadsAustalia.com.au.

53. Madden, M. (2010) 'Older Adults and Social Media: Social networking use among those ages 50 and older nearly doubled over the past year', http://pewinternet.org/Reports/2010/Older-Adults-and-Social-Media.aspx, accessed 12 May 2011.
54. Davis, M. (2005) 'Raising the Bar for Higher Education', in S. Heller (ed.) *The Education Of A Graphic Designer*, New York: Allworth Press, pp.13–18.
55. Brown, T. quoted in Pourdehnad, J., Wexler, E.R. and Wilson, D.V. (2011) 'Systems & Design Thinking: A Conceptual Framework for Their Integration', paper presented at the International Society for the Systems Sciences (ISSS), 55th Annual Conference, All Together Now: Working Across Disciplines, University of Hull, Hull, UK.

Shoshi BAR-ELI

College of Management, Academic Studies, Dept. of Interior Design, Israel

SKETCHING PROFILES: AWARENESS TO INDIVIDUAL DIFFERENCES IN SKETCHING AS A MEANS OF ENHANCING DESIGN SOLUTION DEVELOPMENT

Introduction

The research that forms the foundation for this chapter is based on two main principles: the first is that acquiring a personal process of design, i.e. a way of thinking about making design, is a central objective of the design process; and the second is that understanding the differences between designers is key to optimising the design process of each designer, by allowing each to trust his process and share it with others.

In this chapter we focus on two issues: sketching and design behaviour profile. When addressing the issue of sketching, we chose to examine the conceptual phase of the design process. This phase, in which the student tries to understand the design problem and generates his initial response, is extremely important to both the continuation and the direction of the entire design process. Sketching serves as a tool for both thinking and communicating. It is one of the main forms of external representation and plays a key role in the way designers formulate ill-defined problems and develop solution ideas. This chapter innovatively considers sketches as a tool to evaluate and monitor the designers and their unique way of approaching a design problem and developing a solution.

The design behaviour profile is shaped by a combination of design characteristics, which generate the individual's innate way of designing. We define a design characteristic as a single aspect of behaviour in the context of designing, which demonstrates the individual's habitual mode of solving design problems. A particular combination of design characteristics that is shared by a group of designers in the way they design is defined as a design behaviour profile. Design behaviour profiles represent various approaches to formulating design problems and developing solutions.

The two main goals of the research are:

- To identify individual sketching characteristics of interior design students on the basis of previous research;
- To identify sketching profiles of students based on the combination of their sketching characteristics.

Sketching and the Design Process

The way we represent our thoughts and actions while designing is an important topic in the research of the design process. Sketches are 'a way of turning internal thought public, of making fleeting thoughts more permanent'; or again, 'a sketch is a literal model of an idea, an existence proof' [23, p.1]. There is a large volume of research on the utilisation of sketching as a tool for thinking and communicating. Some emphasise the role of sketching in design cognition [12]. Rogers et al. [13], Goel [6], Goldschmidt [7, 8] and Suwa et al. [20, 21, 22] focus on different aspects of the use of sketching in the conceptual stage of design and on the way it can provide insight into the designer's mode of thinking. Suwa et al. [21, 22] focus on the role of sketches in allowing the designers to interact with their sketches and make unexpected discoveries. Others, like Kokotovich and Purcell [10], emphasise the role of drawing as a tool for developing inventions. Tversky [23] writes about the nature of sketches and how they resemble different kinds of self-expression. Schön and Wiggins [18] show how the designer develops an interactive conversation with the sketches and Ferguson [5] and Goel [6] write about various types of sketches. Most of the existing research emphasises the issues and components of sketching as a phenomenon with little regard to the differences between designers in relation to these issues.

One of the primary notions, when addressing the role of sketching within the design process, is the interactive, dynamic and flexible role of the sketch within the design activity. The challenge of observing sketches in this way can be due to its ambiguous nature, which is open to various ways of interpretation. The dynamic nature of sketching also depends on the ability of the sketcher to 'take considerable liberties when making study sketches, such as prioritising of certain projection, shortcuts and incomplete representations, hybrid representation and so on' [8, p.81].

One of the main important topics of investigation into sketching, that reflects the concept of flexibility and interactivity, is the notion of 'reflection in action' [16, 17].

The notion of the design process as 'reflection in action' considers designers as active players in the structuring of the problem and relates to the fact that, during the design process, they do not evaluate concepts but rather evaluate their own actions in structuring and solving the problem. This topic underscores the subjectivity of the designer, his personal view of the design problem and personal goals in developing solutions. Schön [16] reinforces the central role of drawing in design and the way solutions and problems are explored together through this medium; he sees this exploration as almost a conversation between the designer and his materials.

Goldschmidt [7] suggests the term 'dialectic of sketching': a dialogue between 'seeing that', which is the rationale for a design choice, and 'seeing as', which is the proposal of a tangible feature of a physical nature related to the entity that is being designed. A sketch reveals the relationship between these two kinds of seeing. She also adds that both children and designers 'read' new information in their sketches or drawings and use it to define or refine the rationale for their representations [8, p.72]. This ability to see and discover new information depends on the attentiveness of the designer.

Suwa et al. [20] reinforce this phenomenon of interactivity in their analysis of design protocols. They found that through their interactions with sketches, designers can achieve a higher level of interaction between functional and perceptual actions. The functional action refers to non-visual information that relates to the designed artefact, such as interaction between people and the artefact, proposed function, circulation of people, views and the psychological reactions of people. The perceptual action refers to all the actions that focus on the spatial issues that are detectable in the sketches such as shapes, sizes, textures, relationships among elements and their organisation. They propose a bottom-up process of advancement, in which designers 'perceive spatial features from sketches and use them as cues for thinking about non-visual information, such as functional issues or psychological effects' [20, p.481]. Suwa and Tversky emphasise the fact that designers and architects still turn to freehand sketches for naïve concept framing 'due to the inflexibility of conventional design tools' [19, p.401] and that sketches serve as an 'interface' through which one can discover non-visual functional relations underlying the visual features. In asking how external representations function in people's problem solving and concept framing, they establish the need for better understanding of the differences between designers.

In order to be able to discuss the notion of sketches as a tool for defining and differentiating between designers and design approaches, we need to establish the criteria through which we analyse sketches. Cross [3] argues that the difference between designers can be clearly exhibited in their internal and external representations. Designers may attend to different aspects of the same event and gain different information from it. They often have multiple alternative representations for dealing with a single problem. Goldschmidt refers to the fact that 'designers vary in respect to their sketching activity, both in terms of how much they sketch (and their preferred style of sketching) and how useful they find it' [8, p.85].

Identifying the types of sketches and how they serve designers in different ways can assist in identifying the differences between designers. Ferguson [5] recognises three kinds of sketches: the thinking sketch, the talking sketch and the prescriptive sketch. A thinking sketch is made when designers use the drawing surface in support of their individual thinking processes; a talking sketch is made when designers use the shared drawing surface in support of the group discussion; and a prescriptive sketch is made by designers who communicate design decisions to people who are outside the design process. Van der Lugt argues that 'Ferguson's sketching type has its limitations, as each type of sketch solely covers one type of design activity' and that 'in practice, a single drawing can have various functions at different moments in the process' [24, p.40].

Goel found that 'designers make extensive use of representations, and that these representations encompass many symbol systems' [6, p.128]. He illustrates this claim by using examples of systems of representations that are used in the repertoire of architectural design. These examples can be associated with various kinds of sketches, such as the bubble diagram, which highlights functions and the relationship between them; the layout diagram, which specifies the positions and orientations of the various functional elements; the preliminary sketch, which attempts to give size and shape to the functional elements; the conceptual sketch, which the designer may sometimes create in the very early stages of a new problem; and the freehand perspective, freehand section, detailed sketch and detail sketch executed with drafting instruments. Do and Gross [4], found that designers' working sketches are characterised by actions such as drawing and redrawing, seeing and interpreting. Designers draw repetitive traces, use different tones and often use symbols. The act of redrawing and over tracing is used as a mechanism of focus and selection, emergence, shape interpretation and shape refinement.

Another direction of research relates to the question of how to apply the unique quality of sketches to the world of the computer, or how the computational design media can support design. Researchers such as Gross [9] and Do and Gross [4] developed various computer aided design tools that can '"see" the same emergent shapes in a drawing that a designer does' [9, p.62]. As Gross explains, 'the system does not fully exploit the opportunities that emergent form recognition provides, nor does it solve all the representational issues that emergent form raises from computer aided design' [9, p.64]. Researchers such as Sezgin et al. [14], Sezgin and Davis [15] and Plimmer and Apperley [11] developed a user interface for design that feels as natural as paper. They claim that digital hand-drawn sketches provide a new and unique way of interacting with a prototype user interface design, while it is still rendered as sketch.

Design Behaviour Profiles

The goal of identifying design behaviour profiles is to reveal, in a comprehensive and detailed manner, the differences between designers with respect to two phases of the design process: problem formulation and solution generation. The design behaviour profile is shaped by a combination of design characteristics that generate the individual's innate way of designing. Bar-Eli [1] defines a design characteristic as a single aspect of behaviour in the context of designing, which demonstrates the individual's habitual mode of solving design problems. A combination of design characteristics shared by a group of designers in the way they design can be defined as a design behaviour profile.

The identification of design behaviour profiles was based on 'think aloud' design experiments, in which fifty participants – all interior design students – were assigned two design problems. The students executed the assignments individually, while talking out loud. Both qualitative and quantitative methodologies were implemented in the analysis of the data, consisting of the protocols of the participants' verbalisations. The primary goal of the research was first to determine designing characteristics; and subsequently to derive design behaviour profiles by combining designing characteristics found to be interlinked.

Several profiles were identified in the manner of addressing the two phases of the design process (problem formulation and solution generation). For the purpose of sketch analysis, three of the solution generation profiles were selected: Realisation Oriented Profile; Learning Oriented Profile and Designer Oriented Profile. The reason behind this decision was that during this phase more sketches are used than in the problem formulation phase. The solution generation phase is longer and includes multiple stages, making it easier to follow and analyse. The **Realisation Oriented Profile**, which is directed at the end solution, focuses on applying said solution to reality. The profile displays designing characteristics such as developing a relatively detailed solution, the use of examples from the design world and thinking in a concrete manner. Designers whose behaviour matches this profile tend to test the design idea in reality. The **Learning Oriented Profile**, which is directed at the given problem, and focuses on solution generation as a learning experience. The profile displays designing characteristics of emphasising functional issues and rules, the use of examples from reality (experiential examples) and the use of spatial issues and rules. Designers whose behaviour follows this profile tend to test design steps during the solution generation process. The **Designer Oriented Profile** focuses on the personal design process and on theorising design ideas. The profile includes designing characteristics such as using abstract thinking, using examples from one's personal world and placing emphasis on strategic issues and rules. Designers who behave according to this profile tend to show a greater personal awareness throughout the design process.

In the process of identifying the above design behaviour profiles, the designers' sketches were also included as part of the data collected, supplementing the protocols of the participants' verbalisations. The sketches complimented the understanding of the verbalisation of the design process but were not analysed in depth. However, the sketches comprise a rich source of data and expression and an opportunity for enhancing the understanding of the differences between designers.

Although the design behaviour profiles may be detected by recognising the various characteristics that construct each of them, their identification requires a great deal of effort from both the designers themselves and from others who are external to the design process, such as educators and other designers. The sketches, as opposed to verbal descriptions, are usually available and visible to all. However, they are ambiguous and are therefore difficult to break down into components in order to detect a clear pattern of sketching behaviour. By using the already established design profiles we can utilise the sketches in order to detect repeated patterns and to develop sketching profiles. In the 'Modern Age' experiment, we were able to examine whether the sketching profiles can be used as a tool to differentiate between groups of designers on the sole basis of their sketches, without characterising their design behaviour.

Research Design

The research included two phases:
1. Phase 1: preliminary qualitative analysis based on previous research:

   a. Mapping and formulating sketching characteristics on the basis of previously conducted experiments on design behaviour profiles [1], and prior research on sketching type [4, 6, 24].

   b. Identifying sketching patterns on the basis of combinations of sketching characteristics. This phase was also based on previous research and on the use of design behaviour profiles of groups of students. The results of the analysis served as the basis for the current research.

2. Phase 2: Design problem solving experiments:

   a. The design team comprised interior design students. They were given two design problems: the first was similar to that of the design behaviour profile research; the second was the 'Modern Age' design problem, written in the symposium brief*.

   b. Qualitative sketch analysis: all of the students' sketches were collected and analysed. The purpose of the analysis was to enable to construct individual sketching profiles on the basis of the hypotheses and the combination of sketching characteristics.

The Experimental Procedure

The design team in this experiment comprised second-year undergraduate interior design students studying in the same studio class. The participants chosen for the

---

* The brief: 11% of the world's 6.9 billion people are over the age of 60. By the year 2050, this figure will have doubled to 22%. If we are to be able to support a growing number of older people, we need to produce products, spaces and services that allow them to remain healthy and well, in and around their own home.

current research were at the same level of studies as the participants in previous research (into design behaviour profiles), to allow comparison. Choosing the same population also allowed conducting a preliminary analysis of the sketches in order to map the sketching characteristics and identify general sketching patterns.

Phase 1: Preliminary Qualitative Analysis

For the analysis, we chose a group of students, the members of which together represented all the design behaviour profiles. They were chosen on the basis of their score in the Factor Loading Analysis[*]. The students with the highest score in each design behaviour profile factor were the ones with the greatest inclination to behave according to the profile design characteristics. By using the established design behaviour profiles and analysing the sketches according to categories that were derived from the profiles, we were able map the sketches and consequently formulate sketching categories and characteristics (Table 1). Subsequently, we were able to establish patterns of sketching characteristics that corresponded to each design behaviour profile, which could serve as the basis for the development of sketching profiles. Based on the analysis, we assumed the following sketching profiles could be identified:

Realisation Sketching Profile: The designer uses sketching and writing in order to develop an optimal and actual detailed solution. The emphasis is on detailed sketches, using plan, section and perspective. The designer refers to scale by placing furniture and openings within the sketch. When analysing the progression of the sketches, addition of information is used as means of assessment.

Learning Sketching Profile: The designer uses sketches in order to develop a variety of options for solutions, from diverse points of view. These focus on plans and sections as a representational tool. They sketch in scale and occasionally use people and openings as an additional reference to scale. The emphasis is on multi aspect sketches with a tendency for repetition as an assessment tool.

Designer Sketching Profile: The designer uses abstract sketches in order to theorise ideas and tell a personal story. They use abstract axonometric drawing or abstract plans and sections with a vague reference to scale. Since they focus on a personal design process, an assessment procedure could not be identified in the sketches.

Phase 2: Design Problem-solving Experiments

The students were requested to participate in a design problem-solving experiment involving two design problems (Table 2). A time frame of 60 minutes was allotted for solving each problem. After the problems were solved, the sketches were collected and analysed using the categories pertaining to sketching characteristics.

---

[*] The factor loadings, also called component loadings in Principal Components Analysis (PCA), are the correlation coefficients between the variables (rows) and factors (columns). Analogous to Pearson's r, the squared factor loading is the percent of variance in that variable, explained by the factor.

Table 1: Sketching categories and characteristics

Categories and Characteristics		
Categories	Characteristics	
	Writing	
	Sketching	Detailed
		Spatial Layout
		Abstract Sketch
	Writing and Sketching	Levels and Dimensions
		Labeled Information
Sketching type	Detailed Sketch	
	Abstract Sketch	
	Multi Aspect	
Variation of Representational type	Plan	
	Section	
	Perspective	
	Details	
	Diagram	
	Axonometric Drawing	
Additional Representational Tools	Hatching	
	Colour	
	Shading	
	Line Accentuation	
Reference to Scale	Sketch in Scale	
	Sketch not in Sale	
Scale Representation	People	
	Openings	
	Furniture	
Assessment	Repetition	
	Addition	

Design problem-solving experiment 1: The first design problem derives from the previous research, in which the design behaviour profiles were defined. The purpose of using the same problem was to establish a connection between the previous research and the 'Modern Age' design experiment. In addition, it allowed the students to become familiar with sketching and solving ill-defined (ill-structured) problems under time-constrained conditions. Furthermore, the comparison between the sketches prepared when solving the two problems allowed us to establish a consistency in the sketching activity and to define the sketching profiles more accurately.

Design problem-solving experiment 2 – the 'Modern Age' design problem: The students were requested to participate in another design problem-solving experiment involving the problem that was phrased based on the symposium brief (Table 2). The students were presented with the same spatial data as in the first problem and were asked to design the interior according to the instructions that were specified in the brief. After the problem was solved, the sketches were collected and analysed using categories pertaining to sketching characteristics.

The purpose of assigning the 'Modern Age' problem was to establish the existence of a sketching behaviour pattern that confirms the identification of sketching profiles by comparing the sketching data of the two design problems. The advantage of the 'Modern Age' design problem is its open-ended structure, which enables a variety of interpretations by designers and, as a result, constitutes an effective tool for defining differences between designers.

Results: Qualitative Analysis of Both Design Experiments

The analysis was based on the list of categories representing sketching characteristics. Each sketch was examined and sorted according to the eight categories of sketching characteristics. The sketches of eight students and their complete analysis are presented in the following table (Table 3). The students are grouped into the following sketching profiles:

Students 1–3: Realisation Sketching Profile

The sketches of the students in both problems are detailed. They use both word diagrams and sketching when developing their design solution. The designers use mainly perspective drawings for solution development. These drawings are accompanied by a plan or a section that is not as developed as the perspective. They use people, furniture and openings as a reference to scale and add information to the sketches as a tool for assessment. Unlike the designers in the previous design experiment, they use colour, hatching and accentuation as an additional tool for representation (Figure 1).

Table 2: Design problems

Problem II "Modern Age"	Problem I	
Participants were given a structure:	Participants were given a structure:	Description
See attached plan and section drawings.	See attached plan and section drawings.	
Attached isometric drawing.	Attached isometric drawing.	
11% of the world's 6.9 billion people are over the age of 60. By the year 2050, this figure will have doubled to 22%. If we are to be able to support a growing number of older people, we need to produce products, spaces, and services that allow them to remain healthy and well in and around their own home.	Choose one of the following three problems:	
	Problem 1: Passage space.	
	Design the interior space for use as a place for passage.	
	Problem 2: Space in exile.	
	Design the interior space according to the term – "space in exile".	
Design Problem:	Problem 3: Space for a fugitive.	
Design the interior space to be used as a place for older people, which that surpasses conventional expectations.	Design the interior space for a fugitive.	
PLAN 1:50 (450 × 450)	PLAN 1:50 (450 × 450)	Plan Drawing
SECTION 1:50 (450 × 450)	SECTION 1:50 (450 × 450)	Section Drawing
[isometric cube view]	[isometric cube view]	Isometric View

144 Articulating Design Thinking

Figure 1: Example of Realisation Sketching Profile

Students 4–6: Learning Sketching Profile

The sketches of the students in both problems are multi aspect, i.e. they depict various spatial issues. They mainly use sketches when developing their design solutions. The prominent features in the sketches are that they are in scale and are strongly related to the given data and to the fact that the designer repeatedly traces the plans or sections. Each new sketch serves as a step in the design development process. The repetition is also the assessment tool used by the designer. The characteristics of this profile are evident in the previous and the current research (Figure 2).

Students 7–8: Designer/Reflective Sketching Profile

The sketches of the designers in both problems are abstract. The prominent features of the sketching process are that it produces a small number of sketches. Unlike the designers in the previous research, in some cases the designers use written narrative or a word diagram as a means for developing ideas instead of sketches. There is a vague reference to scale and no evident tool for assessment (Figure 3).

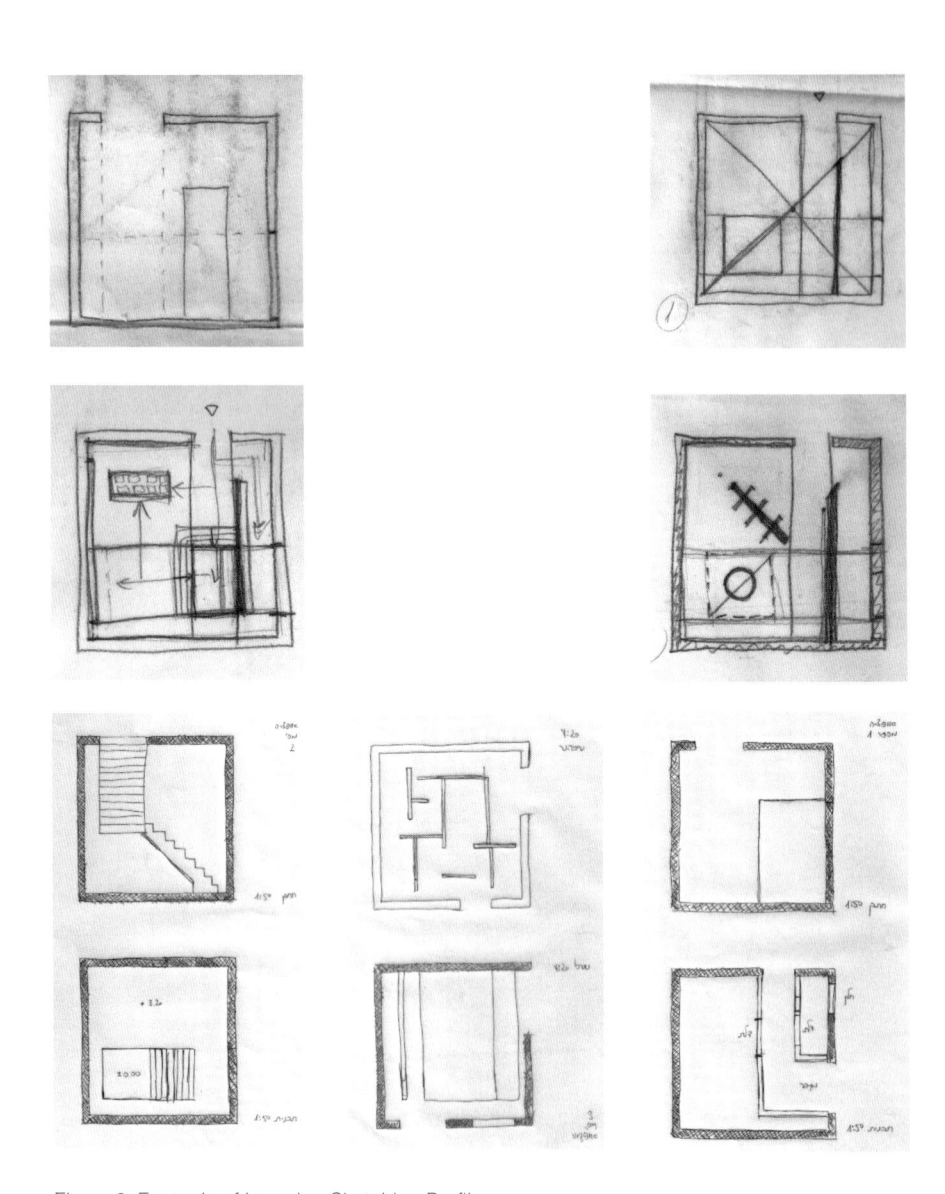

Figure 2: Example of Learning Sketching Profile

146 Articulating Design Thinking

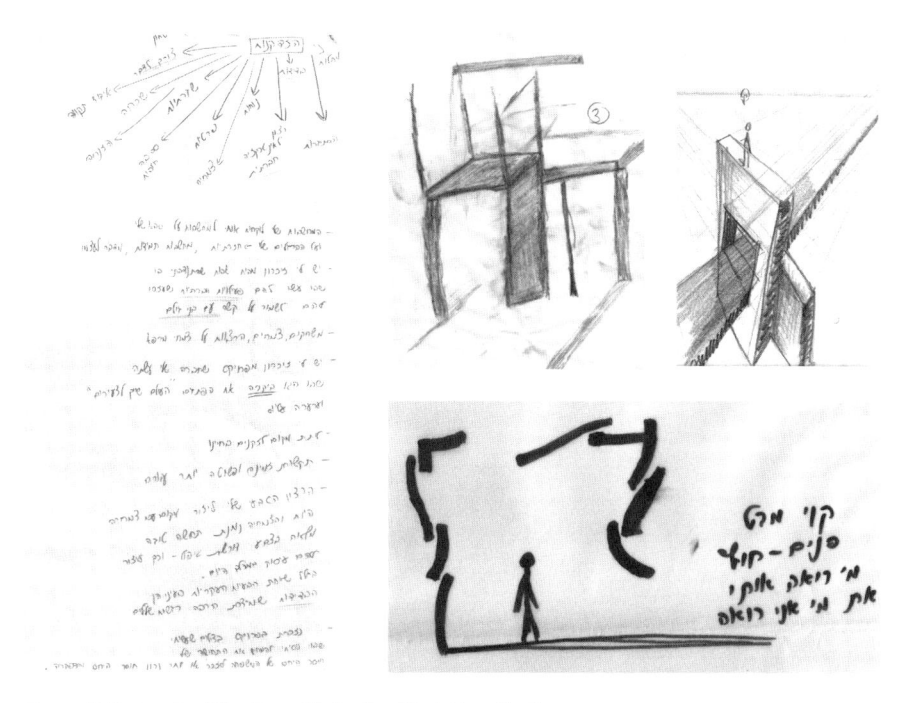

Figure 3: Example of Designer/Reflective Sketching Profile

Discussion: Sketching Profiles
The discussion will focus on an in-depth examination of the specific sketching profiles and the nature of the sketching characteristics of each profile. In addition, the purpose of the discussion is to strengthen the relationship between the sketching profiles and the design behaviour and to propose a comprehensive description of design approaches. Table 4 is a summary of the sketching profiles and the characteristics that comprise them.

Realisation Sketching Profile: Emphasis on an Applicable Solution
The sketches in this profile serve as a platform for understanding and imagining a realistic situation and developing various solutions. The Realisation Sketching Profile relates to designers who aim for solutions that can be tested in reality and implemented in the practical realm. In order to develop a solution that can be tested on the basis of practical criteria, these designers believed that solutions must be detailed and clearly explained. The analysis of the sketches shows that designers who are inclined to behave according to the Realisation Sketching Profile tend to produce highly detailed representations.

Table 3: Qualitative analysis of the two design problems

Student	Problem Number	Representational Sketches	Sketch Type	Variation of Representational Type	Additional Tools for Representation	Reference to Scale	Assessment Tools
1	Problem I	Sketching	Detailed	Detailed Plan + Axonometric drawing	Colour	Openings, Furniture	Adding Information
	Problem II Modern Age	Sketching + Word Diagram	Detailed	Plan + section_perspective detail	Hatching, colour, accentuation	People, Furniture, openings	Adding Information
2	Problem I	Sketching	Detailed	Perspective	Hatching, colour, accentuation	People, furniture, openings	Adding Information
	Problem II Modern Age	Writing + Sketching + Word Diagram	Detailed	Plan + Perspective	General Dimensions, colour, hatching, accentuation	People, Furniture, openings	Adding Information
3	Problem I	Sketching + Word Diagram	Detailed	Perspective	Hatching, colour, accentuation	People, Furniture, openings	Adding Information
	Problem II Modern Age	Sketching + narrative description	Detailed	Plan + Perspective	Hatching, colour, accentuation	People, Furniture, openings	Adding Information
4	Problem I	Sketching + Writing	Multi-Aspect	Plan + section	Dimensions & Levels, Hatching	Sketch is in scale	Repetition of information from one sketch to another
	Problem II Modern Age	Sketching	Multi-Aspect	Plan	Colour, hatching	Sketch is in scale	Repetition of information from one sketch to another

Student	Problem Number	Representational Sketches	Sketch Type	Variation of Representational Type	Additional Tools for Representation	Reference to Scale	Assessment Tools
5	Problem I	Sketching	Multi-Aspect	Plan + Section	Hatching	Sketch is in Scale	Repetition of information from one sketch to another
	Problem II Modern Age	Sketching + word diagram	Multi-Aspect	Plan + section + axonometric drawing + perspective	Hatching + Accentuation	Sketch is in Scale	Repetition of information from one sketch to another
6	Problem I	Sketching + writing	Multi-Aspect	Plan + section	Accentuation	Sketch is in Scale	Repetition of information from one sketch to another
	Problem II Modern Age	Sketching + Word diagram	Multi-Aspect	Plan + perspective	Colour, hatching, accentuation	Sketch is in Scale	Repetition of information from one sketch to another
7	Problem I	narrative description + word diagram + sketch	Abstract sketch	Plan	Dimensions, colour, hatching	Vague	None
	Problem II Modern Age	narrative description + word diagram + sketch	Abstract sketch	Plan + axonometric drawing	Labeled information, colour, hatching, image from previous	Vague	None
8	Problem I	Sketch	Abstract sketch	Plan and section	Hatching	Vague	None
	Problem II Modern Age	Word diagram + sketch	Abstract sketch	Partial axonometric drawing + partial section	Vague	Vague	None

These designers use both word diagrams and sketches in order to define the boundaries of the design solution. Both diagrams and sketches are used as tools for developing a design that corresponds to a situation existing in reality. The written diagram serves as tool for identifying a specific situation in reality that needs to be addressed and resolved. This diagram is accompanied by a detailed sketch that serves as a platform for a continuous process of adding information and details. It is important to note that this type of designer begins to produce detailed sketches right away.

Through the analysis of the designers' sketches, a certain installation strategy can be observed. The designers install furniture and various spatial elements and include written information and other specifications in the sketches. This installation technique allows them to examine and establish the relationship between the various elements in the given space. This technique is also used as a means of understanding, defining and communicating the scale of the design. The installation strategy is identified by Brooker as one that 'heightens the awareness of an existing building and successfully combines the new and the old without compromising or interfering with each other' [2, p.3]. This condition resembles accumulation phenomena, in which different identities emerge into a complexity. The designers use perspective sketches in order to 'see' how the new installed element affects the existing condition and highlights the dialogue between the given and the new.

When relating the notion of the dialectic of sketching [7] to the Realisation Sketching Profile, we can perceive that the designer uses the sketches as an instrument that helps him 'see' a realistic situation and translate this reality according to the potential image of a newly installed interior design. When interpreting sketches as 'spoken words' [23] or addressing the three types of the sketches – thinking, talking and communicating [5] – we can clearly state that the emphasis is placed on communicating. This communication with the sketch serves both the designers and others (educators, fellow designers) who are not part of the process itself, but can be viewed as potential partners.

The Realisation Sketching Profile was identified based on the analysis of the design behaviour profile – in this case, the Realisation Oriented Profile. This design behaviour profile represents a realistic approach to the design process and is manifested in various behaviours. Bar-Eli describes the behaviour of the design as the following: 'Throughout the entire process, they tended to use within-domain knowledge resources – from the design world and from the profession, which suited the type of solution they chose to develop' [1, p.112]. She adds that 'these resources helped designers to detail their solutions by repeatedly referring to examples as they developed their design. Moreover, it affected the way they assessed their advancement by continually asking themselves whether the solution could be implemented in reality, and whether it could actually be built' [1, p.113].

Learning Sketching Profile: Emphasis on the Given Problem

The sketches in this profile serve as a platform for understanding design problems and developing various options for design language. The Learning Sketching Profile is the profile of designers who remained strictly within the parameters of the given problem and regarded the assignment as a learning experience. They were not interested in arriving at a final detailed solution, but rather in presenting the best linkage between function and space. Throughout the entire process, they emphasised the functional and spatial aspects, using rules and themes associated with functionality and spatial language. The analysis of the sketches reveals that designers who are inclined to behave according to the Learning Sketching Profile tend to produce multiple options for solutions by using conventional forms of representation.

The designers start by copying the given plan and section; this allows them to define the work space required for the solution of the given problem. In addition, they use words to break down the problem into function specifications. Throughout the entire process, the designers develop a series of optional solutions, each of which is accompanied by a plan and a section. They move back and forth between plan and section in order both to develop the actual space and to assess their decisions based on the problem specifications.

The analysis of the designers' sketches reveals a certain insertion strategy. The process of insertion, for this type of designer, is closely related to the precise spatial parameters and dimensions of the given space. The designers aim to maximise both their understanding of the given space and their ability to design a new interior that will take the spatial quality of the space into consideration. The accurate performance of the sketch is achieved by using drafting tools such as rulers, a scale bar and an eraser. The precise representation is important, since it is indicative of the designers' approach to understanding the complete space and the spatial variables. The designers' sketching behaviour reflects the definition of the insertion strategy explained by Brooker as: 'the process that establishes an intense relationship between the original building and its adaption and yet allows the character of each to exist in a strong independent manner' [2, p.3].

When relating the notion of the dialectic of sketching [7] to the Learning Sketching Profile, we notice that the designers use the sketches as an instrument that helps them 'see' the actual properties of the space and translate it according to the potential image of a newly inserted interior design. When interpreting sketches as 'spoken words' [23] or referring to the three types of the sketches – thinking, talking and communicating [5] – the emphasis in the use of the sketch in the Learning Sketching Profile is clearly placed on the act of talking. Although the designer doesn't actually talk, we can interpret his actions as if he were using the drawing as an interface for discussion.

This sketching profile resembles that of the perceptual–functional model of Suwa et al. [20] which highlights the higher-level interaction between functional and perceptual actions through the use of sketches. In this research, we broadened this model by identifying the sketching characteristics and demonstrating how they operate in unison when forming the designers' complete performance.

The Learning Sketching Profile was identified based on the analysis of the design behaviour profile – in this case, of the Learning Oriented Profile. This design behaviour profile represents an information-driven approach that focuses on the given assigned design problem and can be seen as a combination of both the designers' 'objective intentions' [25, p.100] and 'experiential intentions' [ibid., p.97]. The objective intentions are represented by the continuous analysis and description of the spatial attributes and the functional rules. The experiential intentions are represented in reference to the designers' experience in situations evoking the desired atmosphere within the current designed space. Bar-Eli adds that '[t]he focus placed on the relationship between function and space, and the use of experiential examples, affects the manner in which the assessment is performed – in this case, repeat testing of design steps throughout the solution generation phase. Testing plays several roles, including keeping track of the design moves; checking the spatial aspects of the design and inspecting its uniformity, as manifested in the relationship between the functional, spatial and experiential aspects of the design. Testing often sets a pace for the progression of the solution generation process' [1, p.114].

Designer/Reflective Sketching Profile: Emphasis on the Personal Design Process

The sketches in this profile serve as a platform for personal thinking through the understanding of a design idea and the development of personal design processes. The Designer Sketching Profile relates to designers who were mostly preoccupied with their own personal design process. Their objective was to develop a general solution that was personal and that could serve as a basis for future development based on their design ideas, processes and tools. These designers, as opposed to designers behaving according to the previous sketching profiles, were neither interested in arriving at a detailed solution, nor in relating to the specific data of the given space.

These designers begin with two types of 'written sketches': a word-association diagram and a narrative description, in which they describe their personal experience and thoughts. The designers then choose a certain part of the 'written sketches' – a word or a situation – and use this as a trigger for the creation of sketches. This activity can be identified by the proximity of the sketch to the chosen word or, in some cases, by the insertion of the actual word into the sketches themselves. In cases where the designers relate to the given space, they usually draw it in a highly schematic manner. The designers may also add a written narrative that explains both the sketch itself and their own thoughts.

Throughout the process of solution generation, the designers use a rich vocabulary of personal examples in the form of visual images, analogies and personal stories. These examples help them to enrich their design ideas and produce a formal design language. This language is manifested in the sketches through the use of abstract forms that are either autonomous or relate to the given space.

Table 4: Summary of sketching profiles

Categories and Characteristics			Sketching profiles		
Categories	Characteristics		Realisation Sketching Profile	Learning Sketching Profile	Designer/ Reflective Sketching profile
Representational preferences	Writing		−	−	+
	Sketching	Detailed	+	−	−
		Spatial Layout	−	+	−
		Abstract Sketch	−	−	+
	Writing and Sketching	Levels and Dimensions	−	+	−
		Labeled Information	−	−	+
Sketching Type	Detailed Sketch		+	−	−
	Abstract Sketch		−	−	+
	Multi Aspect		−	+	−
Variation of Representational Type	Plan		+	+	+
	Section		+	+	+
	Perspective		+	−	−
	Details		+	−	−
	Diagram		−	−	−
	Axonometric drawing		−	−	+
Additional Representational Tools	Hatching		+	+	−
	Colour		+	−	+
	Shading		−	−	+
	Line accentuation		+	−	+
Reference to Scale	Sketch in Scale		+	+	−
	Sketch not in Sale		−	−	+
Scale Representation	People		+	N/A	−
	Openings		+	N/A	−
	Furniture		+	N/A	−
Assessment	Repetition		−	+	−
	Addition		+	−	−

In contrast to the other sketching profiles, one cannot identify a clear designing strategy, since the designers are more occupied with their own thinking process than with generating a solution. The extensive use of written information leads to the creation of a general sketch, which often cannot be understood without the written information. It can be assumed that the words written and the effort invested in them replace the actual production of clear sketches.

When relating the notion of the dialectic of sketching [7] to the Designer/Reflective Sketching Profile, we discern that the designers use the sketches as instruments that help them 'see' their personal ideas and stories. When referring to the three types of the sketches – thinking, talking and communicating [5] – the emphasis of the use of sketches in this designer profile is clearly placed on the act of thinking. The designers make use of the drawing surface in order to support their individual thinking processes.

The Designer Sketching Profile was identified based on the analysis of the design behaviour profile – in this case, the Designer Oriented Profile. This profile represents a personal approach, which focuses on the designers and their individual process of idea generation. Bar-Eli describes the behaviour of the design as follows: 'Throughout the process, they used a rich vocabulary of personal resources in the form of abstract visual images and analogies. These resources helped them enrich their design ideas and produce a formal design language. These participants also relied on procedural knowledge, referring to design tools and processes that they used in the process' [1, p.114].

Conclusions and Implications

In this research, we identified the differences between students' sketching performances based on combinations of sketching characteristics. The sketching profiles we identified represent different ways in which sketches are used as a tool for thinking and communicating throughout the conceptual phase of the design process. In each of the profiles, the designers interact differently with their sketches; each sketch serves as a different interface, which helps the designers to develop solutions. We also demonstrated how each sketching profile relates to a specific design behaviour profile and therefore allow identifying different approaches to solution development.

This research underscores the need to examine sketching in a more flexible and dynamic way. Such dynamic observation broadens the notion that designers read new information in their sketches and that the manner in which designers look at and translate their own sketches can be used to distinguish between them.

The use of sketching as a tool for identifying differences between designers can be applied in various ways. On the personal level of the individual designer, it can strengthen the legitimacy of using and showing a variety of sketches and emphasise the way they sketch. It can also influence education and the development of computational interfaces and tools that maximise the potential of different designers.

With regard to implications on education, we believe that both students and educators stand to benefit from the identification and clarification of the differences between design students in terms of their way of sketching and its influence on their design approach. A better understanding of sketching and design behaviour patterns may serve as a basis for the development of various pedagogical concepts, strategies and tools, and may allow students to understand better the relationship between their world of thought and experience and their design process. Additionally, as a result of the unveiling of the differences among individual designers with respect to their sketching, we may anticipate that students will develop a sense of trust in their teachers, which would encourage them not only to listen more attentively but also to show and communicate through this medium and act upon the instructions they are given, thus improving both their design process and its outcome.

We believe that innovation, in the context of academic teaching and learning and during the design practice, occurs when designers are able to maximise their manner of translating design problems and develop solutions. Furthermore, in order to develop innovative ideas, design problems should be examined from diverse perspectives. Sketches may continue to serve as a key medium for examination, detection and communication between diverse approaches to design.

References

1. Bar-Eli, S. (2010) *Design Behavior Profiles: Similarities and Differences in Design Students' Processes*, Saarbrucken, Germany: LAMBERT Academic Publishing.
2. Brooker, G. (2006) 'Infected interiors: remodeling contaminated buildings', *IDEA Journal*, pp.1–13.
3. Cross, N. (1992) 'Research in design thinking', in Cross, N., Dorst, K. and Roozenburg, N. (eds), *Research in Design Thinking: proceedings of a workshop meeting held at the Faculty of Industrial Design Engineering, Delft University of Technology, May 29–31, 1991*, Delft: Delft University Press.
4. Do, E. and Gross, M. (1996) 'Drawing as a means to design reasoning', in *Visual Representation, Reasoning and Interaction in Design Workshop* notes, Artificial Intelligence in Design '96 (AID '96), 22–27 June 1996, Stanford University.
5. Ferguson, E.S. (1992) *Engineering and the Mind's Eye*, Cambridge, MA: MIT Press.
6. Goel, V. (1995) *Sketches of Thought*, Cambridge, MA: MIT Press.
7. Goldschmidt, G. (1991) 'The dialectic of sketching', *Creativity Research Journal* 4 (2), pp.123–43.
8. Goldschmidt, G. (2003) 'The backtalk of self-generated sketches', *Design Issues* 19 (1), pp.72–88.
9. Gross, M. (2001) 'Emergence in a recognition-based drawing interface', in Gero, J., Tversky, B. and Purcell, T. (eds), *Visual and Spatial Reasoning in Design II*, Key Centre of Design Computing and Cognition, University of Sydney, Australia, pp.51–65.
10. Kokotovich, V. and Purcell, T. (2001) 'Ideas, the embodiment of ideas, and drawing: an experimental investigation of inventing', in Gero, J., Tversky, B. and Purcell, T.

(eds), *Visual and Spatial Reasoning in Design II*, Key Centre of Design Computing and Cognition, University of Sydney, Australia, pp.283–98.
11. Plimmer, B. and Apperly, M. (2004) 'Interacting with sketched interface designs: an evaluation study', *CHI 2004*, April 24–29, Vienna, Austria.
12. Purcell, T. and Gero, J. (1998) 'Drawing and the design process', *Design Studies* 19 (4), pp.389–430.
13. Rogers, P.A., Green, G. and McGown, A. (2000) 'Using concept sketches to track design process', *Design Studies* 21 (5), pp.451–64.
14. Sezgin, T., Stahovich, T. and Davis, R. (2006) 'Sketch based interface: early processing for sketch understanding', *Proceedings of SIGGRAPH 2006*, AMC SIGGRAPH 2006.
15. Sezgin, T. and Davis, R. (2008) 'Sketch recognition in interspersed drawings using time-based graphical models', *Computer & Graphics* 32 (5), pp.500–10.
16. Schön, D.A. (1983) 'The Reflective Practitioners: How Professionals Think in Action', Basic Books, USA.
17. Schön, D.A. (1987) *Educating the Reflective Practitioners: Toward a New Design for Teaching and Learning in the Profession*, San Fransisco: Jossey-Bass.
18. Schön, D.A. and Wiggins, G. (1992) 'Kinds of seeing and their function in designing', *Design Studies* 13 (2), pp.135–56.
19. Suwa, M. and Tversky, B. (1997) 'What do architects and students perceive in their design sketches? A protocol analysis', *Design Studies* 18 (4), pp.385–403.
20. Suwa, M., Purcell, T. and Gero, J. (1998) 'Macroscopic analysis of design processes based on a scheme for coding designers' cognitive actions', *Design Studies* 19(4), pp.455–83.
21. Suwa, M., Gero, J. and Purcell, T. (1999) 'Unexpected discoveries: how designers discover hidden features in sketches', in Gero, J. and Tversky, B. (eds), *Visual and Spatial Reasoning in Design*, Key Centre of Design and Computing and Cognition, University of Sydney, Australia, pp.145–62.
22. Suwa, M., Tversky, B., Gero, J. and Purcell, T. (2001) 'Seeing into sketches: regrouping encourages new interpretations', in Gero, J., Tversky, B. and Purcell, T. (eds), *Visual and Spatial Reasoning in Design II*, Key Centre of Design and Computing and Cognition, University of Sydney, Australia, pp.207–19.
23. Tversky, B. (2002) 'What do sketches say about thinking', AAAI Technical report SS-02-08.
24. Van der Lugt, R. (2001) 'Sketching in Design Idea Generation Meetings', Doctoral dissertation, Delft University of Technology.
25. Downing, F. (2000) *Remembrance and the Design of Places*, College Station, TX: Texas A&M University Press.

ADVİYE AYÇA ÜNLÜER

Yıldız Technical University, İstanbul, Turkey

AND

OĞUZHAN ÖZCAN

Koç University, İstanbul, Turkey

LEARNING NATURAL USER INTERFACE DESIGN THROUGH CREATIVE DRAMA TECHNIQUES: NEW APPROACHES TO DESIGN EDUCATION

Introduction

Natural User Interface

As the complexity of digital information increases, standard devices and Graphical User Interfaces (GUI) grow inadequate to cover all user needs. While conventional interface devices such as mice, keyboards and WIMP interface elements are widely used, new devices and interface elements are rapidly developing. This new generation of interfaces – NUI – aims at facilitating interaction and control of digital information for users [1]. These interfaces must be within an organic structure that is suitable for human ergonomics, easy to learn and easy to use [2]. Technologies such as touch screens, flexible screens, 3D displays, retinal monitors, geospatial tracking, gesture recognition, haptics, tangible UIs, speech recognition, sub-vocal recognition, eye tracking, electrotactile stimulation, bionic contact lenses and brain–computer interfaces mean that human–computer interaction is changing into human–human interaction [3, 4].

NUI is a contemporary concept in Interactive Media Design; the term is used to describe interfaces that let users interact with devices through everyday actions and gestures, which distinguishes it from a GUI. This new type of interaction has already found many critical uses within interactive media design and even more in theoretical studies. With the use of both hands and many other interaction abilities, NUIs offer many options for preparing, manipulating and viewing data-visualisation applications in the fields of medicine, geophysics [9], finance [8] and molecular biology [10]. In the field of education, gestural interaction supports thinking and learning, and contributes to child development by addressing all five senses [5, 6, 7]. Tangible interfaces used in urban planning support spatial problem solving by interpreting the physical restrictions of urban features [8].

NUIs bring features such as education, fitness and imagination enhancement to entertainment, computer gaming and edutainment applications by combining maximised physical input with digitally augmented reality, enabling users to interact with devices easily. Nintendo Wii, Microsoft X-Box Kinect, Sony PS Move, Neurosmith musicblocks, Brain Opera, Glasgow Science Museum can be given as recent examples to such devices. Many artistic applications have been developed using NUIs, such as creating experimental sounds with the manipulation of virtual or real objects or playing digital instruments by body gestures [11, 12, 13]. In social communication, the use of gestures enables emotional expression, abstract messages and task sharing [14, 15]. Interactive way-finding applications are being developed in order to help a user reach their destination, introduce the environment, or view and upload spatial data (Geo-wand) while driving or walking [16, 17].

Natural User Interface covers several research fields, particularly: augmented reality, which covers virtual spatial information and objects [18, 19]; interactive surfaces, which rely on interaction between body gestures and tangible objects [20, 21]; environmental monitors, which are visualisations projected over physical objects [22]; and tangible UIs, which are data and applications that are embedded into physical objects and manipulated by physical guidance [23, 24].

NUI Education

Interactive Media Design is a field that must catch up with the newest interaction possibilities coming out of technological developments. We believe that not only must these areas be explored within Interactive Media Design education but that designers must take an active role in guiding future developments. It is with this opinion that we set off to implement Natural User Interfaces, which we see as the most significant area of interaction development, into Interactive Media Design education in a way that puts innovation in the first place.

There is no commonly accepted syllabus within NUI education, no right or wrong way of teaching and learning this technology. Our main challenge is that most design students, along with the rest of the community, lack experience with these new interfaces as a user. Furthermore, many NUI examples remain deficient and unreliable [25].

Learning to design for NUI requires the exploration of many subjects and technologies as well as embracing user centred design principles. However, these alone will not suffice for innovation in NUI design. One needs to be able to imagine technologies that are not yet developed.

Typically, design students who are used to studying with the more stereotypical technologies of GUIs get confused in their initial exploration of NUI. This is because their previous Graphic UI experiences do not guide them toward adapting features of NUI into their designs. For example, it is observed that students tend to keep old interaction habits while they are sketching with a computer [26]. Yet it would be wrong to conclude that this confusing period of learning is a waste of time. We observed that students are in fact at their most creative level while exploring the *concept* of NUI. If we provide them with existing examples, they tend just to imitate them, mostly because they lack the agility to diversify. Therefore, we believe that continuing this exploratory period throughout the education process, somehow, will increase students' creative interests by building up the concept and understanding of NUI through innovative idea generation.

Through our studies, we concluded that creative drama techniques are a convenient way of developing NUI-based design thinking because these techniques require the use of body language, something on which NUIs depend [27]. However, during the first term of our NUI education class, we saw that the most extensively used technique, role-playing, resulted in more of a design-solution focused process as opposed to the exploratory process that we aimed to achieve.

At this point of the chapter, we shift to a discussion around techniques that are inspired from creative drama and how they may be implemented into interactive media design education in order to produce innovative and creative ideas for developing NUIs.

Use of Drama in Interaction Design

It is worth noting that the earlier studies using role-playing techniques were built upon user-centred design principle [28, 29, 30, 31, 32, 33]. In one of the most important studies, which are mostly from Interaction Design, Simsarian drew attention to the benefit of using role playing in all phases of design (understanding, observing, visualising, evaluation, representation) and noted the most important outcomes as:

- Maintaining group focus on the activities at hand
- Bringing teams onto the 'same page' through a shared vivid experience that involves participant's muscle memory
- Deferring judgment and building on the ideas of others
- Building deeper understanding within context
- The ability to explore viscerally possibilities that may not be readily available in the world.

It is remarkable that most role-plays that have been used in such projects have been recorded. These records are used as video scenarios of the to-be-designed products.

Another notable method used is 'bodystorming', a method derived from brainstorming where ideas emerge from the unconscious and tacit experiences of body, instead of the memory.

In pervasive computing design education, the emphasis is that students should learn ubiquitous interaction independently of computers. Because of this, sketching methods for screen-based interactions are not suitable for this new area. Video-sketching techniques, which are inspired by video scenarios in the industrial design field, are composed of playing photographs or images sequentially [26]. This method was used by interaction design doctoral students and positive results were observed within user-centred design principles. The belief is that this method enables students to make more detailed designs that the users interact more easily.

Method

In the first term of our NUI education class, we used several drama techniques as a way of introducing students to this new concept. We started by creating a persona in detail and then applied it to several role-playing, mime and improvisation exercises. Our aims were to: (1) define the problem space, (2) create different viewpoints of the problem, (3) suggest solutions and (4) test the usability.

We had positive feedback throughout the term. Most notable were the students' adaptation to the concept, the cohesiveness of group work and discussion amongst students, increased interest and motivation, and viable project outcomes. We also, however, observed several inadequacies of the applied techniques. The students could not come up with many diverse ideas and many became stuck within cultural boundaries. Also, there was a lack of flexibility in their design concepts.

We observed that, overall, the techniques *were* successful in convergent design aspects such as framing, defining and constricting, but we cannot say the same for the divergent design aspects, especially increased point of view and rule breaking. While we did adapt the students to the concept of NUI and obtained original and utilisable results, we believe that flexibility in design thinking is essential to our design education and that therefore there is a need to improve upon this element.

As we investigated the reason behind this lack of flexibility, we found that it was because our drama exercises were mostly solution oriented: students sooner or later fell back on a failsafe design solution instead of pushing the limits of interaction further.

In light of our observations during that term, we decided to take a new approach in order to push students to explore the interaction possibilities of NUI. We did this by protecting the positive sides of the previous term's study but, for the second term, we would treat this education problem as a design problem itself.

We created a series of empirical creative drama exercises with the goal of obtaining completely different and diverse points of view. Our intention was to shift from solution-oriented to exploration-oriented exercises.

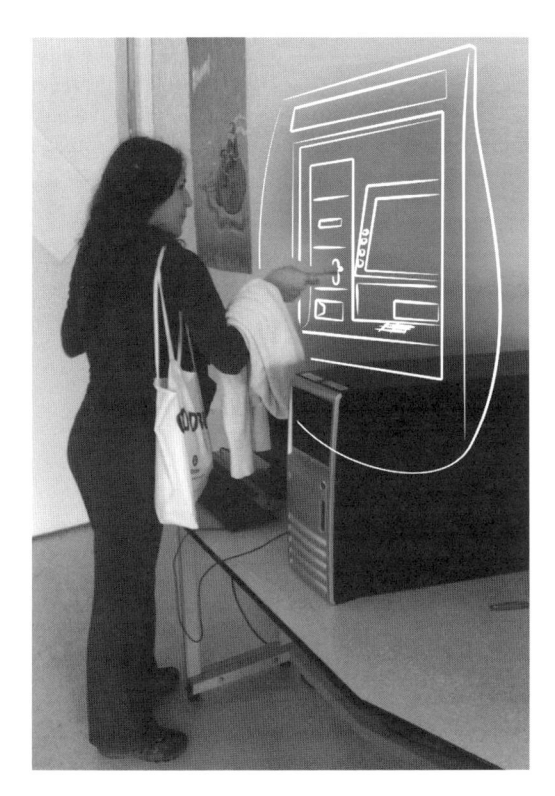

Figure 1: 'Disabled environment bodystorming'

This study project was on a Multi-User Natural User Interface consisting of gestural, visual and voice interactions that allow users to create their virtual natural environments with other users. The emphasis was on graphical and sound elements. The class consisted of five students, different from those involved in the previous term and all new to NUI education. The studies included several drama studies from the previous term in addition to other creative exercises that were outside the realm of role playing. In what follows, we will mostly discuss these drama-based exercises and leave out the rest of the process.

Initial Exploration to NUIs and Gaining Flexibility

This first phase begins with the exploration of full-body interaction, with a glance at different possibilities future technologies may bring. One exercise used several branches inspired by the bodystorming technique. Students were given different tasks in respect to several disabled environments: communication in a noisy environment, ATM transactions that required privacy in a crowded environment, and trying to use an automated info-kiosk while carrying numerous bags. The purpose was to force students to make use of different senses in order to overcome physical handicaps. We encouraged the students to concentrate on their tacit body experience and benefit from conscious idea generation.

Our next application consisted of several alternant versions of role-playing with the goal of expanding students' view to design problems. We created several different design problem scenarios and had the students take on roles in each scenario. But, instead of putting the student in place of the user as design role-plays are usually played, we distorted one element at a time. For example:

1) We replaced the user with a non-human living creature (e.g. an animal) with emphasis on the difference of its physical and cognitive structure, in order to realise human physical and cognitive features better.
2) We imagined looking through the eyes of an observer while letting the scenario run in expected terms.
3) We looked through the eyes of a person or an item that was the source of the problem.
4) We looked through the eyes of a product-to-be-designed that would help the user achieve their task. (The students called this exercise 'the machine'.)

Our goal was to make students see design problems from completely different points of view, to illustrate that there is never just one definition of a design problem, and solutions may be derived from different perspectives.

We called these exercises 'distorted role plays' because of the way we bended the standard methods in a different way each time.

Exploring the Problem Space

During this phase, our aim was to have students generate ideas to overcome different communication problems within different constraints. It is worth noting that, up until this point, students were not aware of the project subject and would not be for a while longer. The scenarios we created reflected different design problems than the one that would come up with the project subject. The purpose was to make the students explore different ways of communication and human–human interaction.

These applications were:

Drama Setup 1: Prehistoric People

In this exercise, students took on the persona of people in a prehistoric society. In other words, there was to be no technology or preset tools and no spoken language. They were given the task of socialising around a camp fire using only body language, sounds and natural objects. The students were asked to collect simple natural materials such as stones or branches beforehand. They were free to dance, build things from objects, or make sounds with objects or their body, and make music together. Because their only goal was to communicate and entertain, they needed to concentrate on doing things that would cause interest and lead other students to join them or watch them.

Figure 2: 'Drama setup of prehistoric people'

Drama Setup 2: A Train Trip with People of Different Cultures

In this exercise, we elaborated upon the level of detail from the previous exercise and built detailed personas for each student. These details included occupation, culture, age, social status and, finally, the items carried in their handbag, which would be in accordance to these other attributes. They were not told what they would be asked to do in the exercise so they wrote down items that their persona is expected to carry along in a train trip. The students were asked to play the role of a person who is making a long international train trip along with people from different countries and cultures, which were played by other students. We prepared a scene with a roughly drawn ground plan of tables and chairs set up to represent a train compartment. Technology was limited to the items they carried in their bags and spoken language was to be limited due to cultural differences. They were asked to introduce themselves to others with items they brought along, share knowledge about the reason for their trip and simply spend time together.

Project Description: Online Communication of Users with the Use of Natural Sounds and Visuals

In the light of the outcomes of the exercises, we moved on to discuss contemporary social communication in digital media, where it stands and which direction it may/should develop.

Figure 3: 'Drama setup of train trip'

We then identified the term's project as the development of a social tool that is controlled by body gestures with no verbal input in which the students were free to use contemporary or future digital technologies. Users in different locations would be able to interact online. The tool would let the users create a natural environment with its graphical and sound elements. Multiple users would be able to create sound compositions.

First, we listened to several natural sounds and compositions made with natural sounds. The students tried to create gestures that could identify natural objects with diverse physical aspects. They tried to classify these objects according to their physical and vocal aspects (such as plants, animals and motions like waves or wind). We asked them to define these objects with gestures according to their form, imagery, their best-known specification (as gestural icons) and so on. Our aim was to expand their view of gestural definitions and move beyond cultural habits.

Non-Verbal Definition: Games to Define Scenes with Gestures and Sounds

This phase was intended to make the students re-explore the basic principles of GUI-based design on human perception, intuition and memory within the context of Gestural Interfaces. This was a phase that occurred prior to introducing project ideas; the exercises were not intended to test usability or create solutions to design problems but to enhance creativity within the field of gestures by forcing the students think of different types of gestures.

We applied a set of different exercises with different types of inputs, feedbacks and outputs. In all the exercises we gave the students a set of nine different scene photographs, some of which had different natural themes (a palm beach, an underwater scene, a tornado, a jungle at night, a cave) and some of which included human-made objects (a watermill, an urban traffic scene, a helicopter creating a sand storm, a ferry, seagulls). All scenes were selected to have both visual and audial identities that are separable from each other.

The exercises used one student who would define the scenes to other students. All the students had taken the definer role in all of the four exercises, which were:

1. Gestural definition, verbal feedback (such as the game of charades)
2. Vocal (non-verbal) definition, verbal feedback
3. Gestural and vocal (non-verbal) definition, no feedback (the students drew their outcomes on paper)
4. Gestural definition behind a curtain, only with silhouette, no feedback (the students drew their outcomes on paper).

In all of the exercises, students were asked to define the scene using as much detail as possible, including things like object details, composition of objects, light, perspective and time.

Figure 4: 'Non-verbal definition game'

The goal of these exercises was to expand the solution repertoire of students and to gain flexibility within their design processes. The inputs (descriptions), feedbacks and outputs were all recorded and discussed. The outcomes and different points of view were evaluated by the students and educators together and the students were then asked to bring up their first concept projects.

Prototyping

The students were asked to create low-fi prototypes for their concept projects and make role-plays with the aim of observing the usability issues. These role-plays were recorded and then discussed by the students and educators. These discussions focused on the perception of the interfaces, learning curves of gestures, and ergonomic aspects. The students were encouraged to criticise each other's concepts and share opinions. This phase was repeated after each designed concept.

Video-supported Presentation and Evaluation

In this phase, students were asked to make a linear video-supported presentation that defined all the design and interaction specifications of their final projects. The designs were evaluated by a jury of Interactive Media Design educators. The innovation and creativity aspects of all the projects were evaluated among the educators afterwards.

Outcomes

Many of the exercises brought about an instant change in the students' behaviour and long-term improvement was observed throughout the course of the term. In order to discuss the stand-alone effects of the exercises, we will address them one by one.

In the 'disabled environment bodystorming' application, we have observed that students force themselves to bring up numerous unusual solutions to deal with the constraints of disabled environments. Their exploration of their own tacit body experience was worth noting: since it was a new experience for most, ideas were generated quickly along with some surprise.

In our 'distorted role-plays', students had time to observe many elements that make up a design problem. After this exercise, students were asked if their conceptualisation of the problem changed. By and large, the reply was that they previously searched for a solution out of the context but now understood that the solution should change the elements that make up the problem in order to overcome it. They also said they were used to looking through the eyes of the user that they were designing for, but rarely through any other personality. Several weeks after this exercise was done (when students started bringing up their own design ideas), they re-evaluated things they learned in this exercise. We noted that they came up with a wider range of ideas compared to previous terms. Looking through the eyes of the product (or 'the machine', as the students call it) became a much referenced term amongst the students by which they brought up many ideas on how to design intelligent systems that help the user.

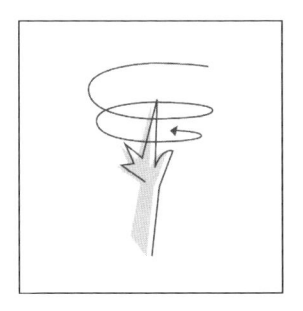

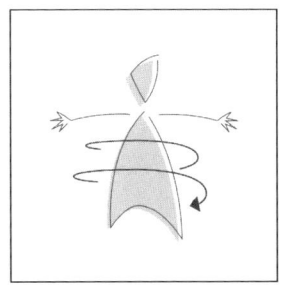

Figure 5: 'Different gestures to define a storm in the non-verbal definition game'

In the prehistoric-people and train-trip drama exercises, students adapted to their personas more than we anticipated. Yet this situation led to several changes in the exercises. For example, because of former knowledge, students tended to think only of survival methods instead of entertainment when doing the prehistoric people exercise. However, both exercises led to idea generation on alternative communication methods as we expected. Gestures, noises and objects were all used for purposes such as introducing oneself, sharing a thought, drawing attention or creating entertainment. Two additional advantages of both role-playing exercises were a deeper interest in the subject and empathy with characters. These are outputs we have observed in role-plays made with detailed personas in earlier terms as well.

In the non-verbal definition exercises, there were two main braches of output. The first one relates to the gestures that were used to define objects. There were several different gestural tendencies that we can classify according to the attributes defined. For example, to define the storm in one of the photographs, some students made storm figures with their hands, some rotated around themselves and others made storm sounds. While the viewers didn't have a problem identifying any of these descriptions, the most important output here came a week later. While we were studying gestures that defined sounds, many students referred to some specific gestures that had been made the previous week. When asked which gestures they brought back from the previous exercise, they put out that they can easily remember the gestures that they could build a bond in their perception. They called these 'meaningful gestures' and this became a principle in their gesture designs later on.

The second branch of outputs in these exercises was how the students defined the spatial composition of the photographed scenes. While in most of the descriptions, the viewers got only a general idea of the composition, in the descriptions made behind a curtain, the describers prevailed in clearly defining the placement of items within the scene. We observed that this was due partially to the curtain acting as a frame but mainly to the students having better control of a 2D surface than a 3D space.

Conclusion

In order to involve new interaction concepts and technologies into design education, innovative approaches are required. As Yıldız Technical University's Communication Design Department, we are trying various techniques that will develop and foster student creativity. We believe that, in order to explore the new possibilities that come along with new technologies and to set forth the development criteria of creating designs for the accurate use of the new technology, we require an education context that emphasises participation and experimentation. While every design problem has its own unique properties, our aim is to make students more aware of their creativity and other cognitive attributes by letting them explore and experience the new research field of the Natural User Interfaces. Throughout the project process, we observed that experiential exercises inspired by creative drama techniques produce effective and innovative points of view by giving students the chance to develop their own ideas around the concept of natural interfaces.

As the supervisors of the class, we observed that these participatory methods brought advantages in creative and innovative thinking ability in addition to their motivating factor for both the student and the educator in comparison to previous terms.

References

1. Yonck, R. (2010) 'The Age of the Interface', *Futurist*, May–June, pp.14–19.
2. Shaer, O. and Hornecker, E. (2010) 'Tangible User Interfaces: Past, Present and Future Directions', *Foundations and Trends® in Human–Computer Interaction* 3(1–2), pp.1–137.
3. Quek, F.K.H. (2002) 'Unencumbered gestural interaction', *IEEE Multimedia* 3(4), pp.36–47.
4. Sato, E., Yamaguchi, T. and Harashima, F. (2007) 'Natural Interface Using Pointing Behavior for Human–Robot Gestural Interaction', *IEEE Transactions on Industrial Electronics* 54(2), pp.1,105–12.
5. Antle, A.N. (2007) 'The CTI framework: Informing the design of tangible systems for children', in *Proceedings of the 1st international conference on Tangible and embedded interaction*, pp.195–202.
6. O'Malley, C. and Fraser, D.S. (2004) 'Literature review in learning with tangible technologies', *NESTA futurelab report* 12, Bristol.
7. Goldin-Meadow, S. (2003) 'Hearing Gesture: How Our Hands Help Us Think', Harvard University Press.
8. Ullmer, B.B., Ishii, H. and Jacob, R. (2005) 'Token+Constraint Systems for Tangible Interaction with Digital Information', *ACM Transactions on Computer–Human Interaction*, 12(1), pp.81–118.
9. Couture, N., Rivière, G. and Reuter, P. (2008) 'GeoTUI: A tangible user interface for geosciences', in *Proceedings of TEI08*, pp.89–96.
10. Gillet, U.A., Sanner, M., Stoffler, D. and Olson, A. (2005) 'Tangible augmented interfaces for structural molecular biology', *IEEE Computer Graphics & Applications* 25(2) pp.13–17.
11. Patten, J., Recht, B. and Ishii, H. (2002) 'Audiopad: A tag-based interface for musical

performance', in *Proceedings of the International Conference on New Interface for Musical Expression (NIME02)*, pp.24–6.
12. Newton-Dunn, H., Nakano, H. and Gibson, J. (2003) 'Blockjam: A tangible interface for interactive music', in *Proceedings of the 2003 Conference on New Interfaces for Musical Expression (NIME-03)*, pp.170–7.
13. Weinberg, G. and Gan, S. (2001) 'The squeezables: Toward an expressive and interdependent multi-player musical instrument', *Computer Music Journal* 25(2) pp.37–45.
14. Greenberg, S. and Kuzuoka, H. (2000) 'Using digital but physical surrogates to mediate awareness, communication and privacy in media spaces', *Personal Technologies* 4(1) pp.182–98.
15. Kalanithi, J.J. and Bove, V.M. (2008) 'Connectibles: Tangible social networks', in *Proceedings of TEI08*, pp.199–206.
16. Counts, S., Smith, M. and Zhao, J. (2007) 'Automated Route Annotation in Support of Community', *Proceedings, MSI workshop CHI2007*, San Jose, California, 2007.
17. Ahern, S., King, S., Naaman, M., Nair, R. and Yang, J.H.I. (2007) 'ZoneTag: Rich, Community-Supported Context-Aware Media Capture and Annotation', *Proceedings, MSI workshop CHI2007*, San Jose, Calif., 2007.
18. Kato, H., Billinghurst, M., Poupyrev, I., Tetsutani, N. and Tachibana, K. (2001) 'Tangible augmented reality for human computer interaction', in *Proceedings of Nicograph*, Nagoya, Japan.
19. Lee, G.A., Nelles, C., Billinghurst, M. and Kim, G.J. (2004) 'Immersive authoring of tangible augmented reality applications', in *Proceedings of IEEE/ACM International Symposium on Mixed and Augmented Reality*, pp.172–81.
20. Kirk, D.S., Sellen, A., Taylor, S., Villar, N. and Izadi, S. (2009) 'Putting the physical into the digital: Issues in designing hybrid interactive surface', in *Proceedings of HCI 2009*.
21. Truong, K.N., Hayes, G.R. and Abowd, G.D. (2006) 'Storyboarding: An empirical determination of best practices and effective guidelines', in *Proceedings of Designing interactive Systems DIS '06*, pp.12–21.
22. Edge, D. and Blackwell, A. (2009) 'Peripheral tangible interaction by analytic design', in *Proceedings of TEI09*, pp.69–76.
23. Fallman, D. (2002) 'Wear, point and tilt: Designing support for mobile service and maintenance in industrial settings', in *Proceedings of DIS2002*, pp.293–302.
24. Fishkin, K.P., Gujar, A., Harrison, B.L., Moran, T.P. and Want, R. (2000) 'Embodied user interfaces for really direct manipulation', *Communications of the ACM*, 43(9) pp.75–80.
25. Norman, D.A. and Nielsen, J. (2010) 'Gestural Interfaces: A Step Backwards in Usability', *Interactions* 17(5) pp.46–9.
26. Zimmerman, J. (2005) 'Video Sketches: Exploring Pervasive Computing Interaction Designs', *IEEE Pervasive Computing*, 4(4), pp.91–4,
27. Johnstone, K. (1999) *Impro for storytellers*, Routledge.
28. Burns, C., Dishman, E. and Verlpark, W. (1994) 'Actors, Hairdos & Videotape – Informance Design', *Proc. CHI'94*, pp.119–20.
29. Binder, T. (1999) 'Setting the Stage for Improvised Video Scenarios', *Ext. Abstracts CHI'99*, pp.230–1.

30. Buchenau, M. and Suri, J.F. (2000) 'Experience prototyping', *Proceedings of the conference on Designing interactive systems: processes, practices, methods, and techniques*, New York City, New York, United States, pp.424–33.
31. Simsarian, K.T. (2003) 'Take it to the next stage: the roles of role playing in the design process', in *CHI '03 extended abstracts on Human factors in computing systems*, pp.1,012–13.
32. Svanaes, D. and Seland, G. (2004) 'Putting the users center stage: Role playing and low-fi prototyping enable end users to design mobile systems', *CHI 2004 Proceedings*, pp.479–86.
33. Türkmayali, A. (2008) 'Forum Theater and Role play in Interaction Design', MA Thesis, Kadir Has University, Faculty of Communications.
34. Ahern, S., King, S., Naaman, M., Nair, R. and Yang, J.H.I. (2007) 'ZoneTag: Rich, Community-Supported Context-Aware Media Capture and Annotation', *Proceedings, MSI workshop CHI2007*, San Jose, Calif., 2007.
35. Bucciarelli, L. (1994) *Designing Engineers*, Cambridge, MA: MIT Press.
36. Nardi, B.A., Schiano, D.J. and Gumbrecht, M. (2004) 'Blogging as social activity, or, would you let 900 million people read your diary?' *Proceedings of the 2004 ACM conference on Computer supported Cooperative Work*, Chicago, Illinois, USA, pp.222–31.
37. Larsson, A. (2007) 'Banking on social capital: towards social connectedness in distributed engineering design teams', *Design Studies* 28 (6), pp.605–22.
38. Peng, C. (1994) 'Exploring communication in collaborative design: co-operative architectural modeling', *Design Studies* 15 (1), pp.19–44.
39. Erickson, T. and Kellogg, W.A. (2000) 'Social translucence: an approach to designing systems that support social processes', *ACM Transactions on Computer–Human Interaction* (Special issue on human–computer interaction in the new millennium, Part 1) 7 (1), pp.59–83.
40. McAfee, A.P. (2006) 'Enterprise 2.0: the dawn of emergent collaboration', *MIT Sloan Management Review* 47 (3), pp.21–8.
41. Joel, S., Smyth, M. and Rodgers, P.A. (2005) 'An ethno-methodological approach to product design practice', in Rodgers P.A. et al. (eds), *Crossing Design Boundaries*, London: Taylor and Francis, pp.157–62.
42. Dykes, T., Rodgers, P.A. and Smyth, M. (2009) 'Towards a new disciplinary framework for contemporary creative design practice', *CoDesign* 5 (2), pp.99–116.
43. Ulrich, K. and Eppinger, S. (2007) *Product Design and Development*, 4th edition, London: McGraw-Hill Higher Education.
44. Adams, R.S., Turns, J. and Atman, C.J. (2003) 'Educating effective engineering designers: the role of reflective practice', *Design Studies* 24 (3), pp.275–94.
45. Valkenburg, R. and Dorst, K. (1998) 'The reflective practice of design teams', *Design Studies* 19 (3), pp.249–71.
46. Smith, D., Hedley, P. and Molloy, M. (2009) 'Design learning: a reflective model', *Design Studies* 30 (1), pp.13–37.

Oliver BREUER, Agnese CAGLIO, Frederik GOTTLIEB, Sergejs GROSKOVS, Anette HILTUNEN, Miguel NAVARRO SANINT and Brian SCHEWE (in alphabetical order)

SPIRE, University of Southern Denmark

THE FACETS OF DESIGN THINKING

Introduction

Design thinking has become a popular label for the practices that, in many respects, have long been staples of the design disciplines: architecture, industrial design and so on. It has entered into popular currency and has been recently heralded as a (or *the*) potential new movement to improve/radicalise fields such as management. In this chapter we document a number of the roles and consequences of applying design thinking practices to the brief issued as an invitation to this conference. One of the contributions of this chapter is the presentation of a set of spectra of the various ways in which design can be mobilised in service of such an open brief. We use this to help create a rudimentary map of various approaches existent in design practice and their kinds of consequences, and to paint some of the heterogeneity of the very idea of design thinking.

The Project

The design concepts that will be described in this chapter have been developed by a team of seven design students at the University of Southern Denmark. The team is composed by interaction designers, industrial designers, multimedia designers and business graduates, who brought together their individual visions and perspectives in the project. Our aim was to develop some design concepts that could contribute in addressing or understanding the issues related to aging in general. The brief was deliberately open in order to allow an exploratory process that would help to investigate aging issues from different perspectives.

Challenging Assumptions: Aging as Seen by the Young

What the team tried to address, during the four months of the project, is an approach that tries to stay away from preconceptions and assumptions – above all, the assumption that a person could be considered 'old', and therefore considered a 'user' of our design, simply by being above a certain age limit (i.e. 65 years old).

One of the first choices of the team, moreover, has been to explore aging not only from the traditional perspectives of the older person but also in relation to the wishes, fears and interpretations related to aging of younger adults. This has been carried on with the intention to understand not only what aging is, or how it is perceived by aging people, but also what it is supposed to be, how it is imagined and interiorised by the people who gravitate around the ecosystem of an elderly.

The project had a strong focus on user research, conducted through interviews and workshops. The research started with an extremely wide spectrum of possibilities and themes, and has been narrowed down during the phases of the investigation, until it has been concentrated on three main themes (relationships young–old, memories, self-fulfilment) that inspired the design concepts presented.

Global Perspectives

Firstly, we explored the concept of aging as it is conceived in different parts of the world and in different cultures and age groups. Fifteen people, from 15 to 83 years old, with diverse experience with aging people (from nurses to young caretakers, to people with no experience) have been interviewed via VoIP on themes that ranged from their perception of aging and growing old to the challenges (or imagined challenges) of everyday activities and life.

Interviews have shown how complex aging has to be considered, since the themes that could be recognised in the patterns of answers ranged from very practical and physical issues (cleaning, dealing with sickness) to more abstract considerations about values (role of memory, the sensation of self-fulfilment, relationships and societal concerns). Younger people, particularly, have been shown to have very different opinions on aging and extremely different degrees of awareness; but, in most of the cases, they considered aspects related to self-knowledge, achievement and pride important.

A phase of analysis, together with the development of some personas, highlighted a series of themes and patterns, some of them overlapping in the different perspectives of younger adults and older adults. Of the many themes that emerged, the team selected some for further development: the role of memories, communication between generations, the perception of the role of elderly in society and the theme of physical impairment versus mental awareness and desires.

These themes were then developed more during a workshop held in Denmark, which involved 10 participants, between old and young people and comparing their positions, expectations and perception of the issues related to the themes with the help of participatory design techniques, like tinkering, activities and role play.

The Concepts

The activities described led to the development of the four concepts presented in this chapter: 'Giulia's Black Box', 'Memory Jewels', 'Forget Me Not' and 'Legal Age'. In the process of developing these concepts, some common dimensions arose. The ways to address the brief are implicit in the research and design process, along with different roles that design itself can have, each one with a specific rationale and seen on a different scale, producing consequently a different outcome.

The intention here is to describe the different concepts highlighting their similarities and differences. This will be done by comparing them on the basis of:

- The *role of design* implicit in the product/service
- The *rationale* of the concept
- The *scale* on which the product will have its effects
- The *outcome*, consequence of the choices taken in relation with the previous dimensions.

In the following paragraphs we briefly introduce the four concepts developed in our research and design process. The purpose is to give an overview of the material produced, in order to move towards an exploration of the different outcomes that a process of design thinking can lead to.

The Giulia's Black Box Concept

Giulia's Black Box is a cube-shaped device that will help a young person with a need for achievement to establish a reflective practice and maintain a constant dialogue with him- or herself. This dialogue will in turn lead to better decisions throughout life and ultimately to a more enjoyable retirement, with a sense of pride about one's life

Figure 1: Extract of a storyboard related to the Giulia's Black Box concept

achievements. The small black box looks inviting and precious, like a piece of fine art at home. Once stroked gently, it asks its user 'What do you want to share with me today?' It records the user's feedback, plays it back to the user and asks 'How do you feel about it?' If the user records what he or she did, listens, responds with a recording of her reflection, and then listens to this same reflection, the device will indicate that the future is safe. However, if left abandoned for a long time, the device will blink erratically thus warning the user about the passing of time and the uncertainty of the future.

The Memory Jewel Concept

Memory Jewel is a small handheld device equipped with a camera and a voice recorder. The device saves the file to a jewel-like memory hardware with a spherical and shiny shape. The sphere has a reduced capacity (30 minutes of sound and six pictures) and, being of small dimensions and pleasant aesthetics, can become an object to be shared or given as present. The files contained on the memory jewels can be uploaded to a computer via a shelf-like device. The areas of the shelf correspond to particular categories: memories can therefore be private (personal diary, thoughts), shared with the family (a recipe, a nice picture) or with a broader community (memories of the past, the story of the town). Once uploaded, shareable memories can be distributed as 'memory spheres' e.g. on the streets or in the metro stations, providing people with an opportunity to download the files and listen to them during a sightseeing tour in the town, or while going to work. A website allows, moreover, to add stories to the stories, comment on the memories or contact the storyteller.

Figure 2: Concept design of the handheld recording-camera device of Memory Jewels

The Forget Me Not Concept

Forget Me Not is an installation that exposes an existing gap that appears with aging due to technological literacy and the perceived usefulness of the elders in the modern world. The product consists of two parts. One part is an iPad application that allows

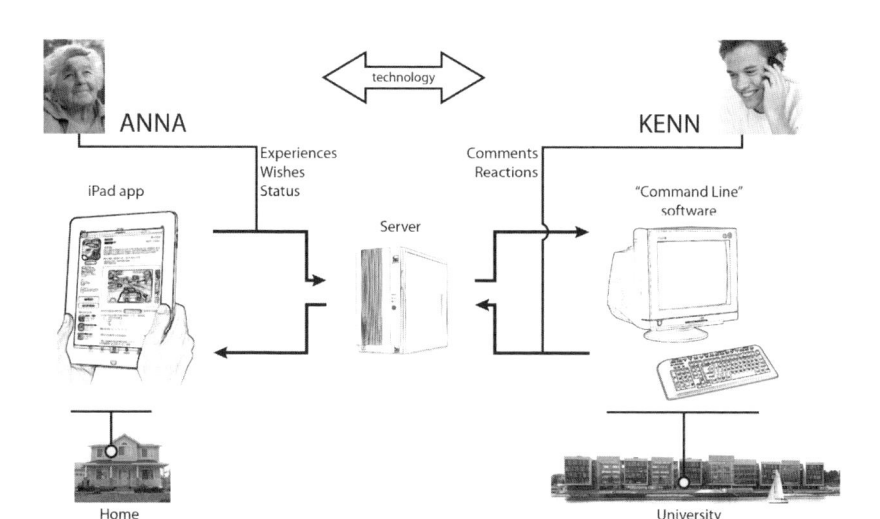

FORGET ME NOT
connecting service for elderly people

Figure 3: Forget Me Not conceptual operation scheme

an elderly user to write down his or her happy thoughts and achievements. Another part is an old computer with keyboard and command-line interface, placed in a public space where youngsters spend their time, e.g. at a university. The old computer invites a young user to read and reply to the posts from elder users. Technology is used as a bridge between both generations contradicting the common idea of technology as a gap maker. The installation takes elderly people to the university context bringing them to a privileged place in the young's mind map.

Anna is a 73-year-old woman, with low technological literacy; she likes to paint, to do crochet and to play cards with her friends. She uses her iPad to write about her experiences and wishes. Kenn is a 19-year-old teenager, with high technological literacy; he studies for a bachelor's degree in engineering and likes to party with his friends and play football on the weekend. While walking around the university, he discovers on his way an old computer surrounded by vintage objects that catches his attention. Everything is working perfectly, even if it looks old, and the space seems to be alive. When he comes closer to the screen he reads a stream of statuses including Anna's. Kenn is touched by the wisdom expressed in the experience shared by Anna and decides to write her a message. Later that day, Anna reads Kenn's message and feels part of the active society for a short but cheerful time, just before sharing with everyone a picture of her latest painting.

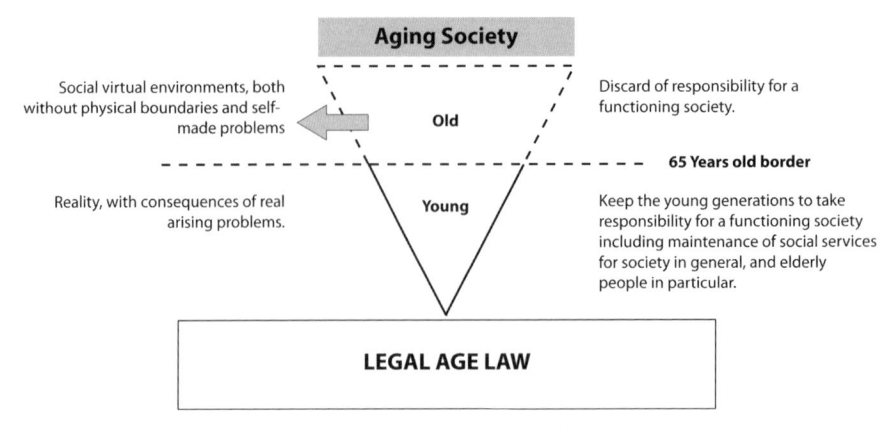

Figure 4: Legal Age concept

The Legal Age Concept

Legal Age is a visionary idea of a new legal age, similar to the age of consent. Children and teenagers often look forward to reaching a certain age to be allowed to drive a car, enter dance clubs, buy alcoholic beverages and so on. An additional threshold of such a kind further down the path of life with corresponding benefits could put people in great anticipation of growing old. Of course, installing such a system would require instances of, for example, control and enforcement, hence raising a range of issues on a large societal level.

Facing the Brief

Designing products, spaces or services in order to support an aging population, to allow the elderly to stay healthy and well, and to make growing old seem more attractive, raises many questions as many concepts are brought up.

First is the idea of being old versus growing old. When do you start being old and why? Second is the idea of attraction. What is attractive and what is unattractive about aging? These two questions open possibilities for varying understandings, making it possible to address the brief in many different ways. Our design team left these decisions to the personal interpretation of the results of the fieldwork activities such as interviews and workshops.

The brief invites empathic design, since everyone is gradually getting old. Hence personal experience was also useful as a first look into the aging concept – although the fact of the team being composed by people under thirty years old made the empathic method a narrow vision of what aging means. To extend the user perception about aging, 25 interviews were conducted. We took advantage of the cultural diversity of the design team and acquired access to the people in different countries – Denmark, Finland, Germany, Latvia, Italy and Colombia – to bear out our starting hypotheses. On one hand, the idea that the unattractiveness of growing old revolves around physical and mental disabilities and a gap with society, that starts pushing people aside as they age; on the other hand, the idea that the attractiveness turns around experience, i.e. memories and family. Here it is important to distinguish between two different visions: the youngsters' vision of being old and the elders' vision of being old.

Who is the User?

It is noteworthy that the unattractiveness related to physical and mental disabilities was mainly the youngsters' vision of being old, while the attractiveness of wisdom was mainly the elders' vision of being old. This contradiction presented one of the main dilemmas of developing a product or a service concept. Who would be the user? Someone young? Or elderly? Or both? Will the product change the current experience of what being old means? Or will it change the youngsters' perception of their future days when they will be old themselves?

In the Giulia's Black Box, the Memory Jewels and the Forget Me Not concepts the users are both young and elderly, although the last one is focused on modifying the attitude of youngsters towards current elders, while in the Legal Age concept the user is an elder and the concept intends to improve the condition of being old. Therefore, the user varies between the different concepts not only in age group, i.e. elderly or young, but also in its role, e.g. changing the attitude towards the elderly or changing their perception of themselves.

Figure 5: Young and elderly workshop participants construct and describe their relationships with family and friends using wooden building blocks

Testing the Initial Concepts

The initial findings were materialised in a number of preliminary concepts and tested in a workshop with young and elderly participants in Denmark. Issues such as the relation between growing old and losing validity, e.g. losing technological literacy; the importance of memories and achievements for a good elderly life; and the contradiction between what the body allows and what one would like to do, were tested using some initial product and service concepts. The elderly participants were five people from a home for the elderly, all females between 65 and 90 years old, some of them with big mobility compromises; while the young participants were two young 'karateka' men, both bachelor's students. During the activities, the workshop participants had direct contact with prototypes that involved high technology, i.e. iPods and virtual-reality concepts, but had usability characteristics easily understood by elderly participants using simple aesthetics and receiving help from the workshop facilitators for some technological tasks, thus allowing the participants to feel the experience. The response to those prototypes was favourable, proving that the use of technology in a project about aging, in which elderly people are involved, is possible. The importance of memories was also confirmed when testing conceptual presumptions, using a provocative service of preserving someone's brain, allowing people to access stored information after that person's death. The elderly were not shocked by the idea and a young participant welcomed the possibility of finally getting his grandmother's secret recipe.

Defining the New Concepts

After testing the first presumptions, the group proceeded to develop four product concepts based on those findings, each responding to a different problem identified in the process.

First, the participants expressed how achievements and memories are an important part of the attractiveness of growing old – especially one of the participants who suffers from short-term memory loss, although she has good memories from her childhood years; and a participant who struggles everyday with mobility issues and every moment is full of achievements, relating the elderly days to the first years of childhood full of physical achievements, e.g. the first steps, going further to the more general memory of some proud moments in life, like their families as their most important achievements. This brought up interesting questions, such as where is the importance of achieving something – in doing it or in the fact of being aware of having done it? As an example, the Giulia's Black Box invites its user to continuously reflect on her achievements, while Memory Jewels allow for constant awareness of achievements and sharable memories facilitating the sharing act.

Second, technology was recognised in the interviews as a gap generator when growing old, but was also seen as a possible interaction channel between youngsters and elders, as both groups of participants, elderly and young, were capable of feeling the experience and relating to the technology to which they were exposed. As a consequence, the Forget Me Not concept uses technology to provoke a reflection that reduces the gap between young and elderly.

Comparison of the Concepts

Role of Design

The word 'design', though commonly understood in its general sense, is contradictory and somehow vague. According to Simon [1], 'everyone designs who devises courses of actions aimed at changing existing situations into preferred ones'. Also, Jones notes that 'there seems to be as many kinds of design process as there are writers about it' [2]. Design processes are linked to a desired outcome and that outcome is also strongly linked to the designer's intentions. Hence, whatever the definition of design might be, it is connected to both the designer's intentions and a set of expectations on what the outcome should be, represent or do – the role of the design.

Depending on the role that is ascribed to design, outcomes and expected results are therefore different. We find it valuable in this context to compare how the four different concepts differ in their conception of the design's role, in order to map them and better understand the underlying assumptions to each of them.

Aging is an issue that is strongly linked to society as a whole and the public sphere. Therefore these differences in intentions become even more evident and potentially crucial when approaching and framing the design project itself.

Providing Means to the Users

In the interview published in the foreword of *Designing Interactions* [3], Gillian Crampton Smith observes that, just as our everyday life has been shaped by physical objects, so it can be by digital artefacts, 'for work, for play, for entertainment'.

The panorama opened by the research on persuasive technologies and their effect on behaviours has extended this idea. Can digital artefacts and objects also influence and shape our habits, our motivations? Thanks to authors like Fogg [4], models are being developed in order better to understand how technology can actually help us to develop healthier habits and possibly improve our quality of life.

Giulia's Black Box, while not to be entirely considered as a persuasive technology, can be at the same time recognised as a technology that provides the means to improve its human user's life. The purpose and the role of design in this case is not to solve a problem but to provoke the user to behave and live in a healthier way. The design is not the actor here. It is just a helper, a less visible presence, whose goal is to enhance human capabilities by developing an individual's motivation.

Thinking Big

In a well-known sentence, often cited, Buckminster Fuller expresses an inspiring idea: 'You never change things by fighting the existing reality. To change something, build a new model that makes the old model obsolete.' [5] In this spirit, the Legal Age tries to build a field of confrontation on delicate but crucial themes that contemporary society is facing and will have to face in the future.

According to Carl DiSalvo, 'a fundamental challenge in the construction of public is making the conditions and consequences of an issue apparent and known. One way that design might contribute to the construction of public is by the application of designerly means to this task' [6]. He argues that the tactics that design can use, in this framework, are two:

- The *projection*, in which the possible consequences of an issue are made visible. These projections can be predictive (just a representation) or prescriptive (embedding sorts of recommendations, a vision of what should happen).
- The *tracing*, which is basically the act of making explicit the set of assumptions and structures that define an issue.

The Legal Age concept, in this perspective, works in developing a vision of making visible all the relationships and issues that gravitate around the aging concept itself. The concept could be considered as the building of a vision, or a utopia, a suggestion to debate or, in the words of Julian Bleecker, 'objects (non-humans) around which stories/conversations ensure and imaginary words come into being' [7].

According to this point of view, we can consider the Legal Age concept as aligned with the experience of other collectives and projects like Future farmers, a platform for artists, designers and researchers developing projects that challenge current systems on various grounds (social, political, economic) [8], and the Massive Change project with its objective of mapping and emphasising the changing of design to generate change itself, and explore future utopian and dystopian possibilities [9]. Whereas design, and the design of the future, are made with the development of strong visions, debate and the intention of raising a more general and shared commitment in order to reach for big results and build the world with our own hands.

Provoking Reflections

Forget Me Not follows the role of provocation, almost outside the boundaries of the common understanding of design, since the nature of the installation makes it more similar to a piece of art than to a proper critical product.

In *The Secret Life of Electronic Objects* [10], Dunne and Raby divide the design landscape into two main areas: an affirmative design that accepts the current state of things in terms of cultural, social and technological values; and a critical design which, on the contrary, argues that the current state of things is not the only possible way.

Critical design, and the Forget Me Not installation in particular, borrows techniques and attitudes from contemporary art and makes them more powerful thanks to its closer position to popular culture and everyday life activities.

The Forget Me Not concept's goal, coherent to the critical attitude of Dunne and Raby's design, is to foster thoughts and reflection in the user; and not this only: it is also meant to challenge common understandings, to make visible the issues that are often taken for granted in a provocative attitude that intends to make problems explicit in order to solve them – in this case, the possible role of technology as a seclusion and inclusion tool.

Improving Activities, Designing New Ones

Interviewed by Lorenzo Imbesi in 2009 about his opinion on the new paths of interaction design research [11], Donald Norman answered: 'Long live the body, the physical world, reality. The world of computers led to an unfortunate diversion away from reality to the confining sterility of screens and keyboards, mice and other artificial animals… We human beings have bodies. We evolved in a world with three dimensional sounds, sights, objects and experiences.'

Memory Jewels can be recognised in this sentence and in the last development of Interaction Design research, focused on the goal to go out of the digital world and bring computing to the materiality of real objects.

A well-known example that could be considered as the symbol of this practice is the marble answering machine, developed by Durrell Bishop in 1992, one of the first explorations of how an answering machine could be transformed into a tangible product. Research has developed further in order to bring computing outside the desktop. As Dourish highlights, 'we need better ways to interact with computers, ways that are better tuned to our needs and abilities.' [12]

Memory Jewels' role is to continue on this path of research, proposing a way of physically sharing what has always been intangible (memories) and also of giving objective properties back to what once was tangible but, with the advent of digital technology, has become immaterial (photographs, for example). By giving a corporeal shape to these things and making them shareable thanks to technology, design attempts to influence and enrich human practices.

Rationale

In this section, the rationale behind each of the concepts will be briefly described. Concept development, in-group work, can be a shared process based on fieldwork findings and concept interpretation; but it can also be dependent on a series of often-complex interactions and negotiations between group members. It is then of interest to explore how the development of a product can be determined by often-conflicting dynamics. For the development of the understanding of design thinking, we think that this is a matter that has crucial importance, since it focuses the attention not only on designers' attitudes and methodologies in problem solving but also on the social and personal influences that arise in teamwork projects.

The process has shown how the development of a concept idea in a design project can be initiated by a specific concern expressed by a respondent (Giulia's Black Box), by the synthesis of several findings (Forget Me Not, Memory Jewels), by a team member's particularly strong interest (Legal Age) or by building upon a previously proposed concept (Memory Jewels based on Giulia's Black Box). Further concept development within the design team, before the first tests, can be influenced heavily by other team members' attitudes towards the idea, especially if they do not share the enthusiasm of the original creator (Legal Age), by the technical expertise within the team (Forget Me Not) or even by not offering other alternatives and thus leaving the original concept intact (Giulia's Black Box, Memory Jewels).

Rationale behind Legal Age

Legal Age is a concept that evolved from an example of a perfect virtual world in which only elderly people would be allowed to spend time. The example of a virtual world, like the Matrix [13], had been articulated and heavily defended by one of the design-team members who was willing to exceed the conventional expectations as required by the conference brief. Other team members were somewhat hesitant towards a well-known and science-fictional idea, but agreed to test it in a workshop with elderly and young participants.

The demonstration at the workshop involved a simulation of a virtual reality mixed with the 'Wizard of Oz' [14] technique. Two elderly participants, one after another, had a cardboard box placed over their heads with an iPhone attached on the inside at eye level. A video call was established with another iPhone, operated by a design-team member and used as a walking camera. Whenever the operating team member reached out for an object with his hand, another team member provided the participant with similar objects to touch and feel in her hand.

Although the workshop participants called the invention 'interesting' and said they would like to try it out once available in real life, the design team argued for not sticking to science fiction and defining a broader concept instead. Thus Legal Age, as a way to raise the wish of reaching a certain age to be able to use something (such as a virtual world), has become the broader concept.

Rationale behind Giulia's Black Box

The Giulia's Black Box came to life as a direct response to the concern expressed by a respondent during one of the interviews, formulated as 'I'm afraid of having become old without having done anything important'. Based on this finding a designer empathised with the young respondent and brought Schön's seminal work [15] to help her prevent the problem from ever happening. A rather open concept of the Black Box was presented to the design team, which questioned the validity of it and urged the creator to elaborate the concept in more detail. An alternative way to help the user establish a reflective practice would be to let her take an educational programme where such principles are taught. The effort, however, involved in taking a course would be much more significant compared to the use of a dedicated device for just several minutes every other day.

Since no other alternatives were offered, the team kept the idea of a black box. With the help of another team member, detailed interaction scenarios were worked out – an acquisition scenario, a first-use scenario and a regular-use scenario – clarifying the concept for the rest of the design team.

Rationale behind Memory Jewels

The Memory Jewels concept was proposed by another design-team member who was inspired by Giulia's Black Box. The inspiration, coupled with findings from the interviews and the workshop such as the problems of memory loss and the desire to share past experiences with relatives and friends, produced a new concept that addressed several of the identified problems simultaneously.

Existing alternatives, considered as somewhat similar in their attempt to address those issues, include Facebook as a website that allows sharing of photos, videos and written comments. However, the Memory Jewels are meant to make interaction with digital memories more tangible and accessible, and to break free from the constraints of desktop computing.

Rationale behind Forget Me Not

The Forget Me Not concept is similar to the concept of Memory Jewels in the sense that it addresses multiple problems identified during the field studies. Problems addressed here are the boundaries created by technology between younger and older generations, and the awareness (especially of the youngest side) regarding this topic. The concept development was handled by two design-team members, just as Giulia's Black Box and Legal Age were. The initial idea involved different artefacts, such as, for example, an old typewriter for the university installation. However beautiful the idea with the typewriter might be, it was turned down for the reason of feasibility: no-one in the team could make a software interface for an old typewriter to receive incoming messages and print them as a typical old typewriter would do. Thus another 'old-school' technology was proposed – a CRT monitor with a command line interface from the 1980s.

Scale

When addressing the previously exposed problems, one, as a designer, can define the limits of action of the intended product, identifying a key element in the entire system and focusing on interactions between them or intervening into the entire system in a holistic approach. On the first level the user is seen as an individual, regardless of

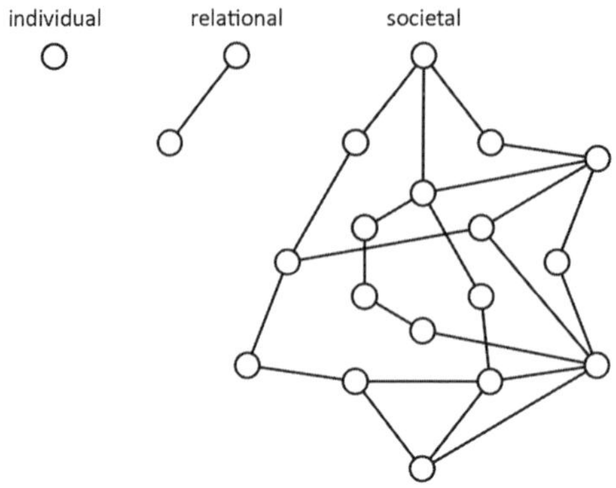

Figure 6: The different scales of effect of the concepts presented

his surrounding society. The second level is the relation between those individuals as emerging properties of a society. The third level is a society as a whole.

The Particular Scale

The particular scale appears from focusing on the individual reflections of the interviewees, as they expressed some personal emotions that don't depend directly on external circumstances but on an inner reflection. For example, Maria Cecilia, a 67-year-old Colombian woman expressed: 'I don't care how people see me. They can see me however they want. I want to see myself.' Giulia's black box approximates the user as a system on itself, composed by memories, feelings, experiences and dreams; the product is in the centre of those elements as a link between them and conscience.

The Relational Scale

The relational scale is based on inserting the interaction as an intervention between two parts of the system as an emerging property of society, facing the entropy that appears in intergenerational interaction, especially between the elderly and the young. The elderly depend on the young, not only for economic reasons but also because of a need for care that increases with years; yet they also feel the need to be free and self-supporting. However, this relationship between the young and the elderly seems to exist only in one direction and, therefore, creates a low synergy of the young–elderly system. Memory Jewels provides a possibility of sharing memories and experience with others while remaining independent, while Forget Me Not aims to create a reflection on the existing entropy.

The Societal Scale

The societal Scale refers to society as a political community, meaning, amongst other things, people ruled by the same laws. This holistic approach responds to a dilemma found during the research between improving the quality of life of the elderly, making it attractive to the young and keeping them from having an active life. The Legal Age concept approaches the problem proposing a law that controls the entire society in a top-down approach.

Outcome

The outcome of the design is highly dependent on designers' assumptions while framing the problem and the role that they imagine design should play in addressing social issues. In the following paragraphs, the different outcomes of the concepts are compared, together with their characteristics.

Increasing Awareness

Providing people with critical artefacts can lead to a breakdown of order, to an increased awareness of and challenge to mundane behaviour patterns and assumptions. It is possible to draw a comparison, for example, with the Electro-draught Excluder placebo project made by Dunne and Raby in 2001 [16]. The product was made to test whether its owner would feel more comfortable if he or she thought that the draught excluder absorbs radiation when near to electronic objects in the home. In regard to a particular outcome, this product made the test persons aware of the invisible electromagnetic waves that their home devices produce, resulting in a feeling of insecurity in one of the users.

Similarly, Forget Me Not is encouraging reflection on existing assumptions about old age being a negative phase. The installation is made to test whether a provided opportunity for an intergenerational contact can alter attitudes. Through discussion and sharing experiences via iPads that synchronise with an installation placed in a youngsters' environment, members of two generations become more aware of each other. The installation is also expected to raise discussion about whom present-day communication media and technology is mainly serving and to provoke people to consider these issues.

Creating Visions and Raising Debate Topics

Visionary design's goal [17] is postulating the possible and seeking to understand what is likely to come by using the understanding of past and present to predict the future-oriented outcome. The most common outcomes are, for example, scenarios, which help to plan strategically or to test the causal relationship between factors, or utopias, ideal societies or communities with perfect social, political and legal systems.

As a utopia, Legal Age is a prediction of a potential law that weaves new ideas into a society – one being a virtual reality into which people, in this case old people, prefer to retreat.

Fostering Actions

Proactive design solutions refer to anticipatory, change-oriented and self-initiated behaviour. Instead of just reacting, the object aims to act in anticipation of potential future situations. For example, the iPhone has a light sensor that measures the amount of light and automatically adjusts the brightness of the screen. Likewise, Giulia's Black Box adjusts to its owner's behaviour by blinking erratically to warn the user about the passing of time and the uncertainty of the future. Its proactiveness is not adaptable to many peoples' needs. The outcome for the user is a more enjoyable retirement with a sense of pride about one's lifetime achievements, because the self-awareness the product has helped to build enables them to take charge of situations.

Memory Jewels

Practical design outcomes aim to solve today's needs. They are functionally oriented in their sense of and focus on the possible and actual. A door handle can be considered as practical in its fundamental sense. In its tangibility it is solving a basic function – opening a door. Memory Jewel is a tangible sharing system that solves the need for a memory-collecting device in a comfortable size.

Conclusions

This chapter intends to be a contribution to the panorama of design thinking on multiple perspectives. Starting from the teamwork experience, its goal is to highlight the complexity and variety of results depending on the framing and interpretation of a design problem. As Rittel and Webber highlighted in 1973 [18], a great part of the process of addressing a public issue is dependent on the goal formulation, which is in itself an 'extraordinarily obstinate task'. This definition brings along several other steps, decisions and a definition of frameworks that can lead to extremely different solutions. The other contribution of this article is indeed on these differences between the solutions, their implications and the assumptions behind them, connected to the role of design, the scale, the rationale and the outcome.

The attempt is to explore the panorama of possible approaches to such a big issue as aging, since the authors are convinced that the comparison between different effects, goals and means of design could bring a useful overview and hopefully the possibility of identifying important aspects of the contribution of design thinking to problem solving in delicate societal situations.

A broad brief such as the one that the design team faced in this chapter is open to a broad spectrum of answering projects. This highlights how design is mainly a matter of where one draws the limits and why. In this case, there was a shared creation of limits, being strongly influenced by the dimension of the team itself, composed of seven members. At the same time, however, the possible users had a considerable influence, as they were the ones who laid the foundations for team discussions and introduced themes that the design group had never before considered as central. Their influence was clearly taken as an inspiration for three of the concepts: Giulia's Black Box, Memory Jewels and Forget me Not; while Legal Age was introduced by one of the team members, users from the field research helping as support for the idea. This created some tensions among the team members, mainly based on the argument of how design-driven or user-driven design should be. Should we, as designers, decide for the users or should they decide for us? In our case, a numerous team made it difficult to take decisions and therefore we relied on the users to decide for us, as they were the source for a shared authorship of ideas. The discussions were provoked basically by the design-driven concept, e.g. Legal Age. This difference had also consequences in the proximity of the concepts to the users and the role played by designers. The user-driven concepts, i.e. Giulia's Black Box, were close to the personal and more private elements of the user bringing solutions to personal recurrent dilemmas; while the design-driven concept ended as an impersonal solution that did not consider particular users but rather took the whole of society as a target, giving the opportunity for a visionary approach that allows exceeding expectations. It is worth noting the large number of concepts created by the same team and how the inclinations of different group members can tilt the concept generation to artistic, functional or visionary fields, in order to create or increase awareness, to raise debates or even completely to rethink the entire social system around the team creation.

References

1. Simon, H. (1969) *The Sciences of the Artificial*, 1st edition, Cambridge, MA: MIT Press, p.129.
2. Jones, J.C. (1970) *Design Methods: seeds of human futures*, London: John Wiley & Sons Ltd., p.77.
3. Moggridge, B. (2007) *Designing Interactions*, Cambridge, MA: MIT Press.
4. Fogg, B.J. (2009) 'A behaviour model for persuasive design', in *Proceedings of the 4th International Conference on Persuasive Technology*, Claremont, California: ACM, pp.1–7.
5. Cited in Bleecker, J. (2008) 'Design Fiction: something and the something in the age of something', *Design engaged*, Montreal, p.9. http://www.slideshare.net/bleeckerj/design-fiction-design-engaged-julian-bleecker-presentation-638179
6. DiSalvo, C. (2009) 'Design and the Construction of Publics', *Design Issues*, vol. 25, no. 1, pp.48–63.
7. Bleecker, J. (2008) 'Design Fiction: something and the something in the age of something', *Design engaged*, Montreal, p.45. http://www.slideshare.net/bleeckerj/design-fiction-design-engaged-julian-bleecker-presentation-638179.
8. Futurefarmers (n.d.) retrieved 24 October 2011 from http://www.futurefarmers.com/.
9. MASSIVECHANGE (n.d.) retrieved 24 October 2011 from http://www.massivechange.com/.
10. Dunne, A. and Raby, F. (2001) *Design Noir: The Secret Life of Electronic Objects*, Basel: Birkhäuser.
11. Imbesi, L. (ed.) (February 2009) Interview on DIID Disegno Industriale Industrial Design n. 39 RDesignPress, Italy, pp.23–4.

12. Dourish, P. (2004) Where the Action is: the foundations of embodied interactions, MIT Press, p.2.
13. Wachowsky, L. and Wachowsky, A. (1999) *The Matrix*, DVD, Warner Bros.
14. Kelley, J.F. (1984) 'An iterative design methodology for user-friendly natural language office information applications', *ACM Trans. Inf. Syst.* 2, 1 (January 1984), 26–41.
15. Schön, D. (1983) The Reflective Practitioner: How professionals think in action, London: Temple Smith.
16. http://www.dunneandraby.co.uk/content/projects/70/0
17. Fuller Buckminster, R. (1970) *Utopia or oblivion: the prospects for humanity*, Allen Lane, The Penguin Press.
18. Rittel, H.W.J. and Webber, M.M. (1973) 'Dilemmas in a General Theory of Planning', *Policy Sciences* 4, Elsevier Scientific Publishing Company, Amsterdam, pp.155–69.

Janet KELLY

*SPIRE Centre for Participatory Innovation,
Oticon AS and Novo Nordisk AS, Denmark*

CRAFTING 'SOLVABLE' PROBLEMS IN THE DESIGN PROCESS

Introduction

The concept of 'wicked problems' was introduced by Rittel in the 1960s [1] to describe a societal class of problems, differentiated from the problems being addressed by of the natural sciences. Unlike the 'tame' problems of the natural sciences which 'are definable and separable and may have solutions that are findable', wicked problems are ill-formulated, involve information that is confusing, have many stakeholders with conflicting values, produce unforeseeable consequences and, although addressable, are not solvable. 'Social problems are never solved. At best they are only re-solved – over and over again.' [2] This idea has resonated within the design community as it recognises issues at the very core of much of design practice. As Buchanan points out regarding the first published report of the idea, the description of wicked problems was in fact an 'amusing description of what confronts designers in every new situation.' [2]

The wicked-problems approach was outlined by Rittel and Webber in their 1973 paper regarding the professional practice of planning where they put forward ten properties of wicked problems, highlighting their indeterminate nature. Later Buchanan offered an explanation as to why design problems specifically are so wicked, arguing that this is because there is no subject matter particular to design, leaving the designer both free and obliged to define their own. 'Design problems are "indeterminate" and "wicked" because design has no special subject matter of its own apart from what a designer conceives it to be. The subject matter of design is potentially universal in scope, because design thinking may be applied to any area of human experience. But in the process of application, the designer must discover or invent a particular subject out of the problems and issues of specific circumstance' [2]. Design is not confined by any one way of doing things but can consider any possible path in order to make a transformation, leaving us with a potentially infinite number of possibilities as to how to respond to any given task.

In contrast to classical problem-solving models, which suggest that the clear definition of a problem comes first followed by the search for a solution, due to their indeterminate nature 'wicked problems' become defined through the forming of a solution, the response determining which elements will comprise the problem being addressed. 'To find the problem is thus the same thing as finding the solution; the problem can't be defined until the solution has been found. The formulation of a wicked problem is the problem! The process of formulating the problem and of conceiving a solution (or re-solution) are identical, since every specification of the problem is a specification of the direction in which a treatment is considered.' [2] Creative design involves an exploration of both problem and solution, and this interdependency of development between the two has become intrinsic to how we currently understand design practice; acknowledging that design exploration is as much about finding problems as solutions. As Cross describes it, 'Defining and framing the design problem is therefore a key aspect of creativity.' [3] Problem formulation is part of the creative design process – we construct a problem out of aspects of the circumstances we are trying to transform, in order to make them solvable.

Maher presented a model of this exploration process as a form of 'co-evolution' [4], in which the problem and the solution spaces are two distinct search spaces that interact over time and where the problem leads to the solution but, in turn, the proposed solution can refocus the problem; meaning that designers define what to change (the problem) and also how to go about it (the solution) in parallel, developing and refining them through constant iterations in search of an apposite concept [5]. 'Creative design involves a period of exploration in which problem and solution spaces are evolving and unstable until (temporarily) fixed by an emergent bridge which identifies a problem-solution pairing' [6]. This exploration phase involves both searching for solutions and potentially solvable problems until they can be matched together. There is a subtle difference then between the problems that our overall goals derive from in most projects and the ones we formulate to solve. The initial and underlying problems that project goals derive from, except in the most trivial of design cases, as Buchanan points out [2], are usually those that can be considered wicked problems, ill-defined and unsolvable; while the design problems we formulate through our exploration must be defined sufficiently in order for solutions, no matter how tentative, to present themselves.

Although these problems may evolve beyond recognition throughout the process of exploring problem-solution pairs, it is necessary to formulate that initial 'solvable' problem from an unsolvable wicked one in the first place. Without the designer's skill in doing this, the exploration would have no starting point to evolve from. Steve Harfield, in the cases of architectural design that he is studying, argues that the architects do this by formulating an architectural or design problem based their own personal views of what constitutes appropriate 'designerly' problems [7], in addition to the problem in the brief: 'By imposing upon the problem-as-given their views, positions and preferences, architects construct the problems they seek to solve while at the same time defining and limiting the solution possibilities available to them.' In the case of a user-driven process such as this presented here, I will attempt to demonstrate how I chose and defined a 'solvable' designerly problem, attempting to take into account stakeholder perspectives as well as my own views as a designer.

The Case

This design project was carried out as part of a research project that is sponsored by two medical devices companies, Novo Nordisk, which produces injection devices for diabetes drugs, and Oticon, which produces hearing aids. The project was initiated because both these companies perceived they had a similar problem in that a large proportion of their potential market, people diagnosed with the medical conditions whose health and wellbeing could benefit from using these treatment devices, are reluctant to begin doing so. In this project we are referring to this group as 'pre-users' of medical devices [8]. The initial aim of this research project has been twofold: firstly, to identify the reasons that prevent people from becoming users; and secondly, to involve the device pre-users in order to develop outcomes that facilitate the transition from pre-user to user. Both these conditions are complex and progressive, making it difficult for people suffering from them to understand what exactly they are being treated for. The project group includes me, a designer, and an anthropologist. The brief for this task asks for designs that surpass conventional expectations but what I would like to present here is a case where I attempt to develop design responses that change conventional expectations, to be better aligned with the actual experience of using the technologies, demonstrating how this became one of the main objectives of the process. Through presenting this case I will also try to demonstrate how the problem I address is typical of Rittels' wicked-problem concept and to explicate how I as a designer try to tackle this; in particular, focussing on the practice involved in constructing a problem formulation in order to create outcomes that respond to a range of different stakeholder interests. For practical reasons, this case involves two similar design projects, one for each of the company sponsors, which were run simultaneously.

The main project goal in this case derives from the commercial interests of the two companies that are sponsoring it. Both hearing loss and diabetes type 2 are conditions that are becoming increasingly more common with an aging population. These medical conditions can have a significant effect on people's health, wellbeing and social life, as well as their ability to stay independent as they grow older. Fortunately, there already exist medical technologies to treat them which are easily available across the developed world and that can allow people with the conditions to achieve a high quality of life. Type 2 diabetes can be treated in many ways, one of the most effective being insulin injection treatment, and hearing aids have been shown to ameliorate many of the problems of hearing loss significantly. The issue both companies have is that they believe they have a large untapped market as, despite the medical benefits of the technologies they produce, many people delay the uptake of these treatments long past the point where they would be of medical benefit to them. Their goal in initiating the research project from which this case is taken, in collaboration with the SPIRE Centre for Participatory Innovation at the University of Southern Denmark, has been to see what could be learnt from people who have the conditions but were not yet using the devices, who had not yet held them in their hands; and to innovate with them in order to 'solve' this (the companies') problem.

Although the goals driving the project are commercial, it is not possible to separate them from the two health-care issues with which they are associated. There are 285 million people worldwide with type 2 diabetes [9], a figure which is increasing rapidly. It is a gradually developing condition that is characterised by insulin resistance and relative insulin deficiency, which in turn causes high blood-sugar (glucose) levels. Although it is often preventable through lifestyle changes, once developed it must be treated to control blood-sugar levels, because sustained high sugar levels will eventually lead to tissue damage, often resulting in serious complications. This tissue damage can occur in many organ systems but the kidneys, eyes, nerves and vascular tree (blood vessels) in particular manifest the most significant, and sometimes fatal, diabetic complications. Diabetes is ranked among the leading causes of blindness, renal failure and lower-limb amputation in most developed countries. Diabetes is also now one of the leading causes of death, largely because of a markedly increased risk of coronary heart disease and stroke (cardiovascular disease). In addition to the human suffering that diabetes-related complications cause, their economic costs are huge [10]. Studies show that failure to begin insulin therapy promptly when it becomes necessary is likely to result in needlessly reduced life expectancy and compromised quality of life [11].

Although the consequences of hearing loss may not be as dramatic as those of diabetes, the condition can still have a drastic effect on the lives of those have it and the people around them. There are 31 million people with hearing loss worldwide, many cases of which are age related [12]. As with diabetes, gradual hearing loss is an incurable condition but most of its effects can be ameliorated with hearing aids. Hearing impairment has been associated with depression [13] and social withdrawal, and can be damaging to personal relationships as it affects communication. It is also shown to have a significantly detrimental effect on work experience and the workforce, with people with hearing loss being significantly more likely to report sick, almost exclusively due to stress-related complaints. In addition, a Danish study has also linked hearing loss with a higher likelihood of taking early retirement [14]. Yet despite a very high satisfaction rate amongst people who use them, in the developed world only one in four people who could benefit from a hearing aid actually uses one [15]. From a medical perspective, both hearing aids and insulin injection devices have significant benefits and, although they will not cure either condition, are able to help prevent some of their worst consequences. Yet despite this the health-care problems have not been 'solved' – the wickedness remains – as people who are supposed to be able to be benefit from these treatments do not.

The circumstances of this wicked problem are thoroughly confusing when considered only from this point of view, which is why gaining an insight into the rationale of the potential users of these devices was important. We chose to take a user- (or, in our case, a pre-user-) driven approach to design in this project. Most of the work presented in this case is based on a pilot study we conducted in Autumn 2009 and follow-up events of Spring 2011, which followed a period of leave from the project. In the pilot project, we interviewed two people with hearing loss but no hearing aids and three people with type 2 diabetes not yet on insulin treatment, in their homes, and invited two of each group to a co-design workshop. In addition to this, based on a hypothesis that the clinical interaction between doctor and patient was important to the decision to adopt the devices, we visited two general-practitioner doctors and two ear-nose-and-throat doctors, for interviews and recorded consultations between them and patients with the condition [8]. After the project leave we were able to go back to one of the people with diabetes for a follow-up workshop. We also revisited one of the people with hearing loss, who had since acquired hearing aids; he was joined in the workshop by his wife who also had hearing loss but was resisting to getting hearing aids.

Formulating a 'Solvable' Problem

Insights into the Problem

Our initial interviews involved going to visit each of the pre-users in their homes and conducting hour-and-a-half, semi-structured interviews with them, focusing on the condition and the way it affected their daily lives. Additionally, we conducted semi-structured interviews with the health-care professionals (HCPs), focusing on their experience of treating these patients and introducing the treatment technologies to them, and recorded consultations where the treatment of the conditions was discussed. One of the conclusions we were able to draw from these was that the perceived benefits offered by the technologies were being weighed against recognised problems the conditions created in people's lives and interpretations of how these might develop in future. For the people who suffered from these conditions, the treatments as 'solutions' to the medical problem were seemingly more problematic than the conditions themselves.

This was partly because the symptoms of the conditions were not necessarily immediately felt by those with them. In the case of type 2 diabetes, most people experience very few symptoms. The condition is treated to prevent long-term damage to the body and to lower the risk of events such as heart attacks but, in general, before these complications emerge there are few things to indicate a person is sick; and once symptoms become apparent, it is often too late. As one GP we talked to explained, it is challenging to explain to people that we treat diabetes for the risks of complications in the future as people do not feel sick now so they are not addressing immediately felt problems. Similarly, gradual hearing loss is a condition which normally develops over many years and so many people may not even be aware they have it for a very long time. It is often the case that they themselves will not be the first to notice their hearing difficulties; frequently, their partner, friends or colleagues notice first [16]. As one of our participants expressed it, 'I do not notice what I don't hear'. Consequently, when people do recognise they have hearing loss, they don't necessarily see it as a problem significant enough to require treatment. One ENT specialist explained to us that people often come to see him because someone else wants them to. In these cases, he is reluctant to offer hearing aids as, in his experience, these people are less likely to use them.

The participants in our study did not feel that the conditions were necessarily causing them any problems in their daily lives; but they did feel that the treatments would. For people with diabetes, taking insulin was presented more as a symptom of the disease than as a treatment, a point in the progression of the disease that suddenly meant it became serious. One of our participants, Marie, explained that to her taking insulin 'means it is now serious, no going back', and even that taking insulin would mean there was nothing more that could be done: 'when I start taking insulin it means the end of my life'. With hearing loss, concern was related to the stigma of having the condition. One participant, Ole, expressed concern that if people saw the hearing aid they would think, 'that poor old man, he can't hear'. The concern was that the hearing aid would make the condition more evident, rather than alleviating the symptoms.

Reluctance to adopt the treatment technologies was not explicitly related to problems with the design of the devices: people associated the treatments with the problems of having the conditions rather than seeing them as the solutions. With type 2 diabetes, the treatment is mainly to prevent future complications rather than current symptoms. With gradual hearing loss, it can be hard for people suffering from the condition to differentiate between problems caused by their environment and those caused by the condition. Additionally, many of the consequences (tiredness, social isolation) can seem completely unrelated. In both cases, people did not feel like they were experiencing problems in their everyday lives caused by the conditions; and so they felt the treatment would actually be more problematic. This insight gave a greater transparency to the nature of the problem from which the project-goal derives; but it did not tame it.

Finding a Problem that Seemed 'Solvable'

The stakeholders' conflicting values, particularly as to what constituted the problem in these circumstances, are a significant aspect of the 'wickedness' of these problems. It appeared to me that finding a way to align these would be one way to respond to this. I considered that if I could make the consequences of not treating the conditions clearer to the pre-users – and by doing so transform their expectations of becoming a user of the technologies from a problem into a solution – then the project goal could be met. Yet I still was not able easily to search or recognise interesting responses from this formulation alone. It was still too broad and indeterminate to begin looking at how it could be resolved with concrete solution concepts, so I began to look for a way to formulate a more defined problem, taking into account this aspect of the problem.

I became interested in one phenomenon that we noticed during our analysis of our ethnographic data: numbers and measurements were referred to frequently when discussing both conditions. Both of the conditions are essentially defined by a number, obtained by measuring blood-sugar levels or hearing threshold: if the number is above a certain cut-off point, then technically the patient has the condition. For the participants our study, the relationship with these numbers and measurements could be problematic in different ways. For those with diabetes, rises in blood sugar sometimes did not seem to relate easily to what they were eating and doing:

> Flødeboller (marshmallow-filled cake) – when I eat that in the evening then in the morning I have a very high blood sugar. That is hard for me to understand because flødeboller are very easy to digest. If I eat drops (candy) or anything in the evening, it is not very high in the morning, then I have offset it.

In addition to this, for some there were no physical symptoms. 'I don't feel it. I never do, I never feel any different when it's low or high'. The abstract and confusing nature of these readings could also have a profound effect on an emotional level: 'Then I will stop measuring – I get the feeling: No, I do not want to be confronted with it… To be confronted with these numbers that just go up and down – I cannot handle that at all.' The emotional impact seemed to be caused by measurement not just being related to the condition itself but also to being judged as a good patient.

With hearing loss, it seemed that one problem was the discrepancy between the subjective experience of it and the abstract technicality of the diagnosis. Many of our study participants had expressed a suspicion that the problems could actually be being caused by environmental factors: they felt they could hear clearly in some situations but not in others, so the problems were often equated with the environment or due to other people 'mumbling'. Being officially diagnosed did little to help allay the suspicions or clarify that problems were actually linked to hearing loss. When tested, the measurements of their hearing levels were recorded on an audiogram from which the hearing care professional obtains the information needed to decide on a treatment [17]. None of our participants who had had a hearing test could explain to us what their diagram meant in terms of their experience of hearing and, from our observations of ENT specialists trying to explain hearing loss to patients, it was evident that it was not easy to understand. One patient we observed, for example, thought the decibel scale indicated an age range at first. People found it hard to relate the loss of some frequencies as indicated on the audiogram to the hearing problems they were having, causing them to doubt the need for treatment.

Our study participants found it hard to relate the abstract nature of this measurement to any problems, which in turn appeared to be one of the reasons they found it hard to

Figure 1: An ENT specialist explains an audiogram to a patient

accept the need to treat it. Measurement and numbers were in fact closely linked to both the experience of the condition and many of the strategies for handling it. This aspect of the problem was connected to the others and could actually meet the companies' goals for the project: if the numbers were more easily related to the experiences and consequences of the conditions, people might better understand the need to treat the conditions and therefore become more willing to adopt the technologies earlier. I recognised potential bridges between this problem formulation and solution concepts that had begun to emerge and felt this would be a productive area to explore further – a component of the overall wicked problem that was potentially 'solvable'.

Evolving the Problem Through Solutions

Critical Artefacts

Finding ways to make the numbers and measurements involved relate better to the experience of the condition presented itself as a designerly [7] problem, as it both gave me a defined and limited subject matter to work with and allowed me to begin conceiving of potential solutions. The first concepts generated were not conceived as potentially realisable design solutions though, but instead as exploratory tools to enquire further into the problematic aspects of the condition with the pre-users. This method was based on Critical Artefacts Methods [18] which are inspired by Critical Design, the idea of which is to use provocative design concepts to generate critical reflection from stakeholders as part of a design process, not as the outcome of it. 'The critical artefacts produced serve the role of "probes" within human-centred design activity – tools for exploring problem contexts and generating needs-focussed product ideas.' The critical artefacts are instrumental in developing better 'answers'. We

Figures 2 and 3: Critical artefacts – NutriScan visual and soundscape information

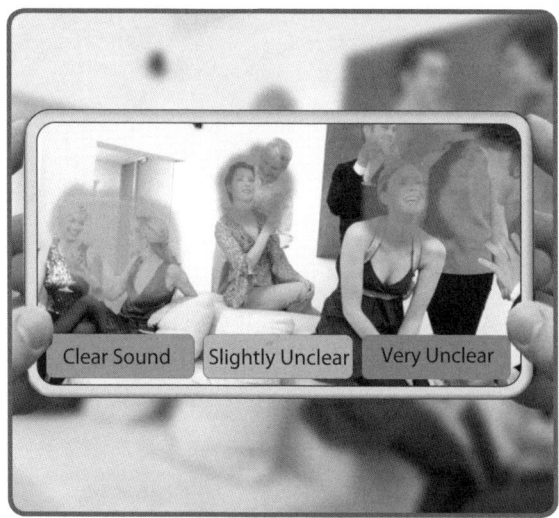

developed critical artefacts, three based around hearing loss and three based around type 2 diabetes and measurement technologies, and presented them in a workshop with pre-user representatives from both disease areas (two of each).

The idea behind the concepts was that, rather than measuring the condition, they would measure aspects of the environment that affected the experience of the condition; technologies that indicated how easy it was to hear in an environment and technologies that indicated how healthy food was. The concepts all varied in the level of privacy they allowed; for example, one concept for diabetes was a plate that would change colour depending on the healthiness of the food, while another was a discreet key-ring-sized device with which patients could 'scan' their food. In the activity, we presented the devices along with a situation, for example a dinner party, and asked the participants to describe how they might use the concepts in that situation.

The discussion in the workshop brought to the surface many of the participants' attitudes towards technology's role in handling their condition and what they felt was acceptable from it. For the participants with diabetes, the artefacts provoked reflection on the role numbers and measurements as indicators of success, showing how well you are controlling it and also what it meant to add a social element by making this visible to others. One participant, for example, discussed how she would try to cheat if she had to use an artefact like the plates; she felt that it would show how unhealthy the food she was eating was, which would be in some way shameful and not something she was willing to make explicitly visible to others.

> Participant – 'The idea that other people could see what I put on my plate, I don't think that's a good idea. I would cheat… if I could.'
>
> Facilitator – 'Cheat? Do you have any idea how?'
>
> Participant – 'No… but I'm sure I would cheat. The green area would be so big on my plate, I would find some way… [uses hands to indicate rearranging food]'.

The artefacts also prompted reflection on the how the numbers and need to measure could be representative of your knowledge about the condition: one participant was quick to label the same idea as childish ('that's for babies') but then realised that it could have a role for people who were newly diagnosed, just starting to learn about managing their condition, highlighting the role of measurement as an existing tool to learn how to control the diabetes through diet.

Figure 4: Pre-user critical artefacts workshop

The reflection provoked by the hearing loss concepts was focused more on how, or if, being able to understand the causes of communication problems in social situations would help to deal with the situation better. In a previous interview, one participant had discussed how he would feel excluded at parties because he could not hear what was going on and would often pretend to understand as a way of coping; when he now considered the use of this concept, he explained that he did not think it would guide him at all: he would still go to the people he wanted to talk with, not the ones he could hear best. This reflection eventually prompted both participants with hearing loss to discuss the advantages of having such a technology as a feature in a hearing aid, so that it would be able to adjust itself automatically without them having to adapt their behaviour in these social situations. The artefact effectively made explicit the role of hearing-loss coping mechanisms in changing behaviour in social situations, which caused the alternative, hearing aids, to appear in a more positive light.

The Second Workshop

After this initial exploration, I began looking at ways in which solving this problem could also address the overall project goal, making the numbers easier to relate to the experiences and consequences of the conditions in order to make people understand the need to treat the conditions better; or more specifically, the benefits of the treatments. For diabetes, the insight from the critical artefacts workshop about the role of measurement in learning how to control the condition with diet made me consider how learning about insulin treatment and other aspects of the condition could be approached in a similar way. I began exploring ways to communicate how changing the three main treatment parameters (diet, exercise and medication) affects blood sugar numbers over time, as a way of relating the treatment of the condition to the way it affected people's bodies. In the hearing-loss case, the workshop had indicated that making the effects of the hearing loss explicit in real situations could make wearing hearing aids seem like a more positive option; so I began looking at concepts inspired by the 'Audiogram of Everyday Sounds' tool, used for counselling on hearing loss in audiological consultations [19], that involved using patients' own audiograms to indicate visually the sounds that they weren't able to hear in real situations.

In order to explore and test these ideas further with the pre-users, we organised two more co-design workshops, one with a participant from the first workshop with diabetes and another with a participant from the first workshop with hearing loss, who had since then started using hearing aids, and his wife who also had a hearing loss. In these workshops, we started by presenting a pre-user scenario, followed by an activity which involved trying to get the participants to forge the links between the measurements and their experiences of the conditions. For diabetes, a graph was presented showing changes in blood sugar over a day; the participant was asked to match cards with meals and activities on them to the peaks and troughs. For hearing loss, we presented a blank audiogram for the participants to fill in by identifying where on it to place the sounds with which they had problems. Finally, we presented concept proposals which the participants critiqued and made development suggestions for.

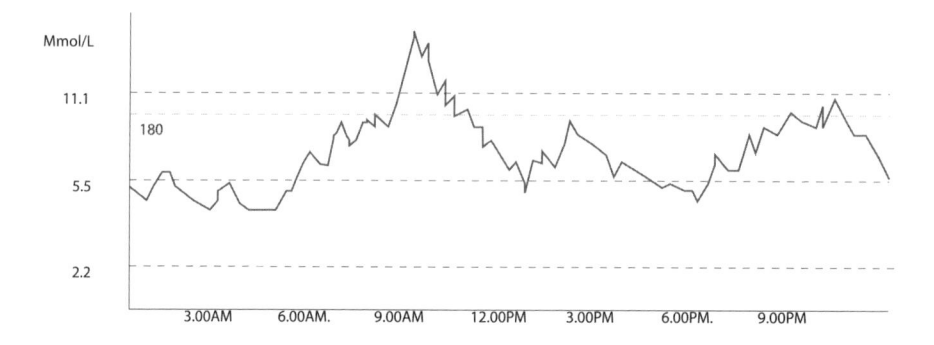

Figure 5: Blood-sugar chart from type 2 diabetes workshop

In the blood-sugar graph activity in the diabetes workshop, the participant was quickly able to make connections between the changes in blood sugar on the graph and the food and exercise images, but struggled to relate the medication options to changes in blood sugar over the day. She really did not seem to need a tool to help her understand the daily changes in blood sugar; but when we discussed the concept

Figure 6: Audiogram activity from hearing-loss workshop

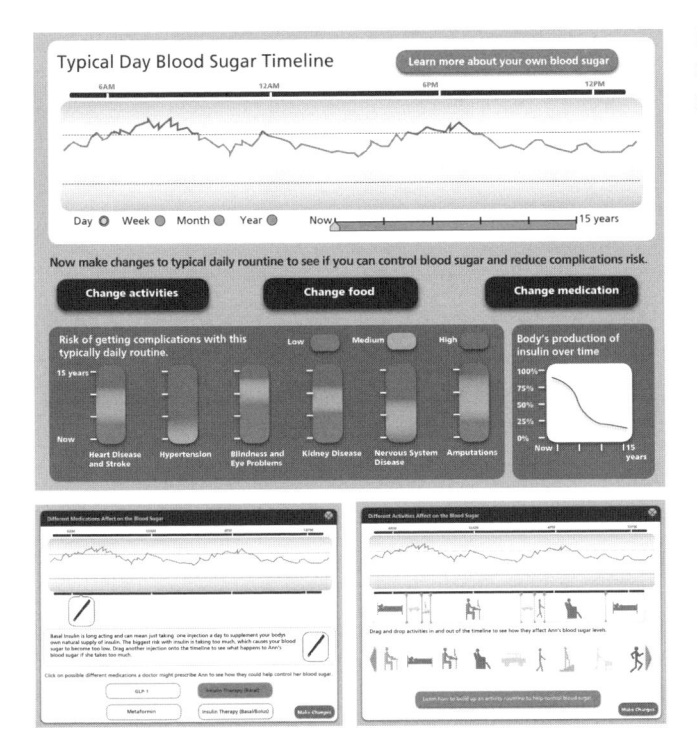

Figure 7: 'Making Sense of Blood-Sugar' interface

afterwards, she discussed the importance of understanding the long-term risks, which put the focus on communicating this, and also the role of medication in preventing them. The participants in the hearing-loss workshop found the audiogram activity more challenging – in particular, trying to identify where sounds they had difficulty hearing would be on the chart or even just trying to work out whether something was a high or low frequency. For example, the sound of bike tyres on gravel was particularly difficult to classify. Although they thought it was interesting to be able to see what they couldn't currently hear, it would be even better if they could *hear* the difference.

The Current Design Proposals

The workshops revealed new aspects of the problems: the importance of understanding the long-term risks of diabetes and being able to hear the difference hearing aids could make in real-life situations. So, based on this, the responses evolved further. The current response for the type 2 diabetes disease area is a concept for an online educational tool, 'Making Sense of Blood Sugar', that helps people discover how food, activities and different medications affect blood sugar, and also indicates the long-term risks involved in maintaining high blood sugar. The concept involves a website, where people with diabetes can learn about how blood-sugar levels can be controlled by the different parameters of medication, exercise and food. By experimenting with changing different aspects of an avatar's daily routine, people can see the extent to which these

Figure 8: 'My Audiogram' smart-phone app

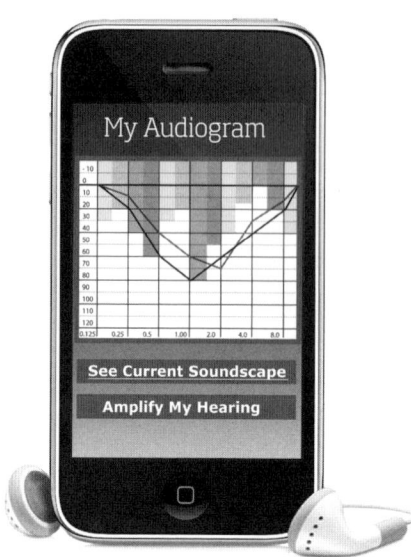

affect the avatar's blood-sugar graph over a day and then how these kinds of numbers would affect the risk of getting long-term complications. The idea is the tool could be developed as part of a training program for people who are newly diagnosed with the condition; but it could also be used by doctors to help explain treatment plans to patients, to help them understand the objectives and relate the treatment to positive consequences for themselves. It seeks to help people to learn how to manage their condition better but also to show how different medications, especially insulin, help to lower and control blood sugar, and why this is worth doing.

The proposal for the hearing-loss area is 'My Audiogram', a concept for a service package that could be provided to hearing care professionals by Oticon. It includes a range of tools that can be given to people who have been newly diagnosed with hearing loss, to help them relate their hearing loss to the problems they are having and to learn what hearing aids could do to help them hear. These tools centre around the audiogram and the main aim of the concept is to give people ways to connect the abstract numbers that are shown on their audiogram to the real-life situations where they experience problems with their hearing by converting electronic audiograms into self-counselling tools. It would include a smart-phone application that would allow people to compare readings of the sounds in their environment to their audiogram, to help them understand how their hearing loss might affect their experiences; they would then be able to convert their phone into a hearing aid, using the phone's own microphone and headset, to be able to hear the difference instantaneously. It seeks to demonstrate to people how hearing aids could help them by demonstrating the benefits in real-life situations both visually and with audio.

Although these concepts could represent ways to resolve the main problem from which the project goals derive, there are questions that require further exploration – not least, would people be motivated to use them and how great an influence would they have on reducing people's reluctance to use the technologies? Prototyping and taking them back to people may help give an indication but only deployment in the specific circumstances for which they are intended will be able to give a true picture of their potential. On reflection, what is most interesting about the hearing concept, I believe, is that it allows people who are having hearing problems to test different situations out to see if a hearing aid would help, which creates another formulation of the problem – and with that indicates another range of potential solutions that could be explored further. Similarly, what becomes interesting about the diabetes concept is how actions now (i.e. initiating insulin) can be linked to preserving health in the future. There may be many other ways to do this. These are not the final concepts but simply the current matching of problem and solution. As the project is not yet complete, and based on the current rate of evolution, it is likely that both problem formulation and solution will change significantly in the search for the apposite concepts.

Conclusion

In this chapter, I have attempted to explicate how problems are constructed as part of a user-driven design process. The given problem in this case is representative of the class of social problems covered by Rittel's 'wicked problem' concept and was addressed through a creative design process where problem formulation and solutions evolved together but, before this was possible, I first had to formulate a problem that was in some way 'solvable'. I have tried to demonstrate that, in a user-driven process such as the one presented here, designers seek to construct such problems that account for both different stakeholder perspectives and their own views on what makes a 'designerly' problem (in other words, a problem that is not only 'solvable' but 'solvable' in a way that creates an experience of value).

In this case, even after gaining deeper insights into the nature of this wicked problem from which the project goals derived, I did not find it possible to explore potential solutions easily without creating a problem formulation that was more defined. I chose to respond to a problem that was both different from and part of the main problem project goals, formulated from different aspects of it where stakeholder interests could be aligned. The choice of this problem was based both on the information I had available to me about the problem space and my experience and instincts as a designer as to what could constitute a 'solvable' problem. Once having arrived at a problem for which I was able to conceive solutions, it was by no means fixed but instead served as a starting point which changed significantly as solution concept generation revealed more aspects of the problem space.

I have tried to demonstrate that in this process there is a difference between the indeterminate, unsolvable, wicked problems which project goals derive from and the design problems that are constructed as part of the process. Here 'design problems' are those which are crafted from aspects of the specific circumstances in order temporarily to create greater determinacy in design processes and therefore give focus to the exploration allowing for potential solutions to become recognisable. I suggest that, as designers, we formulate these problems as tools that allow us to respond with design ideas; to make them defined sufficiently to be able to recognise what a solution might look like and in order to begin exploring further through the co-evolution of solutions. We deliberately formulate these problems in a way that allows us partially to tame them, just enough to begin to identify solutions, but with a flexibility to redefine problem and solution space again and again until an apposite concept emerges as a resolution. By doing this, we are discovering and inventing the particular subject matter in which we will work and I believe it is one of designers' key professional skills, drawing both on their own experience and on the information they have available to them about the problem space, to be able to craft 'solvable' problems.

References

1. Rittel, H. and Webber, M. (1973) 'Dilemmas in a General Theory of Planning', *Policy Sciences*, vol. 4, pp.155–69.
2. Buchanan, R. (1992) 'Wicked Problems in Design Thinking', *Design Issues*, 8 (2), pp.5–21.
3. Dorst, K. and Cross, N. (2001) 'Creativity in the design process: co-evolution of problem-solution', *Design Studies*, 22 (5), pp.425–37.
4. Maher, M.L., Poon, J. and Boulanger, S. (1996) 'Formalising Design Exploration as Co-Evolution: A Combined Gene Approach', in J.S. Gero and F. Sudweeks, *Advances in formal design methods for CAD*, London: Chapman and Hall.
5. Nigel, C. (1997) 'Descriptive models of creative design: application to an example', *Design Studies*, 18 (4), pp.427–40.
6. Kruger, C. and Cross, N. (2006) 'Solution driven versus problem driven design: strategies and outcomes', *Design Studies*, 27 (5), pp.527–48.
7. Harfield, S. (2007) 'On design "problematization": Theorising differences in designed outcomes', *Design Studies*, 28 (2), pp.159–73.
8. Kelly, J. and Matthews, B. (2010) 'Taking transition into account: designing with pre-users of medical devices', in *Proceedings of the 11th Biennial Participatory Design Conference*, PDC'10, New York, NY, USA: ACM, pp.71–80.
9. Diabetes-Diabetes Atlas, http://www.diabetesatlas.org/content/diabetes, accessed 9 May 2011.
10. What is Diabetes – Diabetes Atlas, http://www.diabetesatlas.org/content/what-is-diabetes, accessed 2 May 2011.
11. Goodall, G., Sarpong, E.M., Hayes, C. and Valentine, W.J. (2009) 'The consequences of delaying insulin initiation in UK type 2 diabetes patients failing oral hyperglycaemic agents: a modelling study', *BMC Endocrine Disorders*.
12. Kochkin, S. (2005) 'MarkeTrak VII: Hearing loss population tops 31 million people', *Hearing Review*, 12 (7), pp.16–29.

13. Stephens, D. and Kramer, S. (2009) *Living with Hearing Difficulties: The process of enablement*, Wiley.
14. Christensen, V.T. (2006) *Hard of Hearing*, Copenhagen: Danish National Institute of Social Research.
15. Kochkin, S. (2005) 'MarkeTrak VII: Customer satisfaction with hearing instruments in the digital age', *Hearing Journal*, 58 (9), pp.30–43.
16. Engelund, G. (2006) 'Time for hearing – recognising process for the individual: a grounded theory', PhD dissertation, Det Humanistiske Fakultet, Københavns Universitet.
17. Vogel, D., McCarthy, P., Bratt, G. and Brewer, C. (2007) 'The clinical audiogram: Its history and current use', *Communicative Disorders Review*, vol. 1, no. 2, pp.81–94.
18. Bowen, S.J. and Chamberlain, P.M. (2008) 'Engaging the Ageing: Designing Artefacts to Provoke Dialogue', in P. Langdon, J. Clarkson and P. Robinson (eds), *Designing Inclusive Futures*, London: Springer, pp.35–44.
19. Anon. (2010) 'Maximizing the Patient Counseling Experience with PC-based Audiometry', *Hearing Review*, http://www.hearingreview.com/issues/articles/2010-10_03.asp.

Michael LEITNER
Northumbria University, UK

Giovanni INNELLA
Northumbria University, UK

AND

Freddie YAUNER
Northumbria University, UK

DIFFERENT PERCEPTIONS OF THE DESIGN PROCESS IN THE CONTEXT OF DESIGNART

Introduction

There is a growing group of design practitioners who operate around the fields of conceptual [1] and critical design [2]. The body of work that is being produced aims to challenge assumptions and offer a social critique of the world and design itself: it is this field of work that journalistically and academically can be referred to as DesignArt [3, 4, 5]. In this niche of design, the communication aspect of the artefacts overtakes their physical accessibility and function of use, which remain rather limited [6]. Here designed artefacts convey the designer's opinion and stance; hence authorship is highly valued.

DesignArt practitioners often find themselves in the situation of receiving commissions that are not yet 'confirmed', such as a client inviting a designer to submit proposals which will then be evaluated and hopefully accepted, at which point the commission would be confirmed. This situation puts the designer in an uncomfortable position, as he can't invest too much time or resources on a project that is not certain to happen. However, if the designer does not impress the client with a proposal perceived to have some quality and potential, the designer will lose the opportunity of gaining the commission. This is also a context where briefs are often very broad, intended to give the designer the possibility to express his conceptual process with considerable freedom.

With this work we wanted to understand better the process a designer goes through whilst preparing a proposal and where the client sees value at different stages of this process. In order to get a better insight into what is going on in this creative phase, we conducted a case study which tried to simulate such a setup. Specifically, we wanted to understand how knowledge, process and coherence with the brief are perceived and valued by the different parties involved in preparing and submitting a proposal for a possible commission. We looked at the design process from three perspectives, that of the designer, the client and that of the 'neutral' observer, the traditional researchers. The designer and the client observed the project from the perspectives of their respective involvement, whilst the 'researchers' observed the process but were not involved directly in the making or judging of the outcome. We were interested to see how their different expectations, levels of access to information and roles lead to different understandings and interpretations of the process. The 'researchers' sparked the project by setting up a commission by an appropriate client, which was then sent to the designer. The designer received the design brief and was asked to deliver a concept for an exhibition piece. The set brief specific to the design symposium on the topic of aging was used, with a small adaptation made by the client to include the direction that the outcome should be for an exhibition.

With the results presented in this chapter, we raise questions about types of knowledge used in the communication between the designer and the client in the area of DesignArt. We further report on the perception of process and outcome and how each party perceives these elements. On top of our conclusions, we will discuss which focus we believe design research should take in order to aid communication between designers and clients.

The chapter is structured in the following way: we start with related work drawn from literature, then present and describe the method and study setup before we discuss the results. We finish with conclusions and opportunities for future work.

Literature and Related Work

The question of how designers work and which 'process' they apply – or suggestions on how designers should work and which process they should apply theoretically – has been a matter of much discussion and writing in design research. Whereas it has been suggested and believed that a structured process leads to good design solutions, the value of this rigidity has still to be proven in design [7]. In reality, as Cross discusses, the 'truth' lies somewhere in between. It has been shown that, as with un-systematic approaches, 'unreasonable methodical' approaches affect design outcomes negatively. Often, a structured process is kept alive up to a certain point but is then abandoned in favour of an in-depth exploration of a detailed problem. This, however, does not suggest that designers do not get back on track, more that the route they take is rather opportunistic [7]. Lawson discusses different models of design processes [8], like the RIBA model, which presents four sequential steps (assimilation, general study, development and communication). Markus and Maver's model proposes that designers go through analysis, synthesis, appraisal and decisions on different levels of detail. Lawson, however, concludes that whereas these models have an entitlement, the actual design process in reality is much messier and unstructured. He further raises the problem that 'model makers' are often not designers and vice versa, leaving a gap between those who say how it is or how it should be and those who actually do design but don't really talk about how they do it. Although a gap between theory and practice exists, the mutual understanding of a process and its stages can serve as a 'tool', which helps designers and clients (as well as other contributors) to organise their work and their project communications [8].

There are of course other aspects that influence the design process. The external influences of time, money and information can massively affect the designer and their process, as well as client satisfaction and project outcome [8]. Also, when designers try to describe the design process, the result is often unrealistic, taking the semblance of a recipe. Literally, Bruno Munari described the design process as that of cooking 'green rice', which by the way doesn't sound very inviting as an Italian risotto [9]. Realistically, designers know that the creative process is never so linear.

Designers, in general, seem constantly to define and re-define the 'problem' they are facing; even if they are presented with a well-defined problem, they tend to question it critically, thus starting a continuous process of re-framing the problem. This, however, is not a closed process found at the beginning of a design process but, in contrast, it is an open trajectory or train of thought transcending the design process [7].

Designers in the area of DesignArt tend to apply their own approach and don't often have a need for an externally imposed or pre-given design process. In fact, they often adapt to situations, clients and projects. Rodgers and Smyth interviewed several designers, trying to understand their process. The outcomes gave the overall impression that each designer has his own process, which can only be classified or pushed into models by using 'high level' or general models [10] – which then have little explanatory or descriptive power. Supporting this individuality in design, Dubberly traced different design-process models as they have emerged over the last sixty years and found around hundred individual models, most of which were only related to interactive system design, excluding the countless number of models that have been defined from other areas [11]. Such a multitude of models leaves us with the suspicion that each design process has unique characteristics and that any attempt at modelling has a limited meaning.

The role of information and knowledge used during a design process has been a matter of interest for research. In this area, people have been captivated by the question of how designers inform their creative process and which information they use in doing so. But as Lawson describes, designers often go back and forth in their process, with the research and use of knowledge rarely being structured [8]. Sometimes designers start with a detailed problem which requires specific information research and which raises the need for further knowledge. To investigate decision making and the use of knowledge in the design processes, da Silva Vieira et al. analysed several interviews with designers working in the areas of graphic design, architecture, interaction and engineering [12]. They identified five 'value categories' for decision making, namely emotional-, intuitive-, rational-, experience- and constraint-based priorities. Whereas rational-based priorities (like logic and argument-based reasoning towards a design goal, procedure and user satisfaction) were dominant in all these design areas (although with more emphasis in architecture and graphic design), the researchers could observe differences in value priorities between these areas. For instance, emotion-based priorities prevailed more in graphic and interaction design disciplines and constraint-based priorities (such as technology constraints) were more important in engineering and architecture. Intuition was observed to be on equal importance in all disciplines. Their research suggests that design disciplines share some common ground but that each design has its own priorities.

In general, gathering explicit knowledge to inform the design process is an important task; however, the role of tacit knowledge and intuition-based decision making is crucial too. Both types of knowledge inform the designer's process: whilst the explicit knowledge is easily traceable, the nature of intuition-based knowledge means that often it is concealed and does not emerge, or at least is not articulated [13]. In particular areas of design, like for instance the design of interactive technologies, this lack of rigid 'information and knowledge' gathering methods have led to the emergence of 'Personas' or 'Cultural Probes' (compare Gaver, Dunne and Pacenti [14]) which are intended to deliver inspiration rather than 'hard facts'. However, in the field of DesignArt, more freedom is allowed, to the point that knowledge can rely on the personal experience or assumptions of the designer, without any need for fieldwork.

Communication between client and designer is heavily influenced by their relationship, how well they know each other's 'business' and how much they trust and understand each other [8]. But even beyond a mutual understanding of conduct and expectations, design ideas need to be communicated and made 'accessible' to the different people involved in the design and decision-making process. For instance, storyboarding has proven to be an important 'tool' for achieving such a mutual understanding [15]. Suri and Buchenau coined the term 'experience prototyping' with which they refer to the creation of entities that represent a later design outcome at an early stage, which have been shown to be a powerful form of design communication. An experience prototype can be anything from a model to a tangible object, a visual representation or any other process or performance that is able to envision the 'experience' the design seeks to achieve [16]. But then again, how ideas are communicated and displayed is subject to the area in which the designer and the client operate.

Generally speaking, what has been understood of the design process is that it is hard to understand; designers share some common ground but are still quite individualistic in their approach, especially in areas like DesginArt which tend to have rather open briefs and to require, of necessity, highly creative approaches. Furthermore, it is understood that the role of knowledge and how it is used in design processes is crucial, as is the relationship between the designer and the client and how ideas and designs are communicated throughout the process. These aspects increasingly motivated us to look at the design process from three points of view: those of the designer, the client and the researcher.

Methodology

The aim of this case study was to track the creative process of a designer working towards a commission for a gallery. A design process is a complex construct implying a variety of activities, from issue-raising questioning to interpreting the brief, all the way to the design of the artefacts. However, this study monitors only the information that the designers chose to share through colloquial interactions and the agreed deliverable.

The objective was to identify the process of the designer from different viewpoints, namely those of the involved parties: the designer himself, the client and two neutral observers (Figure 1). The project was conducted in spring 2011 and was set up for this particular research purpose, with no relation to any other commercial or research project. The following paragraphs describe the project as well as the methods used to gather data during it.

Actors

The project included three types of actor: a client, a designer and two neutral observers. The designer and the two neutral observers are also authors of this chapter. The client had a supporting role and was not part of the analysis. The role of each actor is briefly described as follows:

- **Client:** The client's role was that of an exhibition curator; as such, Agata Jaworska – design and content manager at Droog Design – was asked to adapt and issue a design brief. In our case, this was based on a fictional exhibition by Droog Design about 'future ways of living in the home in old age'. The design brief invited designers to submit design proposals of which some would be selected for exhibition. In the design brief, the client asked for proposals in the form of a presentation illustrating the conceptual ideas of the proposed designs. Droog Design is a well-known gallery based in Amsterdam that burst onto the international design scene in the early 1990s. Its approach to design is highly conceptual and provocative, qualities that allowed it to gain visibility on media, including exhibitions [18]. Droog operates mainly in the context of DesignArt.

- **Designer:** The role of the designer was to respond to the design brief issued by the client and to prepare a weekly deliverable describing the current state of the project. The designer was asked to send these deliverables to the client on a weekly basis and the final presentation at the end of the project. Freddie Yauner took the role of the designer. Freddie is a RCA alumnus whose work has been acquired by the public collections of MoMA in New York and the Design Museum in London. For his experience and achievements, Freddie Yauner can be considered a representative of young designers operating in the context of DesignArt.

- **Neutral Observers:** The observers' role was to keep track of the design process, to send out the questionnaires, to observe the weekly deliverables as well as to conduct formal and less formal interviews (i.e. chats) with the designer. The observers, however, did not actively engage with the design process apart from the contact with the designer in the form of interviews.

Basic Project Structure

The project was set up to be a three-week design project starting with the design brief delivered by the client to the designer via email and ending with a design proposal delivered by the designer to the client. The client and the designer did not meet face to face during this period and in fact were located in different towns (Newcastle–London and Amsterdam). Neither did the client respond to the deliverables during the project, which minimised the contact between these two actors. This setup was chosen to simulate a realistic relation between a client and a designer delivering a proposal for a commission. The neutral observers did not interfere at all with the client–designer relationship (Figure 1).

A further note on involvement and possible bias: during the time of the design process, none of the participants had access to the answers and ratings of the other parties, nor was this data analysed or looked at during the design phase by any of the participants.

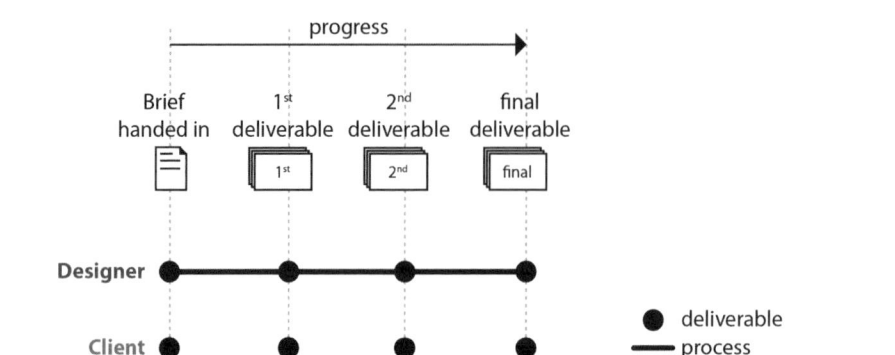

Figure 1: Project setup and access to information by the three actors

212 Articulating Design Thinking

The designer himself was not aware of the fact that he would be part of the analysis team. He was only asked to join the analysis after the last deliverable was sent and the questionnaire was filled out. We were acting as the neutral observers–researchers and did have a double role in this project. We set up the project and acted as neutral observers, and as data interpreters at a later stage. This bias, however, was accepted for this initial case study, although we believe that due to the setup the bias has been reduced as much as possible. Accepting this weakness of the study, the neutral observer–researchers nevertheless tried to be as objective as possible.

Time Structure and Data Gathering

As mentioned above, the project was set up as a three-week project and split into three phases, allowing one phase per week. This structure allowed us to collect data in reference to each of these phases. For each phase, a questionnaire was filled out by each of the actors (designer, client and neutrals). The online questionnaire served as the main tool and the central entity by which data was collected. The questionnaire needed to be answered by each of the actors on a weekly (= phases) basis and contained the following three open questions. In addition, the questionnaire asked participants to rate each of these categories from 1 to 6 according to a Likert scale. In addition, the parties were asked to justify each of their ratings with short textual answers.

- **Knowledge** (1 = not adequate, 6 = highly adequate): The actors were asked to evaluate the knowledge the designer was including and processing at this stage of the project. In the weekly form it was made clear for each actor that: *'As Knowledge you should consider any type of information, experience, data or inspiration taken into consideration by the designer for his creative process'.*

- **Understanding** (1 = not understandable, 6 = highly understandable): The actors were asked to assess how understandable and traceable they found the designer's process at this stage of the project. In the weekly form it was made clear for each actor that: *'As Understanding you should consider the comprehension and traceability of the designer's creative process, as well as the designer's progress towards the final delivery goal'.*

- **Coherence with the brief** (1 = not coherent, 6 = very coherent): The actors were asked to assess how coherent the designer was with the brief at this stage. In the weekly form it was made clear to each actor that: *'As Coherence with the brief you should consider the pertinence of the designer's knowledge, process and deliverables with the brief provided by the client'.*

In order to fill in these questionnaires, different sources of information were used during the project. It is important to note here that the following data sources were used to inform the answers to the questionnaire. Therefore the data gathered via the following means is reflected in the questionnaire, which was then used as the central unit of analysis:

- **Deliverable:** The designer was asked to deliver a current state of the project on a weekly basis. The deliverable was agreed to be a presentation, which should consist of various slides illustrating the current state of the contribution. The questionnaire presented above was only filled in after the designer sent out his deliverable and after the client and the observers had studied the deliverable.

- **Interviews:** During each week, towards the end of a phase but before the designer sent the weekly deliverable, the observers interviewed the designer about his progress, his current thoughts and the concepts he was working on. These interviews were mostly gathered to collect the designer's impressions and thoughts about the project and his progress. The interview data was used and interpreted by the neutral observers. They used the data to fill in the questionnaire. The client was not exposed to any of this interview data.

- **Informal information:** The neutral observers did gather additional information in terms of informal chats with the designers (sometimes over lunch, sometimes when meeting occasionally in the corridor, etc.). For this data gathering, no specific setup was introduced as the official role of the neutrals was defined as 'friends/colleagues' – and in this way, we thought to create a realistic setup. Obviously, in order to inform their answers to the questionnaire, the observers again used this data; but none of this information was communicated to the client.

It is clear that, due to the setup, three different levels of information were created. Firstly, there is the designer, who should know his own process whilst being able to rate his own 'performance' using the questionnaire. Notably, designers are not used to articulating or making their process explicit, especially not while a project is still in progress. We had to accept the possible bias that was created through the designer's involvement in interviews and questionnaire, which in fact are tools for reflection. Secondly, there is the client, who can only use the information in the deliverable that is presented to her to evaluate the designer and his weekly outcome. Finally, there are the observers, who can be considered somehow in the middle between client and designer. They have access to the deliverable, as well as scattered snippets of information that the designer wants to share with them, mainly through informal conversations. This role of the researchers allows them access to more complete information that should allow for objective observation; but at the same time, it increases the risk of being misled and the possibility of wrong interpretations and assumptions. It is exactly this setup of different levels of information and interpretation that we wanted to create as we believe it reproduces a realistic setup, which in the end should allow us to evaluate the different perceptions of each of the parties during the project.

Results and Discussion

Design Outcome

This chapter discusses the actual design outcomes the designer delivered as his response to the given brief. The design outcome of the project is not so important for

Figure 2: A slide from the designer's first deliverable

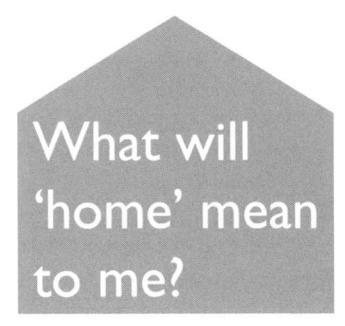

In 2050 I will be 68.

What will 'home' mean to me?

the purpose of the research, but the way the brief has been answered by the designer still has an influence on the flow of the project. In order to provide this context, we discuss the design outcomes briefly. By 'design outcome', we mean the concept the designer worked on and which he presented to the client in the last deliverable.

- **Deliverable 1:** The designer's first presentation consisted of four slides, which introduced the designer's self-centred approach. The designer repeats the brief and states here that he would imagine himself in 2050, when he will be 68, and use that as a source for inspiration (Figure 2).

- **Deliverable 2:** The second presentation is richer in content, as the designer took the opportunity to share some of his 'issue raising'. Questions like 'Living to an optimum age? or living to an optimum wage?', 'Is longevity good?' and 'How important is quality of life?', among others, are clearly visible in the first of six slides together with a disquieting image of the now old-looking designer himself (Figure 3). The questions really serve for the designer as a representation of his search for inspiration.

Every day you survive you add 7 days to your life…

Is longevity good?

Living to an optimum age? or Living to an optimum wage?

How important is quality of life?

Figure 3: The designer's general critical questions in the second deliverable

In the next slides, the designer makes it clear that the space for his design is within the tension of what is possible for physiology (as physical health) and the limits of neurology (as mental health) (Figure 4). This presentation concludes with a slide that doesn't seem to be related to the previous five. The designer introduces his interest for meta-materials, without an apparent relevance to his process (Figure 5).

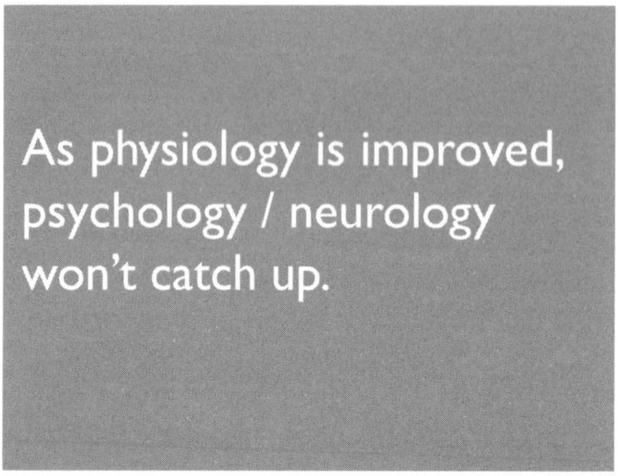

Figure 4: Physiology vs. neurology in the second deliverable

> As physiology is improved, psychology / neurology won't catch up.

Figure 5: Final slide in the second deliverable

What will our tubular steel be?

META MATERIALS...

- **Deliverable 3:** The final deliverable was composed of 16 slides, guiding the reader through the process and the final proposal. The designer draws out a scenario in which people will have to choose between two options. The first is to accept all sorts of medical aids to extend their life, thus leading to a life that lasts so long that they may not have the money to support themselves endlessly. The second option in this scenario is to join the 'Opt-Out Community' and refuse medical support, so retiring at a normal age but dying young (Figure 6).

Life Saving[s] is the start of an archive of paraphernalia and objects that were created during the Opt-Out movement of 2050.

During this period there was wide spread unrest, with many people choosing not to engage with the latest medical science. Choosing instead to stop working sooner and die naturally of old age.

Figure 6: Description Opt-Out movement in final deliverable

At this point the designer introduces his paraphernalia, which is composed of medical devices misused by members of this community as ornaments and futile knick-knacks (Figure 7). In the content of the mail he sent submitting the proposal, the designer makes clearer that the final proposal: 'would be to create a number of the proposed objects and paraphernalia, and create a representation of the outlined archive.'

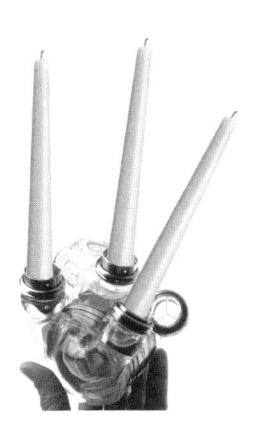

Figure 7: One example of the paraphernalia included in the final deliverable: a cardiovascular prosthesis turned into a candleholder

Data from the Questionnaires
This chapter discusses the outcome of the categories we observed in the study. It tries to highlight perceived differences of knowledge, understanding of the process and coherence with the brief, as they were evaluated by each of the parties.

- **Knowledge**

'As Knowledge you should consider any type of information, experience, data or inspiration taken into consideration by the designer for his creative process'.

The knowledge the designer was using during the project was perceived quite differently by each of the parties (Figure 8). We believe this was due to the different type and amount of information that was available to each party but also to the different expectations of each party towards the project outcome itself. The main difference we could observe here was related to inspirational knowledge, by which we mean the designer's 'questioning' and 'issue raising' as used to help them identify and create topic area(s) they want to explore and work in (compare [7]).

After the first deliverable, the client rated the designer's knowledge as very low, as the designer's communication contained only little, issue-raising content – which made it difficult for the client to interpret the trajectory the designer was taking. Although the designer mentioned a possible direction, namely that of using 'smart materials', this was not valued by the client as satisfactory knowledge. The designer similarly didn't value the knowledge concerning smart materials he had gathered at that point as adequate. The neutral observers did however rate the knowledge as adequate, valuing both the deliberate self-exploratory approach and the designer's intentions to get into smart materials in the following phases.

In the second and third deliverables, it can be observed that the designer's work started being more grounded in the explicit critical questions and attempts of problem framing (compare [7]). This resulted in a better consideration of the designer's knowledge by the client. The designer, however, still valued his own knowledge as very low at the end of the second phase. At this point, he still wanted to incorporate smart materials into his design but, at the same time, he admitted to the neutral observers that due to other commitments he was going to face a severe lack of time to allow deeper research into that area. Despite showing increased aspects of issue raising in the second week's deliverable, which the other parties saw as a positive direction, the designer himself did not consider this as satisfactory design knowledge.

It became quite clear that the designer did not value his self-exploratory approach, nor did he see the questions and issues he raised out of this approach as adequate knowledge. Only after the designer had dropped the idea of working with smart materials, due to time constraints, did he start to value his inspirational knowledge to a greater extent, as reflected by his higher rating of knowledge in the project's last week. The client in contrast did value this type of issue raising and problem framing as something important and adequate. This difference in perception of the process

KNOWLEDGE

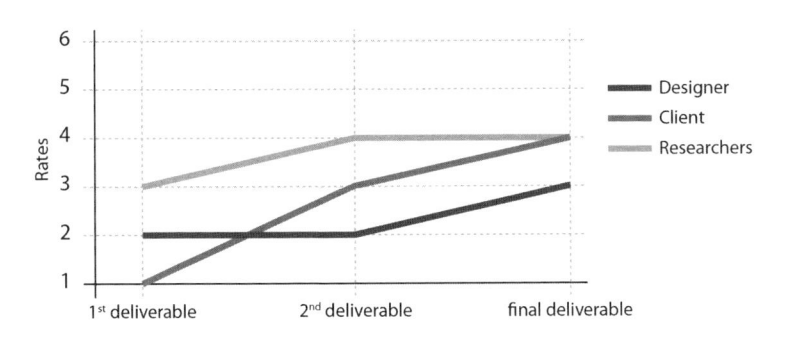

Figure 8: Graph illustrating the perception of Knowledge

at this point is due to the different expectations of, and information available to, these roles. Both the designer and the neutral observers expected some structured research to start the proposal for the commission. Neither put much value on the initial broader critical questions and intuition-based knowledge, whilst the client did put value on this more open and exploratory form of knowledge. However, the more explicit the design outcome became, the less importance was given to this acquisition of new and rather formal knowledge.

- *Understanding*

'As Understanding you should consider the comprehension and traceability of the designer's creative process, as well as the designer's progress towards the final goal'.

After visualising (Figure 9) and analysing how each of the three 'roles' understood the designer's process we conclude the following:

At the beginning of the project, we observed that each party valued differently the fact that the designer didn't have a clear direction towards an outcome. Both the designer and the neutral observers interpreted this as a good sign and a good start to the project. They argued that being in an uncertain situation at the beginning of a project is not a problem, that it opens up spaces and led them to expect an intriguing outcome. The client, however, was concerned by the small amount of information presented and the lack of direct insights. The client found the process harder to understand due to the small quantity of information made available by the designer. This uncertainty about the designer's understanding was still felt by all parties in the second phase but again perceived differently due to their particular roles in the project. The neutral observers assessed this uncertainty as an increasingly good sign for the eventual design outcome ('We expect him to combine these different topics into something intriguing, we expect him to surprise us'), whilst the client also started to understand the designer's process better. Although the client still mentioned the vagueness she saw in the designer's deliverable, her perception of his process becomes more positive. As far as we understand, this was due to the amount of content she could see in the designer's deliverables, even if this content was vague. However, at this point in the project, the designer started feeling some anxiety due to his open approach, largely because he felt that he had too little time to complete a successful proposal. He felt the need of knowing where he was going and his obstinacy in keeping an open direction was not helping in this situation.

We believe these differences in perception of the designer's understanding are clearly explainable in terms of the different roles of the parties. For the designer, time pressure and uncertainty close to the project's mid-point left him unsure of his understanding and concerned about how he would find a desirable outcome in the remaining time. The researchers at this stage did not have any need to see a possible outcome; their role was to observe the process which is where their focus and interest lay. This explains why they still valued the designer's uncertainty as a positive part of his process. This uncertainty was in some ways 'understandable' and seemed to promise an exciting outcome. The client at this stage was also becoming concerned about the final outcome, like the designer. The client still felt there was vagueness in the second deliverable but, due to the increased quantity of content, she started to see some potential towards a possible outcome. We can clearly see that, due to the pressure of being the participant who needed to deliver an outcome, the designer lost confidence in his own understanding as he was unable to see a clear, possible outcome that could have been worked on in the remaining weeks. He did not know exactly where he was in his process and if he was doing well. This clearly illustrates that the perception of the designer's process is heavily influenced by his role in the project.

We observed also that while the researchers kept up quite a strong focus on the actual process the designer was going through, the designer and the client substituted the process for the actual outcome throughout the project. By 'substitution' we mean that the need to understand the design process loses its importance in favour of understanding the actual outcome. This shift continued in relation to the time the project took: in the second and third deliverables, both the designer and the client were largely talking more about the design outcome when they were asked about the process. In fact, when asked about the understandability of the designer's process at the end of the project, the designer did not mention the process at all but instead insisted on the design outcome ('I felt that the scenario that I was spelling out was believable'). Likewise, when asked the same question, the client talked about the clear presentation of the design outcome and about the way the designer communicated his ideas in the deliverable ('His presentation was clear and coherent'). By actually evaluating the outcome instead of the understanding of the process, they both claim to have an above-average understanding of the design process. For the designer and the client, the final deliverable (the outcome) represents the creative process. It became evident that for those two roles the outcome represents the creativity invested. What they actually interpret is not the sequence of traceable actions and steps over time towards the final outcome but the compound of creative thoughts and how the designer put this together. The researchers instead evaluated their understanding of the designer's process at the end of the project as low. They stated that they could not see any incremental growth of the argument or the reasoning. Notably, they mentioned that the designer dropped the topic of smart materials completely without justifying this. Although this display of opportunistic behaviour is typical of designers [7], it does not necessarily devalue the outcome. Nevertheless, the researchers interpreted this negatively. Clearly, the researchers understood the process as a string of logical steps, something that is not at all represented or communicated through the outcome. Process and outcome were considered to be detached from each other.

This result is particularly interesting as we believe it reflects the difference between theoretical and practical perceptions of design projects quite well. Without saying that either delivers absolute truth, it somehow shows that in practical setups the emphasis is on the outcome; and the process that was used to obtain this outcome is just a tool which is often not even articulated. Whereas in theory-speak, the emphasis often lies more on the process and its comprehension.

UNDERSTANDING

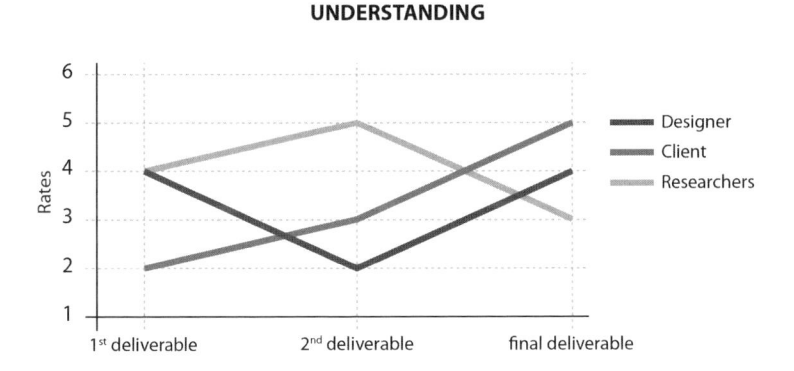

Figure 9: Graph illustrating the perception of Understanding

- *Coherence with the Brief*

'As Coherence with the brief you should consider the pertinence of the designer's knowledge, process and deliverables with the brief provided by the client'.

The brief was very broad and consequently the designer initially didn't seem to take any specific direction, other than to focus on the date 2050. Because of this, both researchers and the designer expressed a positive assessment for the first stage on the criteria of 'Coherence with the brief' (Figure 10). At this stage, the designer basically just stated that he would take a self-centered approach and, as the researchers observed, the brief didn't exclude this. The designer simply repeated the brief, promising that he would stick to it. Likewise, the client didn't have any particular criticism of this aspect; however, her judgment of it was low. The fact that so little was shown ('Yes, it was coherent... because so little was shown') disturbed the client, who was much more focused on what was still to come rather than what had been done.

For the second deliverable, the opinion of the researchers didn't change from the previous stage. The designer, however, started looking towards the next phases and expressed concern about where his process would go. He explicitly declared that he had 'not moved to anything concrete yet'. His mark was low because he didn't know whether he would still be coherent with the brief once those decisions had been taken. The client stated that the designer was on topic; however, her mark was still low (rated as 2). The client didn't know how to interpret the designer's decision to go for meta-materials. This information, thrown in at the end of the second deliverable, disorientated the client, thus leading to a low mark as a reaction ('at the end for example the materials are mentioned and I am not sure what to do with it'). The researchers were not puzzled by such a decision because they had had the chance to chat with the designer who, at various points, anticipated his interest in that area.

The final deliverable resulted in dramatic changes in the judgments of the client and the researchers. The researchers' scrupulous approach meant they found incongruity between the proposal of the designer and the brief. In fact, the brief asked for works 'about the future of living at home in old age'. Freddie's proposal, although very visionary, didn't act on that particular aspect. Interestingly, the client was not concerned about it and the fact that the proposal includes 'various product types and ways of communicating' was enough to cover the brief. The designer's comments served as a clarification of the proposal ('I was proposing that people would opt to make their lives worse as a way to make them better') rather than as an analysis of its coherence. His focus at this stage had totally moved from the brief to the proposal.

The designer and the client both denoted a strong focus on the outcome of the proposal and seem to have been very flexible in accepting formal incoherence with the brief, while the researchers were very meticulous in looking at discrepancies. In this

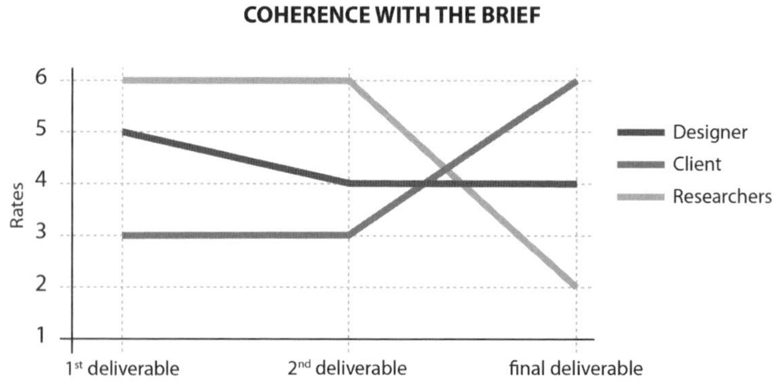

Figure 10: Graph illustrating the perception of Coherence

context of design, incoherence is perhaps even appreciated sometimes as the client expects to be 'surprised' by the designer and led to areas that he didn't consider. The researchers did not expect the designer to 'raise questions' by stepping out of the design brief but rather expected him solely to respond to it.

Conclusion

In this chapter, we investigated the field of DesignArt, in particular the different perceptions of the designer, the client and a neutral observer. The aim was to observe and understand the relationship between the practising designer and the client, in the hope of being able to make some preliminary suggestions for a designer's best practice when undertaking a proposal for a commission. In general, we observe that the client and the designer are much more aligned in what they expect and value, especially when it comes to knowledge, process and outcome. However, as this is a sole case study we cannot draw any definitive conclusions from that; instead we believe that this is a topic for future exploration.

One of our main findings comes from the discrepancies we observed in the perceptions of the designer's knowledge. This relates to 'Inspirational Knowledge' or what has been called issue raising or problem framing [7], examples of intuition-based rather than explicit knowledge. These processes are accepted practice for designers, traditionally associated with idea generation and identification of a project 'space' to work within. However, we found that these explicit critical questions and attempts at problem framing were appreciated by the client as an interesting output in their own right. Likewise, once the designer has realised there is not enough time to complete his search for 'new' knowledge, he starts to see the value of his intuition-based knowledge and builds his final presentation around it.

In our scenario we have a designer submitting a proposal for a commission. Based on what we have seen, we could argue that the right use and presentation of general questions and problem framing is a self-exploratory approach for gaining knowledge. In addition, this can be used not just as a process leading to a good design outcome but as convincing design communication in itself. The client in this scenario plays the role of a contemporary design curator, who is not expecting to be informed by 'new' knowledge but instead looking for an understanding of the spirit of the times and a level of authorship from the designer.

One of the clearest findings relates to the roles within the scenario and their respective focus on outcomes rather than process. It appears that the client is solely focused on outcomes throughout and in fact concerned by the first deliverable, due to the nature of the presentation and the small quantity of output. The client would not usually see the designer's process at this stage and finds it difficult to imagine a satisfactory outcome with so little to go on. The researchers are not concerned with the outcome but with the observation of the design process for said outcome. By the second deliverable, we can see that the designer has become predominantly concerned with the outcome and its quality, especially as it is he who has to produce it, and as a result gives himself a lower mark than the week before.

It is around this point of focus on outcome and in the discrepancies in perception of the designer's coherence with the brief that we see the distinct difference in approach between the neutral observers (researchers) and both the client and designer. The researchers looking at the process from a neutral perspective somehow expected the framing of a problem in relation to the brief, whereas the designer and client are not concerned by these shifts and appropriations towards the final outcome. In this case, our results match other findings showing that designers sometimes act opportunistically seeking solutions, rather than problems [7]. It is around this topic of the quality of the outcome and how it was achieved that we find some interesting observations in the study and potentially in the different research approaches that the study encompasses. The researchers took their role seriously and would not shift away from rigidly looking at the process as something that may be contemplated as a separate entity from the outcome.

After this investigation, what was left in our mind was doubt. We know that DesignArt is a growing phenomenon that, with its visibility, attracts more and more young designers. In this context of DesignArt the design process is respected in its mysterious form and it is very hard, but also arguably less relevant, to attempt to model or represent. It seems that neither the designer nor the client in the realm of DesignArt are particularly interested in the process as a string of actions per se. If they are interested in the process, it seems they are interested in how this process is represented in the outcome itself. In our study, the designer's issue raising and framing of the context was perceived as being one of the most essential parts of the process as it heavily frames the outcome. In contrast, being able to see logical steps towards the final proposal, which is a more traditional understanding of 'the design process', seemed less important for the designer and the client, as this information did not add any value to the proposal itself. In this area of design the process is – so it seems – not something neutral and transferable but rather very unique. Such aspects seem to be important in the client–designer relationship in the realm of DesignArt, whereas the mere representation of knowledge or steps taken seems to be of less value.

We would like here to highlight the fact that the context of DesignArt doesn't present a strong problem-solving approach. Here, outcomes are usually seen as triggers for the audience's thoughts; they have to make people reflect and quickly catch their attention. Therefore DesignArt can't rely on highly specific knowledge but rather must find its foundations in popular culture and offer an original take on it. Although the area claims a conceptual process, these processes have to remain understandable and culminate in effective provocations. In more established commercial fields, a model of a design process can be used to inform interaction between the designer and the client. In contrast, what concerns an independent designer working in the area of DesignArt is actually how the client perceives that process with particular focus on the appeal of the outcome. In order to achieve better understanding of this, we suggest a higher care for studies that look at the way clients perceive a design outcome.

Acknowledgments

We thank Agata Jaworska for her contribution and involvement during the project, Özge Subasi for her feedback on the first draft of this chapter and Alana James for her suggestions and precious proofread of the last draft. We thank the reviewers for their constructive comments.

References

1. Schouwenberg, L. and Staal, G. (2008) *House of Concepts: Design Academy Eindhoven*, Berlin: Die Gestalten Verlag.
2. Zimmerman, J., Forlizzi, J. and Evenson, S. (2007) 'Research through design as a method for interaction design research in HCI', in *Proceedings of the SIGCHI conference on Human factors in computing systems*, New York, NY, USA: ACM, pp.493–502.
3. Coles, A. (2005) *DesignArt: on art's romance with design*, London: Tate Publishing.
4. Coles, A. (2007) *Design and Art*, London: Whitechapel Gallery.
5. Poynor, R. (2005) 'Art's Little Brother', *Icon Eye*, (23). Available at: http://www.iconeye.com/read-previous-issues/icon-023-|-may-2005/art-s-little-brother-|-icon-023-|-may-2005, accessed 27 September 2011.
6. Innella, G., Rodgers, P.A., Spencer, N. and Bohemia, E. (2011) 'Examining the physical to visual shift in how we now experience designed objects', IASDR Conference, Delft (in Press).
7. Cross, N. (2006) *Designerly ways of knowing*, London: Springer-Verlag.
8. Lawson, B. (2006) *How Designers Think: The design process demystified*, fourth edition, Architectural Press (Elsevier).
9. Munari, B. (1998) *Da cosa nasce cosa*, 16th edition, Roma: Editori Laterza.
10. Rodgers, P. and Smyth, M. (2010) *Digital Blur: Creative Practice at the Boundaries of Architecture, Design and Art*, London: Libri Publishing.
11. Dubberly, H. (2004) 'How do you design: A compendium of models', http://www.dubberly.com/articles/how-do-you-design.html, accessed 21 June 2010.
12. da Silva Vieira, S., Badke-Schaub, P., Fernandes, A. and Fronseca, T. (2010) 'Understanding how designers' thinking and acting enhance the value of the design process', in *Proceedings of the 8th design thinking research symposium (dtrs8)*, Sydney, 19–20 October.
13. Wong, W.L.P. and Radcliffe, D.F. (2000) 'The Tacit nature of Design Knowledge', *Technology and Analysis & Strategic Management*, vol. 12, no. 4.
14. Gaver, B., Dunne, T. and Pacenti, E. (1999) 'Design: Cultural probes', *Interactions* 6, pp.21–9.
15. Lelie, van der, C. (2006) 'The value of storyboards in the product design process', *Journal of Personal and Ubiquitous Computing*, vol. 10, issue 2, Springer London; pp.159–62.
16. Buchenau, M. and Suri, J.F. (2000) 'Experience prototyping', in *DIS '00: Proceedings of the 3rd conference on Designing interactive systems*, ACM, New York, NY, USA, pp.424–33.

17. Bruce, M. and Docherty, C. (1993) 'It's all in a relationship: a comparative study of client–design consultant relationships', *Journal of Design Studies*, vol. 14, issue 4, pp.402–22.
18. Moors, A. (2006) *Simply Droog (Revised Edition),* Amsterdam: Droog Design.

Elena NAZZI, Naveen BAGALKOT,
Arun NARARGOJE and Tomas SOKOLER

IT University of Copenhagen, Denmark

CONCEPT DRIVEN INTERACTION DESIGN RESEARCH IN THE DOMAIN OF ATTRACTIVE AGEING: THE EXAMPLE OF WALKY

Introduction

While designing for ageing has been largely focused on making ageing in place possible [15, for instance], designing for making it attractive and desirable by focusing on the social and emotional aspects of ageing is still under-explored [8, 11, 20 and 23, for instance]. Hence in this chapter we take the brief of designing for attractive ageing as an opportunity to focus on supporting social interactions in the everyday life of senior citizens with digital technology.

We approach design for ageing by looking at seniors not only as people in need of care but as citizens in a third, rich phase of their life. While we recognise the importance of and need for research in care technologies, we look at quality of ageing from its social and emotional aspects. We take inspiration from what seniors do in their everyday practice, the more or less mundane activities that compose their everyday life. In particular, we focus on walking as an activity of everyday life in order to design for social aspects of senior life. In this chapter, we present Walky, our on-going design project through which we engage in collaboration with senior citizens, people from the municipal corporation and other stake holders.

As we describe in detail, in Walky we explored if, and how, the everyday objects that the senior citizens use for walking can also support them to share with their friends the fact that they are out walking. We have termed this way of sharing what one is doing, simply by doing, as 'twittering-by-doing' [17]. Our speculation is that, by taking part in this exchange of small pieces of information, the senior citizens can create an additional non-stigmatising way to notice what is going on in their community, to keep an eye on each other and find new openings for quality social interactions. These exchanges would contribute to a stronger sense of community and thus to a better quality of life. This speculation is supported by theoretical perspectives about quality of life when growing older [11, for instance] as well as about social phenomena like microblogging, in which sharing small clues about mundane everyday activities may form a social glue [4, 12, 13, 18 and 19, for instance]. Additionally the theoretical perspective about Embodied Interaction [9] frames our focus on the things and the people involved in walking as an everyday activity.

In this chapter, we present Walky as an example of how we engaged in a dialectic process of exploring these theoretical perspectives in a particular design situation, which led to the design of concrete artefacts. In other words, Walky is an example of applying design thinking in the design of digital technology for supporting social interaction of senior citizens.

Following a concept-driven interaction design research [24], we explicate the design process of Walky as a 'compositional whole'. This process was driven by sketching interactive artefacts to engage senior citizens and other stakeholders in co-design sessions, in settings close to the seniors' everyday life.

We contribute to the interaction design research community focusing on ageing, suggesting that the process of engaging with the theory–situation dialectic be made explicit as valuable knowledge for other researchers in the field. In other words, design researchers need to be explicit about how they apply design thinking to contribute to research knowledge. We support this suggestion by providing the example of Walky and its compositional whole as a demonstration of how we explored abstract theoretical perspectives in particular design situations leading to three concrete designed artefacts.

Below, we briefly provide the background on previous work about concept-driven interaction design research and the role of the design ideal. We then introduce Walky with a brief overview of its compositional whole. We describe the exploration, explicating the relation between theory, concept, design ideal, designed artefact and design situation. Further we present our reflections on how the compositional whole contributes to theorising and to the advancement of the situation. Finally we conclude with a discussion on how this explication of Walky is an example of exploring theoretical perspectives in the particular situation of designing for social interaction of senior citizens; an example of design thinking for attractive ageing.

Background

Within the fields of human computer interaction and interaction design, the inclusion of design as a way of inquiry and research has gained ground. A core aspect of this on-going discourse is to articulate the nature of the research contributions of an interaction design research process. In this respect, there have been proposals arguing for, on the one hand, contributions oriented towards advancing a particular situation towards possible desired states and, on the other, contributions oriented towards theorising.

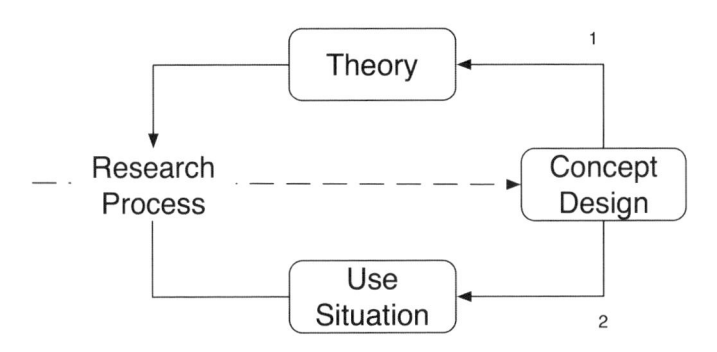

Figure 1: Two complementary cycles of interaction design research
Cycle 1 is concept-driven research
Cycle 2 is situation-driven research
(Stolterman and Wiberg [22])

Talking about designerly ways of knowing, Cross [7] highlights that the work of design practice qualifies as research only if it contain reflections on the work and communicates re-usable results from this reflection. Zimmerman et al. [24] claim that the main contribution of 'research-through-design' is to explore the solutions for a real-world problem through a series of alternatives forming a design space. Elsewhere, Binder and Redström [3] position 'research-through-design' as a co-evolution of design program (philosophical framework) and design practice (design settings) through a series of explorations. They highlight that, for evaluating the research contributions of such design explorations, one needs to evaluate critically the extent to which the knowledge created by the dialogue between the framework and design situations 'suggests viable changes and alternatives to, developments of, etc., both the existing theory and practice' [7, p.11].

Meanwhile, Stolterman and Wiberg argue for an interaction design research process that aims to contribute to advancement of 'theory about interaction design' [22]. They position concept-driven interaction design research as complimentary to the situation-driven interaction design research (see Figure 1). The concept-driven interaction design research is driven by a theoretically constructed concept and the design of an artefact (the designed artefact) that manifests the theoretical concept. The concept and the

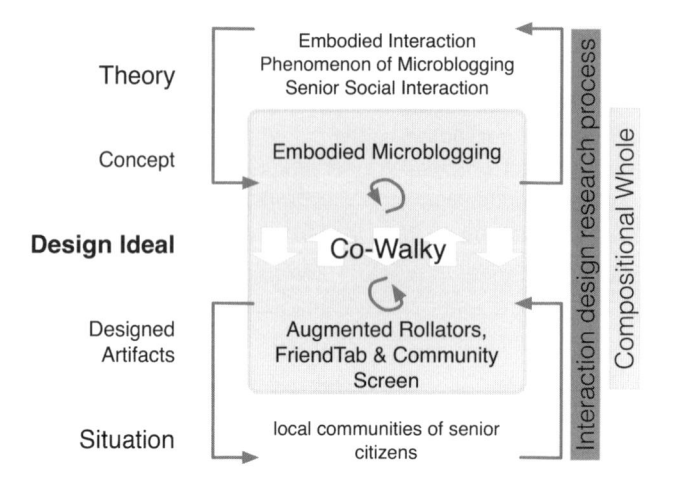

Figure 2: The compositional whole of Walky and its elements

designed artefact form a 'compositional whole'. This compositional whole constitutes a research contribution as an argument for possible new understandings of interaction thereby advancing the current theoretical understanding.

Therefore, there is a responsibility for the interaction design researchers to communicate explicitly the design thinking employed in the research process. In summary, design thinking is the process of engaging with the dialectics of theorising and advancing the current state to desirable states, through an exploration of a solution space driven by the *making* of artefacts. In a recent paper [2], we took this understanding as a starting point to explicate our formulation of a sesign ideal as an interface between theoretical concept and design situation: a formulation that helped us to engage with a dialectic relationship between theorising and advancing the current situation.

Below we explicate how we employed this understanding of design thinking in Walky, starting with giving a brief overview of the elements of its compositional whole.

Walky and its Compositional Whole

the diagram in Figure 2 represents Walky as an example of concept-driven interaction design research pointing at the elements of its compositional whole. In this chapter, we will use these elements to make an account of our engagement in the dialectic between theory and situation.

We understand *theory* as an account of theoretical starting points for design that include – but are not restricted to – theories about interaction design and theories coming from the specifics of the situation or inspiring phenomena from human practice. In Walky, the theoretical starting points are embodied interaction, research on social interaction in ageing and research on microblogging as a social phenomenon.

At the opposite side, the *situation* describes the environment, made of people, places, things, technologies and interactions, within which the design exploration takes place. In Walky, the situation is local communities of senior citizens.

Entering the compositional whole, the *theoretical concept* drives and at the same time is refined by the exploration. The concept incorporates knowledge derived from the theory. It aims to build knowledge about interaction in the design process. In Walky, the theoretical concept is Embodied Microblogging (EMb), an embodied interaction perspective on the social phenomenon of microblogging.

The central element of the diagram is the *design ideal*. It is the interface between concept and situation, the ideal driving the design situation from the current state to preferred states. We understand it as the initial vision that emerges when the interaction design researcher encounters a particular design situation. The design ideal of Walky is Co-Walky, which points to the possibility of making walking an even more social activity by sharing simple clues about walking.

The *designed artefacts* are concrete design objects or often sketches that have been created, developed and experienced during the design process. They serve the purpose of making a concrete manifestation of the theoretical concept framed by the design ideal in the specifics of the situation. In this form they are available for the design researchers and co-designers to explore, discuss and foresee a concrete instance of the design ideal and its possibilities. In Walky the designed artefacts are of three types: augmented bag rollators, four-wheeled walkers able to communicate simple clues to a local walking community; personal tablets, FriendTabs, that display detailed information about the walking activities of our walking friends; and community screens that display anonymous information about activities going on in the community.

The sketching and co-design process with the evolving designed artefacts is the driving engine to explore the design ideal of Co-Walky in this particular situation.

The *compositional whole* is therefore the collection of all these components and the reflection on how they interact with each other in the design process for the final contributions to theory building and situation advancement.

Engaging with the Dialectics

walky broadly explores the design of digital technology to facilitate the creation of new openings for social interaction in local communities of senior citizens. The starting point of Walky is the understanding that everyday activities may act as fruitful ticket-to-talk, i.e. 'resources of information about the state of affairs within a community that may help turn a casual encounter into an opening for social interaction' [23]. Walky is therefore focused on making everyday activities more noticeable and provide additional ways of communicating among peers.

Theory Informing Design

The Walky exploration is informed by three theoretical perspectives: embodied interaction as theory about interaction design; theories on microblogging as social phenomenon; and theories about social well-being in ageing-in-place initiatives and on local communities.

Rooted in Phenomenology, Embodied Interaction is the nature of human interaction with the world through which people make meaning out of their actions [9]. The theory about Embodied Interaction stresses the role of the human body in the interaction with the world, the everyday practices within which this interaction is situated and the nexus of things that the humans employ within these practices, in the meaning-making process. It gives us the perspective that everyday activities of senior citizens, that is, their situated active engagement with everyday artefacts and people, could be resources for design as well as something to design for.

'Microblogging' is a term less than 10-years-old but it reflects a phenomenon of millions of people sharing almost any type of content with their social networks. Although it has been largely defined for its technological structures and analysed with regards to the content type of its posts [16, for instance], research has been theorising about microblogging beyond the technology that enables it [4, 12, 13 and 19, for instance]. Boyd [4] defines blogging practice as 'both a medium and a bi-product of expression': the medium enabling the expression of self, the activity of creating updates and the updates themselves as carriers of self-expression. Microblogging, born as a faster and easier version of blogging, can be similarly described. As a phenomenon that is socially constructed, microblogging practice transcends the limits of the technology that shapes its current functionalities. We therefore look at microblogging as the phenomenon of people sharing their mundane and everyday activities within a social network, contributing together with simple and often trivial clues to form a social glue: the common ground that allows individuals to feel part of a community and engage in occasional social interactions. In line with this, Huberman et al. [12] reflect on social networks-that-matters, while Marwick and Boyd [13] highlight the phatic nature and the social function of tweets in reinforcing connections and maintaining social bonds.

As the third theoretical starting point, we take the area of ageing in place – the initiatives that aim to provide the ability to live in one's own home as long, and as confidently and comfortably, as possible [1]. Despite much research in making ageing-in-place possible, there is a large design space still under-explored that focuses on the social and emotional aspects of ageing. These aspects have been recognised to contribute to quality of life [11] and we believe they are crucial for attractive ageing. Many of the solutions looking at seniors, social interaction and computer-mediated communication [e.g. 11, 14, 15, 20, 21] share a vision of seniors as in need of care. In addition, they explore how to facilitate the communication with caregivers and distant family members. Our work aligns with the research looking at seniors as citizens entering a third rich phase of their life. In line with projects such as the PeerCare [20], we focus on reinforcing communication among peers, stressing the reciprocal support that peers

Figure 3: The situation: local communities of senior citizens – a view of the building where our senior co-explorers live and its garden

can offer to each other. Peer networks often have the dual function of helping members 'keep an eye on each other' and of creating occasions for social interactions, both contributing to a more meaningful ageing in local communities.

From Theory to Concept: Embodied Microblogging

From the above-mentioned theoretical understandings, we constructed the theoretical concept of Embodied Microblogging (EMb). We currently understand it as an embodied way of sharing small clues about everyday activities through direct engagement with everyday objects within everyday practice. EMb aims to inform the design of digital technology that facilitates senior citizens to make their everyday activities more noticeable in their local communities through the active usage of everyday objects, which are augmented to broadcast activity clues. These clues would contribute to build social glue, creating new openings for social interaction and thus contributing to a sense of belonging to a community and a more attractive ageing.

EMb is a perspective on the social phenomenon of microblogging that is informed by Embodied Interaction (EI) [9]. It foresees the possibilities for designing digital technology that go beyond text-based interactions with general-purpose mobile devices and make the act of microblogging more embedded in everyday practice. EMb further points to:

- The possibilities offered by communicating by doing [17], i.e. leveraging the act of communication by embedding it in the actual activity that we want to share
- The nexus of everyday objects and people that seniors engage with in their daily practice
- The possibility of building social glue through the reciprocal exchange of simple clues about everyday activities.

The Situation

Our exploration was part of the Senior Interaction* project, a larger project investigating innovative solutions to support social interaction among senior citizens in their everyday

---

*   http://seniorinteraktion.dk/

life. The situation within which we explored Walky consisted of a local community of senior citizens living in Valby, a suburb of Copenhagen, where 51 seniors live in private apartments distributed in three buildings, with shared common facilities, leisure spaces and a large garden (see Figure 3). Some seniors have lived there for 10 years, some with their spouse and others on their own. They range from 60 to 98 years of age and all have different types of problems due to ageing. The community has access to a good set of common activities and events organised by seniors themselves, from coffee meetings to gym classes.

The seniors we have been working with are a heterogeneous and complex group. Some seniors are more socially active and some others are not. Some of them do not like some people within the group and thereby avoid specific common activities.

Within this situation, we decided to focus our exploration on the activity of walking. Walking enables many other activities – from shopping, to reaching the laundry room or visiting a friend living nearby. With ageing, walking and mobility might degrade, making some activities more difficult to achieve and limiting a person in her everyday life. In Denmark, many seniors have free access to walking aids but, in some cases, the stigma associated with the use of these aids prevents their use. It is therefore important for designers to alleviate the stigma associated with walking aids, instead considering them simply as resources for the senior citizens to use to go about their everyday life. With this understanding, we are collaborating with a design firm based in Copenhagen, AKP Design, producer of the PROMENADE BagRollator (see Figure 4). The motto of this new type of rollator is to 'make it easy to get out and about in style!' The BagRollator is designed to reduce the stigma associated with the aid itself by making the design aesthetically appealing and more functional for shopping activities. In this collaboration, designers from AKPDesign are looking for possibilities to expand their design with digital technology. As researchers, we considered the BagRollator as

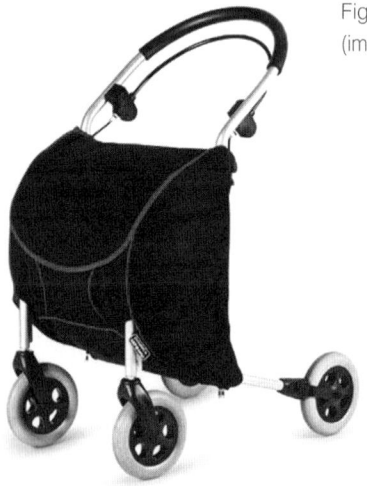

Figure 4: PROMENADE BagRollator from AKP Design (image from http://www.inclusion-by-akpdesign.dk/)

a platform that already incorporates a shared understanding of designing for ageing: design that is non-stigmatising, that builds on the everyday activities of seniors and that is designed in collaboration with seniors.

From the Situation to the Design Ideal: Co-Walky

The availability of common spaces and activities made these obvious settings for our exploration. The challenges of making tenants more aware of activities going on in the building, or simply making them more curious to participate, were our starting points. We speculated that making people's everyday activities more easily noticeable to each other could be a vehicle for creating new openings for social interactions. These would strengthen a sense of community contributing to a more meaningful and attractive ageing.

From these premises, we formulated the design ideal of Co-Walky, exemplifying the possibility of sharing walking activities within the local community at large or with the members of one's walking group. In this design ideal, the everyday objects used for walking acquired a dual role: they support the on-going activity of walking and at the same time are able to communicate information about walking activity. Co-Walky is based on a bag rollator augmented with sensing and communication technologies. It enables seniors to communicate 'I am out walking' to their walking friends while, and simply, using this rollator for walking, in line with the notion of Twitterido [17].

Here follows the scenario explicating the design ideal in the first stages of the Walky exploration:

> John is 75 years old and he uses a rollator to walk. He is a member of a walking group he initiated with other five seniors friends from his activity centre. John usually walks 30 minutes in the mornings. While he walks, his augmented rollator broadcasts status notifications to his walking friends.
>
> During his breakfast, Peter, a member of John's walking group, sees an update from his walking friends on his digital frame in the kitchen: 'John is out walking'. Peter remembers the usual route John takes in the mornings and decides to reroute a bit from his way to the supermarket and to head towards him.
>
> Simultaneously, John's rollator emits a mild vibration from its handles, making John notice that another of his friends is out walking. Peter and John finally meet and together decide to have a coffee at John's place after Peter's shopping.
>
> Dorte, another member of the walking group, busy doing her laundry, could notice from the community screen in the laundry room that there was someone walking. Back at home, she checks the recent activity amongst her walking friends on her digital frame, where she has access to their status. Among others, she notices that Peter is out walking and decides to call him and check on his recent knee problems. Peter then invites her to join John and him for a cup of coffee.

Co-Walky combines augmented rollators and dedicated displays (like digital picture frames, TV sets, mobile phones, tablets and big screens). The general mechanism behind Co-Walky is communicating by doing. A person, by simply using a rollator, broadcasts the walking activity clues to her walking community. At the same time, through feedback from her rollator, or from dedicated displays, a person can receive notifications from her walking friends and notice their walking activity. Further, through very simple actuators, rollators themselves can also become displays of what is happening in the walking community.

This scenario plays an important role in our exploration. Here we highlight some pointers that define our understanding of the role of digital technology in this situation:

- The role of everyday objects in mediating a situated human-to-human communication
- The role of dedicated displays in helping people to notice what is happening in the community, maintaining anonymity on public displays by separating them from the detailed information of the personal displays
- The situatedness of the technology intended to facilitate seniors in the process of making their activity noticeable for others and others' activity noticeable for them
- The possibilities for social interactions opened up by simple reciprocal exchanges of clues and previous knowledge about each other's routines.

The strategy of Co-Walky for non-stigmatising social interaction is to piggyback on the senior citizens' act of sharing everyday activities for different purposes, without explicitly giving out the purpose.

From the Concept to the Design Ideal

In this situation, Co-Walky as design ideal translates the abstract understanding of the Embodied Microblogging concept into concrete pointers for desirable future situations. Co-Walky points to concrete possibilities of embodied ways for the seniors to make their everyday walking activities noticeable. By means of augmented walking aids and dedicated displays, Co-Walky enables more informal ways of communicating and noticing walking activities within networks of friends. We foresee a future in which common everyday objects facilitate people to stay connected with their friends by communicating simple clues about their everyday activities. In this design ideal, digital technology builds on top of microblogging as phenomenon and has a dual role: enabling self-disclosure and community-disclosure of everyday activities; and enabling situated connectedness, i.e. allowing seniors to feel part of a community when engaged in their everyday activities.

Co-Walky captures the possibility of opening up and supporting the collaborative and communicable aspects of walking as an everyday activity.

Sketching and Co-exploring the Design Ideal

We explored the possibilities brought up by Co-Walky in a living lab that started in February 2011 in our design situation. The explorations reported here are related to the period between February and May 2011, while the living lab runs until December 2012. We organised two types of exploration: workshops open to the larger community (from 10 to 20 seniors); and focused design meetings with a small group of seniors (from two to five seniors). We conducted a total of six workshops and four design meetings (see Figure 5). The workshops were mainly targeted to engage the larger community in discussing the ideas of sharing everyday activities and its possible benefits for the community. The design meetings were instead focused on a more direct engagement with scenarios and sketches as concrete manifestations of our design ideal for the seniors to experience. Discussing with the seniors, and just being there at least twice a month, we understood better the dynamics and tensions present, and therefore the possibilities that the place itself, and the people living there, would allow us to explore.

We concentrated on three settings – the home, shopping and the laundry room – replicating the settings of the scenario described earlier. With a series of sketches, ranging from paper sketches to software and hardware sketches on different platforms, we exemplified Co-Walky and engaged the seniors in fruitful conversations. To support these three settings we developed three main sketches. The first is a BagRollator

Figure 5: Views from the workshops and design meetings

Figure 6: BagRollators and Augmented BagRollators in co-design sessions

augmented with digital technology with the Arduino platform. In this sketch, an accelerometer detects movement as the starting of the walking activity; Xbee modules enable the communication of new states to a central station; and simple actuators signal the presence of activity in the walking network through blinking or stable lights (see Figure 6).

The second sketch is an Android tablet, the FriendTab. This is a dedicated device meant for personal use from which seniors can notice their walking friends and receive notifications of new updates (see Figure 7).

The third sketch is the community screen, a web application available on large screens publicly available in the entrance halls of the building. They allow the senior community to notice what is happening in the community when going out and about.

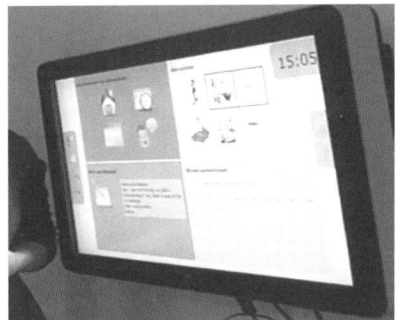

Figure 7: Exploring and discussing community screens (in common spaces) and FriendsTab (at home)

The community screens display anonymous information about everyday activities. As suggested by our senior co-designers, the community screens merge the classic noticeboard with the ideal of Co-Walky, connecting static information about activities and dynamic clues about what is currently going on in the community (see Figure 7).

We explored the three settings in three design meetings. In the first, we introduced the big picture of the scenario and then we concentrated on the home environment by actually moving to the living room of one of our participants. We used the tablet application and paper sketches to trigger discussion and to experience their possible role in everyday life at home. In the second meeting, we focused on the community screens and the possibility of noticing activities in common areas. We used the community screens that were recently built in the three entrance halls of the building of our community. In the third meeting, we focused on the outdoor setting and the shop environment. Here we stressed the role of the rollator for communicating to friends and community (in this case anonymously) the activity of walking and how seniors can feel connected when out walking or shopping.

As we saw, the sketches themselves do not offer direct communication functionalities – they allow for noticing 'if someone is out walking' or 'when Lene was out walking' through animated icons from the community screens or through the text on the tablets. The sketches offer few functionalities and simple information that might trigger openings for direct communication. This communication may happen through other media – as pointed in the scenario when Dorte simply calls Peter with the phone – or in occasional face-to-face encounters.

The three sketches of augmented rollator, FriendsTab and community screens are our designed artefacts.

From Exploring the Design Ideal to Designed Artefacts

Acting on the insights from these co-explorations, we are currently evolving the sketches just introduced; they form an ensemble of artefacts acting together to manifest the design ideal of Co-Walky. The three sketches on their own would not fully represent Co-Walky but it is their interaction and their availability in different social and physical settings that holds the design ideal.

While designing, we realised that our sketches belong to two categories: situated tweeters and situated displays.

Situated Tweeters

The augmented rollators belong to the category of situated tweeters. Situated tweeters are augmented objects enabled to communicate their use and to provide simple clues about activity happening in the network. They serve the role of facilitating the seniors to make their activity noticeable and enable a situated communication to support connectedness in everyday life on the go (see figures 5 and 6).

Situated Displays

Community screens and personal tablets belong to the category of situated displays. Currently implemented with web-based technologies, they aim to facilitate seniors to notice which activities are going on only through anonymous data due to their public availability (see Figure 7). Similarly, personal screens are situated personal displays that range from tablets to phones. They are currently implemented as a simple application for the Android platform (see Figure 7). Differently from community screens, they aim to facilitate seniors in noticing what is happening in their friend group while involved in other everyday activities.

We envision this ensemble of designed artefacts as providing new, technologically enhanced but still situated ways for seniors to notice and make noticeable their everyday activities.

Reflections: the Design Ideal as an Interface

In the previous sections we have described the role of Co-Walky, the design ideal, in driving the research process. We now reflect on how this design ideal acts as an interface between the theoretical concept of Embodied Microblogging and the situation of local communities of senior citizens sharing common spaces and facilities. Co-Walky, as a situated manifestation of EMb, brings the abstract understanding of

EMb to the concreteness of the local community of the senior citizens designing with us. Co-Walky points at advancing:

- The current situation in local communities of senior citizens to a desired one with additional, situated ways for communicating everyday activities that support common ground and stimulate new openings for quality social interaction; and
- The articulation of the theoretical concept of EMb and its role in designing digital technology that supports social interaction in ageing.

Co-Walky resulted in a set of concrete designed artefacts: the augmented rollator, FriendTab and community screens.

In this first phase of the living lab we succeeded in bringing our design ideal to a concrete state through sketching and co-designing. These need to be further explored, investigating how our seniors will include them in their everyday life.

We now report a brief account of points in our explorations that highlight the role of the compositional whole of Walky in advancing the situation and in advancing the articulation of the theoretical concept.

Compositional Whole for an Advancement of the Situation

In the exploration of Co-Walky we investigated possible and desirable states with our senior-citizen co-designers. From the material collected emerged a promising picture in terms of how much our seniors recognised the potentials of the design ideal.

When we presented the senior citizens with the idea that some of the activities going on, for instance billiards or bowling, could be anonymously displayed on the common screens, a senior commented that she could easily see how, given the ability to determine that someone is already playing without having to go to the actual site to see what is happening, they could organise spontaneous events.

Although the process of explaining and experiencing the design ideal has been long and non-trivial, our explorations have contributed to making our senior co-designers see its possibilities. The sketches and the co-design sessions were fundamental in achieving this status. On many occasions the seniors supported our thinking (the design ideal), explaining to each other and actively discussing possibilities. When presented with the possibility of having dedicated technology (the FriendTabs) that provides one function and is dedicated to specific activities, some recognised it to be less scary or intimidating.

In our discussions, the seniors also remarked on the fact that the idea of sharing the shopping activity with the neighbour or going walking with a friend is already part of their everyday life. For example, a senior woman reported her practice of sharing shopping and offers with her neighbour. These discussions support our strategy of building on top of existing activities and practices. Expanding what is already present or encouraging practices that might have stopped for different reasons can be a support for the practices themselves.

We discussed the purpose of sharing everyday activities with the seniors. We suggested it not just as a way to find better shopping offers or to find friends to go for a walk, but also as a contribution to the community. Getting to know what is happening around in the community might trigger the curiosity of the less-active people, or even propagate a sense of community. Our senior co-designers could relate to this, although they were more concerned about the practical benefits they can get by the use of the technology explored.

Compositional Whole for an Advancement of the Concept

During the explorations, we discussed the relation of Co-Walky to the act of 'looking out of the window to see what is happening around', by chance or on purpose. Visiting the local community, we found many seniors enjoying the sun on their terraces while reading or just watching what is going on in the street. When presented with this comparison, a senior woman commented that it is not the same, pointing to the fact that when you turn the corner you disappear from others' view. Walky instead is more persistent and would offer a window always open to others' activities.

This suggests the importance of control over self-disclosure: offering explicit control for seniors to know how they can allow, or not, others to open a window on their activities; and most importantly, ensuring that only the people they select are able to look through that window. This therefore stresses the importance of sharing more detailed and personal information with networks-that-matter, both in terms of people they know but also in terms of what they want the others to know.

In this regard, reciprocity plays an important role to motivate seniors in participating in sharing. This reciprocity should allow for asymmetrical reciprocity so it could then become a practice within the community to encourage participation.

During the explorations, we faced the big concern that people have towards privacy and the low trust that they have towards sensing technology. They mention how easily these technologies turn into monitoring tools – and none of our seniors see themselves as in need of being monitored to feel safer. This design exploration has taught us that reciprocity in self-disclosure within networks-that-matter is crucial for tracing the boundaries between monitoring and social networking that involves pervasive communication technologies.

Engaging in this co-exploration has therefore refined our understanding of the complexities that EMb implies when we want to design for embodied ways of microblogging to support the creation of new openings for social interaction.

The compositional whole therefore creates pointers towards refining EMb, indicating the importance of control on self-disclosure, and of reciprocity-in-networks-that-matter as fundamental characters of Embodied Microblogging.

Conclusions

In this chapter, we answered the call for 'designing for an attractive ageing' by designing for supporting the social interaction of senior citizens within their community. In this vein, we presented Walky, a design exploration through which we explored if, and how, augmenting the rollator that senior citizens use for walking could open up opportunities for social interaction within their community. In particular, we reported on the possibilities of how augmented rollators and situated private and personal displays can facilitate seniors in making their everyday walking activities noticeable, and how they can notice others' activities. In a reciprocal exchange of walking clues, they can create a common ground of understanding and open up new opportunities for social interaction. This leads to a stronger sense of belonging to their community and therefore to a more attractive ageing.

We further reported the collaborative design process of exploring these theoretical perspectives with the senior citizens living in a local community in the Valby suburb of Copenhagen, AKPDesign and the members from the municipal corporation of the city of Copenhagen.

Through this, with Walky we presented how we explored abstract theoretical perspectives – of embodied interaction, social interaction in the senior citizen's everyday life, and the phenomenon of microblogging – in this particular design situation. We did this by explicating the process of producing the compositional whole of Walky that consisted of:

- The theoretical concept as a conceptual confluence of the different theoretical starting points
- The design situation of designing for supporting social interaction around the everyday walking of senior citizens
- The Co-Walky as the design ideal, which interfaces the abstract concept with the particular situation
- The augmented rollator, the FriendTab and community screens, as the designed artefacts manifesting the abstract theoretical perspectives in concrete ways
- The detailed description of this exploration driven by sketching and co-designing; and
- The reflection on the relation between these elements, highlighting the contribution to theorising and advancing the situation towards desirable outcomes.

Thus the compositional whole explicates the process of engaging with the theory–situation dialectics in designing for social aspects of ageing. With this, we contribute to the interaction design research community focusing on ageing, suggesting that the process of engaging with the theory–situation dialectic be made explicit as valuable knowledge for other researchers in the field. In other words, design researchers need to be explicit about how they apply design thinking to contribute to research knowledge. We support this suggestion by providing the example of Walky and its compositional whole as a demonstration of how we explored abstract theoretical perspectives in particular design situations leading to three concrete designed artefacts.

Acknowledgement

We take this occasion to thank all the research members of the Senior Interaction Project and the different stakeholders that made our work possible. In particular, we want to thank our senior co-designers for hosting us in their community for our living lab and AKPDesign for the support and the interest in looking further at the possible futures of ageing.

References

1. Wikipedia (no date) 'Ageing in place', http://en.wikipedia.org/wiki/Ageing_in_place, accessed October 2011.
2. Bagalkot, N., Nazzi, E. and Sokoler, T. (2011) 'Magic-Mirror-Spiral: Looking into the role of "design ideal" in interaction design research projects', in *Proceedings of Nordic Design Research Conference*, Nordes.
3. Binder, T. and Redström, J. (2006) 'Exemplary Design Research', http://eprints.sics.se/920/, accessed 17 February 2011.
4. Boyd, D. (2006) 'A blogger's blog: Exploring the definition of a medium', *Reconstruction*, vol. 6.
5. Buchanan, R. (2001) 'Design Research and the New Learning', *Design Issues*, vol. 17, no. 4, pp.3–23.
6. Crawford, K. (2009) 'These Foolish Things: On Intimacy and Insignificance in Mobile Media', in G. Goggin and L. Hjorth (eds), *Mobile Technologies: From Telecommunications to Media*, New York: Routledge.
7. Cross, N. (2007) *Designerly Ways of Knowing*, Board of International research in Design, BIRD.
8. Dishman, E. (2004) 'Inventing wellness systems for ageing in place', *Computer*, 37 (5), pp.34–41.
9. Dourish, P. (2001) *Where the Action Is: The Foundations of Embodied Interaction*, MIT press.
10. Inclusion by AKP design, http://www.inclusion-by-akpdesign.dk, accessed October 2011.
11. Hirsch, T., Forlizzi, J., Hyder, E., Goetz, J., and Stroback, J. (2000) 'The ELDer Project: Social, Emotional, and Environmental Factors in the Design of Eldercare', *CUU '00 Proceedings of the Conference for Universal Usability*, Washington DC, pp.72–80.
12. Huberman, B.A., Romero, D.M. and Wu, F. (2009) 'Social networks that matter: Twitter under the microscope', *First Monday*, vol. 14.
13. Marwick, A.E. and Boyd, D. (2011) 'I tweet honestly, I tweet passionately: Twitter users, context collapse, and the imagined audience', *New Media & Society*, vol. 13.

14. Mynatt, E., Rowan, J., Craighill, S. and Jacobs, A. (2001) 'Digital family portraits: supporting peace of mind for extended family members', in *Proceedings of the SIGCHI conference on Human factors in computing systems, CHI '01*, Seattle, pp.333–40.
15. Morris, M., Lundell, J., Dishman, E. and Needham, B. (2003) 'New Perspectives on Ubiquitous Computing from Ethnographic Study of Elders with Cognitive Decline', *UbiComp 2003*, pp.227–42.
16. Nardi, B.A., Schiano, D.J. and Gumbrecht, M. (2004) 'Blogging as social activity: or, would you let 900 million people read your diary?' in *Proceedings of the 2004 ACM conference on Computer supported Cooperative Work*, Chicago, Illinois, USA, pp.222–31.
17. Nazzi, E., Bagalkot, N. and Sokoler, T. (2010) 'Twitterido: designing for transitions in communicating through doing', in *Proceedings of Create 2010 the interaction design conference*, pp.83–4.
18. Oulasvirta, A., Petit, R., Raento, M. and Tiitta, S. (2007) 'Interpreting and acting on mobile awareness cues', *Human-Computer Interaction*, vol. 22, pp.97–135.
19. Oulasvirta, A., Lehtonen, E. and Kurvinen, E. (2010) 'Making the ordinary visible in microblogs', *Personal and Ubiquitous Computing*, vol. 14, pp.237–49.
20. Riche, Y. and Mackay, W. (2010) 'PeerCare: Supporting Awareness of Rhythms and Routines for Better Ageing in Place', *Computer Supported Cooperative Work* (CSCW).
21. Rowan, J. and Mynatt, E.D. (2005) 'Digital Family Portrait Field Trial: Support for Ageing in Place', *Technology*, pp.521–30.
22. Stolterman, E. and Wiberg, M. (2010) 'Concept-Driven Interaction Design Research', *Human–Computer Interaction*, 25 (2), pp.95–118.
23. Svensson, M. and Sokoler, T. (2008) 'Ticket-to-talk-television: designing for the circumstantial nature of everyday social interaction', in *NordiCHI '08: Proceedings of the 5th Nordic conference on Human-computer interaction: building bridges*.
24. Zimmerman, J., Forlizzi, J. and Evenson, S. (2007) 'Research through design as a method for interaction design research in HCI', in *Proceedings of the SIGCHI Conference on Human Factors in Computing Systems*, CHI '07, ACM.

Author Index

Naveen Bagalkot *(IT University of Copenhagen, Denmark)*	227
Shoshi Bar-Eli *(College of Management Academic Studies, Israel)*	135
Oliver Breuer *(SPIRE, University of Southern Denmark)*	171
Agnese Caglio *(SPIRE, University of Southern Denmark)*	171
Ryan Daniel *(James Cook University, Australia)*	107
Parag Deshpande *(Umeå Institute of Design, Sweden)*	9
Ian Ewart *(University of Reading, UK)*	89
Katja Fleischmann *(James Cook University, Australia)*	107
John S. Gero *(Krasnow Institute for Advanced Studies, USA)*	73
Gabriela Goldschmidt *(Israel institute of Technology)*	55
Frederik Gottlieb *(SPIRE, University of Southern Denmark)*	171
Sergejs Groskovs *(SPIRE, University of Southern Denmark)*	171
Richard Herriott *(Aarhus School of Architecture, Denmark)*	39
Anette Hiltunen *(SPIRE, University of Southern Denmark)*	171
Giovanni Innella *(Northumbria University, UK)*	207
Birgitte Geert Jensen *(Aarhus School of Architecture, Denmark)*	39
Janet Kelly *(Novo Nordisk, Denmark)*	189
Michael Leitner *(Northumbria University, UK)*	207
Rachael Luck *(University of Reading, UK)*	89
Arun Narargoje *(IT University of Copenhagen, Denmark)*	227
Elena Nazzi *(IT University of Copenhagen, Denmark)*	227
O uzhan Özcan *(Koç University, Turkey)*	157
Morteza Pourmohamadi *(University of Sydney, Australia)*	73
Paul A. Rodgers *(Northumbria University, UK)*	55
Miguel Navarro Sanint *(SPIRE, University of Southern Denmark)*	171
Maria Antonietta Sbordone *(Seconda Università di Napoli, Italy)*	27
Brian Schewe *(SPIRE, University of Southern Denmark)*	171
Tomas Sokoler *(IT University of Copenhagen, Denmark)*	227
Adviye Ayçça Ünlüer *(Yıldız Technical University, Turkey)*	157
Gemma Visini *(James Cook University, Australia)*	107
Christopher B. Williams *(Virginia Polytechnic Institute & State University, USA)*	73
Freddie Yauner *(Northumbria University, UK)*	207